Deliberative Gov
Development

Deliberative Governance for Sustainable Development argues that governance has become the core problem of sustainable development and identifies deliberative democracy and governance as a path forward for Western societies.

In this book the author puts forward three messages. Firstly, while sustainable development theoretically is a common good of all people, it is in practice constantly associated with a multitude of smaller and larger conflicts. These conflicts arise repeatedly because, in practice, the benefits, costs and risks of sustainable development are unequally distributed and therefore form a massive barrier to sustainable development. As a result, sustainable development depends on the ability of the social and political institutions of societies to accommodate these conflicts. Second, within the framework of their established institutional structures, Western societies do not have the sufficient tools for conflict resolution that are adequate to the conditions of modern diversified societies and the complex challenges of sustainable development. They need to implement institutional reforms that switch institutional structures towards deliberation. Third, by switching to deliberation, Western societies can reach the high level of governance that enables them to achieve environmentally sustainable development that will bring them significant economic and social benefits and, as a result, may reach far beyond their borders.

This volume offers a novel, transdisciplinary approach to sustainable development and governance in Western societies. It will be of great interest to students and scholars of sociology, economics, politics, environmental studies and philosophy, as well as professionals and policymakers working in the area of sustainable development.

Franz Lehner is Professor Emeritus of political science and of applied social research at the Ruhr-University of Bochum, Germany. For more than 20 years he was President of the Institute of Work and Technology, Gelsenkirchen, Germany, a public institute for applied research on economic and social change.

Routledge Studies in Environmental Policy

Mainstreaming Solar Energy in Small, Tropical Islands
Cultural and Policy Implications
Kiron C. Neale

EU Environmental Governance
Current and Future Challenges
Edited by Amandine Orsini and Elena Kavvatha

The European Union and Global Environmental Protection
Transforming Influence into Action
Edited by Mar Campins Eritja

Environmental Policy and Air Pollution in China
Governance and Strategy
Yuan Xu

Climate Change Law and Policy in the Middle East and North Africa Region
Edited by Damilola S. Olawuyi

European Foreign Policy in a Decarbonising world
Challenges and Opportunities
Sebastian Oberthür, Dennis Tänzler, and Emily Wright, with Gauri Khandekar

How to Successfully Encourage Sustainable Development Policy
Lessons from Germany
Günther Bachmann

Deliberative Governance for Sustainable Development
An Innovative Solution for Environment, Economy and Society
Franz Lehner

For more information about this series, please visit: www.routledge.com/
Routledge-Studies-in-Environmental-Policy/book-series/RSEP

Deliberative Governance for Sustainable Development

An Innovative Solution for Environment, Economy and Society

Franz Lehner

Routledge
Taylor & Francis Group
LONDON AND NEW YORK

from Routledge

First published 2023
by Routledge
4 Park Square, Milton Park, Abingdon, Oxon OX14 4RN

and by Routledge
605 Third Avenue, New York, NY 10158

Routledge is an imprint of the Taylor & Francis Group, an informa business

© 2023 Franz Lehner

British Library Cataloguing-in-Publication Data
A catalogue record for this book is available from the British Library

Library of Congress Cataloging-in-Publication Data
A catalog record has been requested for this book

ISBN: 978-1-032-19842-2 (hbk)
ISBN: 978-1-032-19867-5 (pbk)
ISBN: 978-1-003-26142-1 (ebk)

DOI: 10.4324/9781003261421

Typeset in Goudy
by Taylor & Francis Books

To Friedrich Schmidt-Bleek and Jürg Steiner

Contents

Preface   ix

1   Sustainable Development: The Real Challenge   1

   The Misunderstood Commonality 2
   The Logic of Social Transformation 6
   A Changing Context: Knowledge Society 13
   The Key Problem: Governance 17
   Regaining Common Grounds 23
   The Institutional Solution: A Deliberative Switch 26
   The Deliberative Way: Threefold Sustainability 31

2   Sustainability: A Threefold Challenge   37

   A New Approach to the Common Good 38
   The Threefold Challenge 43
   The Environmental Dimension: Resource Productivity 46
   The Economic Dimension: Living Standard 49
   The Social Dimension: Cohesion 53
   A Key Issue: Radical Innovation 58
   The Deliberative Way: Activating Government 61

3   The Economic Charm of Ecology   66

   Resource Productivity or Climate Neutrality? 68
   Factor 10, Rucksacks and Footprints 73
   The Driving Force: A Dynamic Resource Tax 78
   The Environmental Promise of the Knowledge Society 82
   A Key Actor: The City 86
   The Deliberative Way: An Ordered Chaos 91

4   From the Wealth of Nations to the Wealth of People   95

The Neglect of the Greatest Happiness Principle 96
The Logic of the Distributive State 101
The "Nickel-and-Dime Economy" Revisited 106
A New Economy 110
A Key Issue: The Future of Work 116
The Deliberative Way: Making Small Beautiful Again 119

5   A Social Contract for a Sustainable Society   124

The Underpinning of Cohesion 125
The Shaping of Social Development 129
Western Societies in the Face of Decline 133
New Topicality for Milton Friedman 137
Representing Pluralist Societies 142
A Key Issue: Culture 145
The Deliberative Way: An Alliance for Reframing 150

6   Mastering the Knowledge Society   155

From Genesis to Telesis 157
Coping with the Janus Face 162
A New Innovation Dynamism 167
A Key Issue: Restructuring Human Capital 170
Winning the Race 174
The Fine Art of Social Learning 179
The Deliberative Way: A New Enlightenment 183

7   The Deliberative Switch   188

The Implementation of Threefold Sustainability 189
Deliberation: A Gentle Revolution 192
Making Pluralism Work 195
Reframing Governance 197
From Deliberative Democracy to Deliberative Society 202

Index   205

Preface

Most societies on this planet are set up to fail at the challenges of sustainable development including climate neutrality. They do not fail because of a lack of knowledge but because of a lack of governance. Governance means the totality of structures and processes for ordering and regulation of societies and other social systems. In relation to society at large, governance includes government, markets and the institutions and organizations of civil society. Simply speaking, civil society refers to all the social interactions which are neither regulated by government nor by the market. This includes non-governmental organizations (NGOs) and other social associations as well as most of everyday life and social communication. To put it in nutshell, I argue in this book that most societies on this planet are likely to fall short of sustainable development because their governments and their markets, and to some extent their civil societies are not up to the challenges of sustainable development. This is particularly true for those societies which use the largest share of the planet's resources and create the largest damage to the planet and its climate, namely Western societies, China, Russia, India, Japan, South Korea and the rich Arab countries.

The reason for the case which I just described is that sustainable development while theoretically a common good of all people is in practice constantly associated with a multitude of smaller and larger conflicts. These are rarely fundamental conflicts on sustainable development, but rather conflicts on the distribution of the benefits, costs and risks of sustainable development. It is precisely these conflicts, which are not fundamental at all, that hinder, delay and ultimately prevent the achievement of sustainable development.

The conflicts take different forms in different systems and different societies. Different systems and different societies also have different ways and means to cope with the conflicts. This also affects the probably inevitable economic, political and ideological competition between these countries. In autocratic systems, conflicts can be prevented from unfolding in the first place by coercive state power, repression and indoctrination. Moreover, the state can also resolve conflicts through imposed solutions. However, these systems may pay a high price in the form of a lower capacity for social learning and innovation, and a lower ability to increase the prosperity of their citizens.

In democratic systems, conflicts can unfold more easily. This applies in particular to Western societies whose openness and social diversity also create high potential for conflict. On the other hand, the possibilities for deciding conflicts by coercive force are much more narrowly limited. At the same time, the openness and social diversity of Western societies also represent a major asset. They considerably promote creativity, social learning and innovation, and society's ability to increase and secure the prosperity of its citizens. I will not further discuss this here, but conclude that different systems and societies face different problems and abilities with respect to sustainable development.

This is the factual reason why I focus this book on the Western societies. There is also a political reason: I want to show a way that will enable Western countries to achieve sustainable development early, that is, realistically, by the middle of this century. This should help them to sustainably secure and improve the prosperity of their present and future citizens. But it should also help them to assert themselves in the economic and political competition of systems and to resist autocratic and populist dangers from within.

Currently, Western societies are, like most other societies, unlikely to achieve sustainable development until the middle of this century. Their institutions are not geared at reaching widely accepted solutions and achieving the common good. In the political system, political representation by elected officials and majority rule regularly exclude a smaller or larger variety of social interests. The competition of interests, euphemistically called polyarchy, rarely leads to the theoretically postulated check and balance of social interests, but rather promotes strong influence of special but well-organized interests and a frequent neglect of general interests. Where competition could in principle lead to widely accepted results, namely in the market, its functioning is massively impaired by poor regulation and a strong concentration of economic power. In civil society, an erosion of common grounds often limits its capacity to solve social problems by social self-organization. The established governance structures of Western societies therefore are often neither capable to adequately cope with the high potential for conflict associated with the openness and diversity of Western societies nor to exploit its high potential for creativity, learning and innovation to solve the problems of sustainable development. Rather than resolving the mostly small conflicts associated with sustainable development they are likely to perpetuate a high level of conflict and thus doom sustainable development to failure.

These are fundamental problems, but they can be solved without having to radically change the entire system. Radical system changes are, as we know from much theoretical knowledge and practical experience, fraught with much resistance and many conflicts. Their outcome is therefore often uncertain or different from what was originally thought. Radical changes of existing institutional structures may therefore prevent, rather than promote, achievement of sustainable development by the middle of this century. Hence, a solution within the existing structures is preferable.

The solution is deliberative governance. It is one of the two pillars on which the strategy for sustainable development which I propose in this book builds up. The other one is threefold sustainability. Both pillars should on the one hand reduce the occurrence of conflicts over sustainable development without endangering the social diversity of Western societies and on the other hand lead to broadly accepted solutions to the probably still remaining conflicts.

In a book published in 1970, Jürg Steiner, a Swiss political scientist teaching at the University of North Carolina at Chapel Hill and one of the pioneers of the concept, described deliberative governance in politics as amicable agreement of conflicts. In this and later books, he demonstrated that this approach may work well in socially diverse and even in deeply divided societies. In the meantime, many scientists and practitioners have concretized the concept in a variety of practical procedures. These procedures have been applied for several years already by national governments, cities and many other actors in the USA, Canada, Australia, France, Denmark, Ireland and other countries to develop widely accepted solutions to complex problems such as technology assessment, sustainable development, abortion or fundamental constitutional reform. Researchers at Harvard University have developed a similar approach for business. I will discuss these practices in more detail in the first chapter and throughout the book.

With Jürg Steiner, I have enjoyed for many decades until his death in 2020 a professional friendship and many, sometimes controversial but always amicable discussions on the governance problems of Western societies and about this book. He has significantly influenced the understanding of governance on which this book is based and helped me a lot in the conceptualization of the book.

The concept of threefold sustainability which is applied in this book has been developed by a group of scholars, which I had the great pleasure to chair, in a study for the German industrialist and member of the Club of Rome, Klaus Steilmann. I refer to the group in this book as the Steilmann commission, or 'the commission'. Threefold means that social development not only must be sustainable in environmental, but also in economic and social terms. More precisely, the concept asserts that under current conditions of modern Western societies environmentally sustainable development is impossible if it endangers the standard of living of the mass of societies' populations and societies' social cohesion. I will further explain this in chapters 1 and 2.

The Steilmann commission has operationally defined the environmental dimension of sustainability by resource productivity. The definition follows the Factor 10 concept of the German chemist and environmental researcher Friedrich Schmidt-Bleek, a member of the commission. The Factor 10 concept argues that Western societies can achieve sustainable development if they succeed in reducing their resource productivity by a factor of 10 within a few decades. In concrete terms, this means that they must manage to produce the same amount of goods with one tenth of the current consumption. The commission made this concept the basis of its work. The concept also plays a crucial role in my argumentation in this book. It shows how sustainable development is possible even under conditions of capitalism. More precisely, it shows a way to decouple economic growth from the consumption of non-renewable natural resources, at least for a longer period of time.

I also had many years of friendly and stimulating cooperation with Friedrich Schmidt-Bleek. We had a lot of fun writing a book together in which we showed that resource productivity can be the engine of sustainable economic growth. I will come back to this in the second chapter.

The social dimension was added by the commission after a long and initially controversial discussion on the importance to be attached to the argument that environmental sustainability is a common good. This discussion was initiated by the British sociologist Anthony Charles with the argument that in modern societies sustainable development, like any other social development, is associated with different and conflicting interests and thus with conflicts. The commission eventually accepted this argument and adopted the social dimension, defining it as ensuring social cohesion.

Tony Charles is another colleague and friend with whom I have many years of close collaboration. He has helped me in the conceptualization of this book and has carefully read the drafts of all chapters, providing me with sympathetic criticism and many interesting suggestions.

Working in the Steilmann commission was an extremely interesting and positive experience in transdisciplinary research from which I benefited a lot. The commission brought together a group of scholars and practitioners from different disciplines. In addition to the members I have already mentioned, the sociologist Anthony Charles and the chemist and environmental researcher Friedrich Schmidt-Bleek, these were Nicholas Ashford, an American who holds doctoral degrees in law and in physical chemistry and who is a professor of technology and policy at the Massachusetts Institute of Technology, the Swiss economist Stephan Bieri, who in his professional life headed, among other things, an energy supply company and then one of the most important scientific organizations of Switzerland, the ETH Board, the Swiss physicist and environmental researcher Willy Bierter who in his professional life has repeatedly alternated between scientific work at prestigious institutions, including the Swiss Institute of Technology and the Wuppertal Institute for Climate and Energy, and practical work as a consultant, the Italian economist Roberto Camagni, a professor of regional science at the Politechnico di Milano and a pioneer in research on innovative milieus, the Greek economist Anthony Courakis, who worked as a fellow in monetary and financial economics at Oxford University, and also was the Greek Ambassador to the OECD, the German industrial engineer, Wolf D. Hartmann, who worked as university professor in the former GDR and after German reunification as a manager, consultant and science journalist, and the German-Austrian economist Friedrich Schneider, a professor at the University of Linz and a specialist in fields as diverse as environmental economics and the shadow economy, but which fit together well in terms of threefold sustainability.

Transdisciplinary research is becoming increasingly important in today's world because, on the one hand, real-world problems are becoming more complex and transcend scientific disciplines and, on the other hand, scientific research owes its performance and rapid development to a large extent to increasing specialization. Therefore, in order to solve real-world problems, knowledge from different disciplines and sub-disciplines often has to be combined, and furthermore has to be combined with experiential knowledge from different areas of society. This is especially true for sustainable development.

That is why this book too offers a transdisciplinary approach to sustainable development. Sustainable development is an important theme for students and scholars in economics, political science, sociology, philosophy, education, the sciences and other disciplines and a variety of different professions, as well as for many other persons. For all these people the book aims at providing a comprehensive understanding of sustainable development which is scholarly well founded but written in accessible prose.

I received a lot of support from colleagues and practitioners while working on this book, for which I am very grateful. I am particularly grateful to Jürg Steiner and Tony Charles, as I mentioned earlier. I am also very grateful to Heinz-Peter Heidrich, a banker, and Hans-Günter Rolff, an educationalist. Both have taken the trouble to read through and comment on the entire manuscript, and with both I have had many stimulating discussions about the book. For the same reason, I am very grateful to my wife Ilse Führer-Lehner and my son David Lehner, who created a small creative milieu for me. Many thanks are also due to Stephan Bieri, who helped me with the conception of the book. I am also indebted to Hanspeter Sauter, a banker, and Ludger Wibbeke, the head of large capital management company, for much sympathetic criticism and many suggestions. I am grateful to Sauter and Wibbeke as well as Heinz-Peter Heidrich for an important suggestion on the relationship between capitalism and sustainable development, which I will present in the last chapter of the book. Finally, I would like to thank my colleagues Ben Dankbaar, Rolf Heinze, Jürgen Howaldt, Stefan Schirm, Uli Paetzel and Hans-Peter Noll who at different stages of working on this book helped me with their advice.

1 Sustainable Development

The Real Challenge

Environmental researchers and activists have argued for many years that time to achieve sustainable development is running out. They are right: Most societies, including Western societies, are indeed on the verge of foundering over the development of a sustainable society including climate neutrality. They may even fall short of attaining the moderate self-defined climate goals agreed at the 2015 the World Climate Conference of Paris – to keep global warming below 2 degrees Celsius. The sad thing about this situation is that there is already enough knowledge available to achieve sustainable development including climate neutrality by the middle of this century at the latest, and in the next few years much more will be added. This is especially true for those countries that are the biggest polluters and that use or waste a largely disproportionate share of the world's natural resources, including Western societies. With the knowledge available now or in a few years Western societies could drastically reduce their exploitation of nature.[1]

The impending failure to achieve sustainable development is a universal problem of social evolution. The problem is that societies will always change out of their existing structures and can only change out of these structures. Sustainable development, too, can only develop out of existing social structures. But these are precisely the structures that have long since ceased to be sustainable and also stand in the way of sustainable development. In modern societies, these structures are associated with a multitude of different understandings, living conditions and interests, and with complicated power relationships. I will explain this in more detail below. At this point, I only want to draw the conclusion from this situation: In modern societies, sustainable development, like any significant social change, is always and inevitably associated with many small and large conflicts. These are rarely fundamental conflicts about sustainable development, but conflicts about specific strategies and measures and about their costs. These many small and larger conflicts probably inhibit sustainable development much more than a fundamental dispute ever could.[2]

The real challenge of sustainable development is thus to solve the many conflicts that are always associated with sustainable development in such a way that, with all the knowledge available now or in the near future,

DOI: 10.4324/9781003261421-1

sustainable development can be achieved within a few decades. This is a governance problem, i.e. a problem of the institutional capabilities of societies to
accommodate conflict, to solve problems and to achieve common targets.[3]

Since the social structures that generate the conflicts about sustainable
development and define concrete governance differ in important respects
between different types of societies I focus in this book on Western societies. This is also justified because Western societies together plus China,
Russia, and the rich Arab countries, are responsible for most of the world's
global consumption and waste of natural resources. Moreover, the Western
lifestyle is widespread globally and is the desirable model for many people in
the world. Western societies therefore have a special responsibility to
achieve sustainable development as quickly and thoroughly as possible.

As I briefly explained in the preface, there is also a political reason for the
focus on Western societies: I want to show a way that puts Western societies at the forefront of sustainable development and that also secures the
standard of living of their citizens and their social cohesion. This should
enable them to stand their ground in the political and economic competition
between systems, and to resist autocratic and populist dangers from within.

In this chapter, I will provide an overview over the argument of the book. It
is intended to give readers from different disciplines, professions and areas of
activity a frame of reference. This should help them to follow the argument
which is written in accessible prose but does not oversimplify the complex
problems of sustainable development and governance in Western societies.

The Misunderstood Commonality

In order to fully apprehend the situation which I just outlined, it is necessary
to abandon a widespread understanding of environmental sustainability. It is
the conception that environmental sustainability is the common good of
mankind. The term common good is used differently, as the common good or
as a common good. The first means the general public interest or the general
welfare. The second denotes a scarce good or resource that can be used by all
members of society or of any other community. Examples are common water
resources in a certain area or common land of farmers. In the way we treat it,
nature is not only the public good of mankind but rather a common good of
mankind, a common resource which is scarce, but we all may use. Common
goods are associated with specific problems of governance.[4]

Environmentalists and other people usually speak of nature as the
common good and assume that nature and sustainable development are in
the interest of all people. This argument is certainly true in theoretical terms,
but practically totally misleading. It fails to recognize that in nearly all activities for sustainable development the general public benefits in abstract
terms, but certain social interest groups gain in very concrete terms while
others first have to pay a high price or to accept high risk of paying this
price in the future. An illustrative example of this is a conflict over a place in

Germany called Hambacher Forst. This is a forest that is threatened by plans for lignite opencast mining. At this place, environmentalists and local residents on the one hand and police and workers of the mining company on the other hand have engaged in bitter disputes and even violent conflict. For many committed environmentalists this is a very clear situation. Good environmentalists are in conflict with people and organizations for whom the pursuit of their own interests is more important than the preservation of our common good – our natural resources. However, it is not that simple.

On the one side, there are mostly people who are committed to the general interest of protecting natural resources but who are not affected by the closure of the mine. In addition, there are also people whose houses have to make way for mining and who may therefore benefit from conservation of the forest. On the other side, there are people whose jobs and the social opportunities of their children are at risk. It does not take much imagination to conceive situations in which people from both camps change sides. For example: citizens who are otherwise environmentally committed oppose a high-voltage power line near their homes which would allow more wind power to be used. On the other hand, power plant workers are campaigning for the power line precisely because wind energy and other renewable energies open up new growth and employment opportunities for their companies. In this situation, the good guys become the bad guys and the bad ones the good ones.

To cut to the chase: the fact that environmental sustainability is a common good of mankind does not imply that this good can be easily produced. As long as the pursuit of sustainability involves, in any concrete situation, significant losses for some people in terms of important or even vital interests while others profit, sustainable development will always face conflicts and resistance to particular strategies and measures for sustainable development. As mentioned above, these conflicts are rarely conflicts over environmental sustainability itself, but conflicts over the distribution of benefits, costs and risks of concrete strategies and activities for sustainable development.

This makes a big difference. Conflicts over environmental sustainability itself can hardly be solved while conflicts on associated benefits, costs and risks are in principle solvable through redistribution or compensation of benefits, costs and risks. There is, for example, little or no chance of an agreement between environmentally active politicians and politicians who deny human made climate change. Conflicts over phasing out of conventional energies, on the other hand, can be resolved by compensating the losses of the concerned companies and providing new jobs for their workers. These are, however, not easy solutions. They require a more or less complicated political balance between different, sometimes competing interests or an environmentally efficient market regime. We return to this in chapter 2.

In the view of Ulrich Beck, the situation described above represents fundamental social change. In his book "Risk Society: Towards a New Modernity", he argues that modern industrial society is generating more and more risks in the course of its production of wealth and its way of living. This is why conflicts about the distribution of social wealth are increasingly overlaid by conflicts about the distribution of environmental and social risks.[5]

This pattern of conflict exacerbates one of the fundamental problems of Western societies in a way that is environmentally extremely harmful. The problem is inequality concerning income and wealth. Inequality is an ambivalent condition. To a certain degree, inequality is, in capitalist societies at least, a positive factor in achievement motivation and risk-taking. The chance to achieve a higher income, a higher standard of living and better education for their children motivates many people to invest more in their own education, to work harder, to invest time and energy in their careers, to start businesses and take the risks of being an entrepreneur, or to invest in radical innovations. Insofar, in capitalist societies inequality is a positive factor in the innovation and competitiveness of the economy and its ability to improve both the current and future potential for satisfying human needs and desires. However, high levels of inequality create adverse effects. As will be discussed in more detail in chapter 4, high inequality is associated with stagnating mass incomes, weak mass purchasing power and domestic demand, weak innovation and slow growth. At the same time, it advances the formation of large fortunes. In a rather strange way, this leads to an abundance of capital, low interest rates and increasing speculation. As a result, the economy loses its ability to produce and distribute wealth in a way that meets people's present and future needs. Even worse, high inequality leads to a fundamental change in the structure of the economy, namely to development of what has been described as a "nickel-and-dime-economy". The concept of the "nickel-and-dime-economy" was coined by Barbara Ehrenreich in her book "Nickel & Dimed: Undercover in Low-wage USA" as a description of an economy with many full-time employed people for wages at the poverty-level.[6]

In this book, I look at the nickel-and-dime economy from a market and production perspective. I therefore define the "nickel-and-dime-economy" as a developed economy that has adapted through fierce price competition and mass production to a prolonged period of stagnating or even falling incomes of a significant part of the population. Stagnating or falling mass income, a significant low-wage-sector and rising income inequality create, as will be explained in chapter 4, attractive markets for low-priced mass products. Falling or stagnating prices for these products have enabled many people to maintain their material standard of living despite stagnating or falling incomes. However, this has a high economic and social price, for example a further increasing low-wage-sector, further deindustrialization and an exploitation of low wages and low social and environmental standards in developing countries.

Environmentally, the "nickel-and-dime-economy" is a real disaster. The often extreme price competition provides strong incentives to produce in an unsustainable way. It also divides society environmentally into "top" and "bottom". At the top, there is an increasing number of non-working rich and people with decent incomes. They can afford sustainable consumption and often benefit from public subsidies for sustainable development, e.g. for photovoltaic installations on the roofs of their houses. At the bottom there is a much bigger number of working poor and other people with low incomes who cannot afford sustainable consumption unless they are willing to pay for it with declining living standards. For these people, sustainable development is nothing they have in common with the more wealthy people. On the contrary, sustainable development disconnects these people and groups even more from the general development of prosperity in Western societies. This amounts to an ecological division of society and conflicts that are difficult to resolve. This is all the more true as the division is exploited by populist parties and movements in several Western countries. In some countries, this leads to a polarization of society, which massively endangers the political ability of these countries to act.[7]

In addition to these many smaller and larger conflicts, sustainable development in Western societies is massively hampered by a second factor. This factor consists in the fact that environmental sustainability is not only a common good but also a collective good. In the social sciences, a collective good is a good that can be consumed without contributing to production costs. If the environmental condition in a city, a region or a whole country is improved by some measures, everyone who lives there and every company that is located there benefits. People and actors, thus, may enjoy better environmental quality even if they do not contribute to its production or even act to the detriment of the environment. They may, for example, benefit from a reduction of fine dust pollution at their place of residence while still driving an SUV. This is known as "free-riding".[8]

Free-riding in environmental protection is not a matter of a few "bad" people, but one of most people in society – not always, but again and again. It is rarely done out of ignorance of environmental problems, but rather out of convenience, for financial reasons, lack of meaningful alternatives and similar, understandable reasons. In many cities, for example, people can still get from place to place more rapidly by car than by public transport. In rural areas there is often no realistic alternative to the car. Products from organic farming are often much more expensive than other products and for some households simply too expensive. It is easier for older people to get into an SUV than into a smaller vehicle.

For most people, even for those who care about the environment, free-riding is psychologically easy. It seems to be justified by the argument that one's own behavior is irrelevant to the world climate or the national consumption of resources – whether one goes into town by car instead of tram does not even change the local climate, not to speak of the global climate. This is absolutely right from the point of view of the individual, but since many people act in the same way, the environment suffers greatly. The easy option of free riding by people and organizations limits the promotion of sustainability through spontaneous action. It limits, for example, the environmentally conscious behavior of consumers and producers which could help to drive sustainable development via market forces. Likewise, it is not conducive to broad civil involvement in sustainable development.

This leads to a somewhat paradoxical situation: although environmental sustainability is in the common interest of the whole society, the chances that it emerges spontaneously within society are currently fairly low. Rather, it depends strongly, and probably too much, on government regulation whether it will be attained in a reasonable time or not. This is not a very hopeful perspective because governments often fail at this task. In order to make the common good a really common good, governments would have to set understandings and rules for sustainable development that are widely accepted and followed because they really and tangibly benefit most people in society. These rules must therefore ensure that the distribution of costs and benefits is perceived to be fair. To achieve this, government must stand up to many powerful special interest groups which it, however, rarely does. A special interest group is a group of people or other actors who have particular interests and seek to influence public policy in their favor. The opposite are general interest groups. These are groups which act in favor of interests which are widely shared in society.

This points to a core problem for Western democracies and their current institutions. Well-organized special interest groups, for example the lobbying associations of the automobile industry in Germany or the arms lobby in the USA, and other powerful actors, for example banks which are considered as systemically important, enjoy a political influence that goes far beyond their economic and social significance. In environmental policy this influence leads to a miserable failure of government to bring together different interests in such a way that broadly accepted and sustainable solutions emerge. It is much more likely that solutions are either highly controversial or they are lazy compromises that solve neither problems nor conflicts.

From what has been said in this part, a conclusion emerges that may be disappointing, but must be faced if we really want to achieve sustainable development. The conclusion is: In Western societies, sustainable development is a process of social transformation that is structurally hindered and perhaps even prevented by many smaller and larger conflicts on one side and by a lack of social commitment on the other. This implies that if we want to achieve sustainable development in Western societies, we have to change this process. To do this, however, we first have to understand this process properly.

The Logic of Social Transformation

At the end of the nineteenth century, the British philosopher Herbert Spencer, one of the founding fathers of sociology, developed a theory that conceived of social development as an evolutionary process. He understood evolution as a fundamental cosmic principle underlying nature and society. His theory was similar to that of Charles Darwin, which emerged around the same time. Just as different variants of a species develop in nature through mutation, different structures or understandings emerge in social systems from social interactions. And just as variants of species are more or less successful in the struggle for survival, some variants of structures or understandings make societies more successful in economic, military, cultural or other terms and are adopted by less successful societies. Some examples: At the beginning of the nineteenth century, Prussia carried out an administrative reform, which created a uniform administration with legal rule and a clear hierarchy. The success of the reform led to many states adopting it. In the 1980s, New Public Management was introduced in New Zealand, the Netherlands and Switzerland, where private sector management techniques were adopted in public administration. This, too, was adopted in whole or in part by many states. Another example: The Japanese automobile company Toyota developed a new management system in the second half of the last century called lean management and lean production. This system increased the competitiveness of Toyota significantly. Therefore, it was adopted by many other companies. Other examples of social evolution are the establishment of successful designs within fashion or the enforcement of theories in scientific competition.[9]

Spencer differs, however, in one crucial point from Darwin's theory. He recognized over a hundred years ago that animals are at the mercy of evolution while humans can anticipate it, react to it differently, learn from it, actively adapt to it and act strategically on it. There is an example of this that is very instructive for any strategy to change society.

In the 1960s and 1970s, in a number of countries, predominantly young people rebelled against the culture and structures of that time. This development was not uniform, but rather varied considerably across countries. The common ground was some vision of a more open, egalitarian, livable and sustainable society with high quality of life, social and cultural diversity, good working conditions, more political participation, better education and more self-realization. These movements have changed a lot. While they did not create an ideal world, they did create one which justified hopes that the world, at any rate Western world, is on the way to livable and sustainable societies. Western societies experienced a period of prosperity in which more people get educated, more people get white-collar jobs and more blue-collar workers become skilled and enjoy a similar living standard and lifestyle as white-collar workers. The middle class has grown and society has developed into a middle-class society. New opportunities opened up for an environmentally more sustainable development of economy and society. Western societies became more open and tolerant.

Much has been accomplished in these years, but half a century later, the good departure came at least for the time being to a bad end. Most Western societies exclude a large part of their population from the aim of a livable and sustainable society. For many people in Western societies, living and working conditions have not improved, but rather deteriorated. In addition, racism, xenophobia, misogyny and homophobia are once again on the rise in the USA and the European Union. Civil rights are also not looking good in some countries.

In Spencer's approach to social evolution, there is a sobering explanation for this. The movements of the 1960s and 1970s were tumultuous and impatient. They forced many changes with narrow majorities and failed to carry many people along. Some parties and other organizations who were defeated in the respective majority decisions accepted some of these changes only formally or not all. Many of the people that were not carried along did not accept the majority decision, but aligned with opposing parties and organizations, became radicalized, lost trust in the established institutions, withdrew from society into social environments with like-minded people, or simply fell into political lethargy. This has resulted in resistance against the changes and in building up counter movements. It also has created lasting social divisions that have been exploited by populist or fundamentalist movements and become effective in a resurgence of overt racism, xenophobia, misogyny and homophobia in many countries today.[10]

This case offers an important lesson for all those who are actively committed to sustainable development: If these actors fail to take most people along, they may end up like the movements of the 1960s and 1970s. They will build up so much lethargy, free-riding, resistance and countermovements which in the end make them fail – and with them sustainable development.

Most modern evolutionary theories in economics and sociology have not incorporated Spencer's argument but straightforwardly follow the Darwinian model. This applies particularly to the bulk of evolutionary theory in economics. A certain exception is Niklas Luhmann's theory of social system, the leading sociological theory of evolution. It differs from Darwin's model in one important point: While with Darwin the environment decides which species will prevail, in Luhmann's theory the selection of the best solutions is done by the respective social system itself. Whether a new norm or value, some new structure or a new understanding prevails in a society is determined by the structures, principles and communication that exist in that society at any given time. Societies are self-referential and self-organized. In a conservative rural milieu, for example, more open views on sexuality or gender are unlikely to be accepted but will rather provoke a reinforcement of fundamental religious values whereas in a secularized urban milieu the same views may gain strong support. To put it much more simply: Societies change out of themselves. This is also the view of the only economic theory which builds upon Spencer, namely the theory of Ulrich Witt. I return to this theory in detail below.[11]

This is a central insight for our problem. It is the theoretical basis for the argument that the real problem arises from the fact that sustainable development must be achieved within the prevailing economic, social and political structures that have hitherto been unsustainable and that inhibit or even prevent sustainable development. Aimed social changes have to emerge from these structures and their underlying principles. This is the meaning of social evolution. In the relevant research, this is also referred to as path dependency. The existing structures do not allow for arbitrary developments but limit future developments to a more or less broad corridor of possibilities. This is, as the above examples indicate, not only a question of objective conditions, but even more one of the values, behavioral patterns, interest structures, power relations, understandings and behavior that are associated with current structures and their underlying principles. The latter, more than the former, are the cause of the many conflicts associated with sustainable development.

This situation points to a controversial issue that comes up again and again in environmental discourse, namely the question of whether sustainable development is possible at all in a capitalist society. In an evolutionary view, the question is wrongly posed. In any society whose development is not yet sustainable, there is a fundamental danger that existing structures will prevent sustainable development altogether. But the structures of modern societies are in a constant state of flux and are, in principle, also changeable in the sense of sustainable development. The interesting question is therefore not whether, but how sustainable development can be initiated and realized in a particular society or type of society. In terms of sustainable development, the most unfavorable answer to this question is that necessary structural changes require a revolution, because in the complex modern societies revolutions are particularly difficult, protracted and unpredictable. The much better answer is to identify major structural impediments and find ways to remove them. Part of this answer also consists in identifying structures and contradictions in the system in question that can be exploited to initiate and drive change. This can be illustrated by two topics that play an important role both in the discussion of capitalism and sustainability and for the sustainability strategy proposed in this book. The topics are growth and technological progress.

In 1972, Club of Rome published a widely recognized study which argued that mankind would reach the absolute environmental limits of growth within 100 years with its way of production and life which is to be precise, primarily the capitalist or Western-inspired way. Since then economic growth has played a prominent role in environmental debates. This has made the compatibility of capitalism and growth an important topic in these debates. It is often argued that capitalism is associated with growth constraints that lead to a systematic exploitation of nature. It remains to be seen whether this is really a compelling economic law of capitalism. But is unmistakable and undeniable that there exists a close, perhaps even inseparable link between capitalism and growth. It is equally obvious and undeniable that so far economic growth has always been accompanied by growing consumption of natural resources and increasing damage to nature. It is, however, precisely this connection between growth and resource consumption that provides a strong starting point for initiating and advancing sustainable development in capitalist societies. The starting point is to decouple growth from resource consumption. Decoupling means that growth does not increase resource consumption. This is only possible if resources are used much more productively than is the case hitherto. This may sound quite simple and easy, but it is an ambitious undertaking. I will further discuss this in the last part of this chapter.[12]

The vehicle for decoupling growth from resource consumption is technological progress. In an evolutionist view, technological progress is the real driver of economic growth in capitalist societies. It constantly creates new ways of satisfying human needs and solving social or technical problems. It also constantly creates new opportunities to develop new products and open up new markets, as well as to improve products and production processes and to increase productivity. Last not least, it stimulates often fierce innovation-competition. In order to keep up in this process, companies have to invest in innovation and in new equipment. All this generates various opportunities to grow and to increase profits. For employees, this often means new job opportunities and wage increases. This further drives growth. Since human needs as well as social problems hardly seem to be limited, these opportunities will exist for a long time – if and only if growth can be decoupled from consumption of natural resources over that time.

The growth impetus of technological progress is part of the strategy. The idea is to turn sustainable development into a growth engine of capitalist societies and by this exploit the capitalist logic to reach sustainable development and the necessary structural changes in the capitalist societies. In the end, this approach may lead to the emergence of structures that decouple the capitalist economy from growth, at least for the next years and decades. This is very important because at least for the next years and decades growth is necessary to achieve sustainable development of capitalist societies. It is necessary for the solution of another strong impediment to sustainable development which is embedded in capitalist structures and their global outreach, namely the high inequality within Western societies and between rich and poor countries. It is also necessary for the elimination of the "nickel-and-dime economy" which in Western societies is associated with high inequality. Last not least, it is necessary for the poorer countries to develop their economies to a level which provides decent livelihoods to all their citizens. We will discuss this question in more detail in the following chapters.

The strategy just outlined, like any other strategy of social change, can only be planned to a limited extent because both the conditions in which it must be applied and its effects can only be predicted to a limited extent. It is even less possible to predict how resilient the capitalist system will be to the strategy. The systematic use of technological progress to decouple growth and resource consumption, for example, links sustainable development to a transformation process that has been underway for some time, namely the development of industrial societies into knowledge societies.

A knowledge society is a society in which knowledge is "becoming the sole factor of production, sidelining both capital and labor". This may, as we will discuss further down, lead to a more or less far-reaching displacement of structural principles of capitalism by structural principles of the knowledge society. This, in turn, could permanently change the role and profits of different forms of capital and create significant divisions within capitalism, e.g. between institutional investors or venture capitalists on one side and people that "invest" money short-timed just to increase their fortunes or speculators on the other one. But it is also possible that existing economic and social structures impede transformation to the knowledge society. Another example: the technologies from which the necessary radical innovations are to spring, namely digitization, biotechnology and microsystems technology, may cause massive job losses in established capitalist corporate structures, but at the same time they may stimulate new forms of enterprise, such as cooperatives or networks of freelancers, and new forms of work and employment. This may lead to a fundamental change in the role of wage labor and thus in the current structures of capitalist societies. It may even lead to a society in which work plays a minor role. Yet, it may also enhance inequality, creating a sharp cleavage between those members of society which have regular work and those that do not and provoke massive conflict. We will discuss this further too in chapter 4.[13]

What will really happen is difficult or impossible to predict or even control. This is the nature of social evolution and is not difficult to understand. The evolution of societies and other social systems is influenced every day by many actions and communications. Many of these actions and communications trigger other actions and communications in response, which in turn prompt responses. The individual actions and communications and the reactions they generate are probably very predictable and perhaps even controllable. However, their interaction is no longer explainable when it extends over a considerable spatial or temporal distance. Then it becomes decisive when, where and in which constellation something happens.

A funny example: you have an important appointment one morning (a job interview, an exam or an important business deal). Before you leave your apartment, you quickly drink an expresso while standing up. The cup falls out of your hand. You quickly clean up the broken pieces and the mess, leaving your apartment a minute or two later than usual and narrowly miss your bus. But that seems to be no problem since the next bus departs five minutes later. Unfortunately, the next bus gets caught in a traffic jam that was caused minutes earlier by a distracted professor who stalled the engine of his car in the middle of an important intersection because he or she was preoccupied with his or her new book. In the end, you miss your appointment. You miss the job you applied for or the deal you wanted to close or you lose an entire semester because of the missed exam. If you had not dropped your cup, or if the professor had been at the intersection just a few minutes later, everything would have been very different.

How complicated social evolution is can only be understood properly if one departs from the Darwinian model and falls back on Spencer's model and the theory of the German economist Ulrich Witt. Witt's theory systematically builds upon Spencer's recognition that human actors can understand and anticipate selections, evade them and influence evolution. It argues that the basis of these capabilities is human learning. Learning generates new solutions to problems that form variations in the social system. In the Darwinian model, variations cause selections. The variations are either adopted or rejected by the system. Afterwards, the system temporarily regains a certain stability. In Witt's model, however, variations do not provoke real selections, but new learning and new variations. Social systems thus remain permanently in flux.

The difference between Darwinism and Witt's theory can be illustrated by a prime example of an evolutionary approach in the social sciences, namely the concept of a process of creative destruction which the Austrian-American Economist Joseph A. Schumpeter introduced in 1942. In this concept Schumpeter argues that innovations which succeed on the market give companies the chance to generate higher profits than less innovative companies while non-innovative companies run the risk of disappearing from the market and going bankrupt. Innovations thus have the same function as mutations in biological innovation: They create better solutions and stronger companies and destroy weaker ones. Schumpeter's model follows the usual Darwinian approach. In the perspective of Witt's theory the case is different. Companies and human actors in general are not at the mercy of the process of creative destruction. Even if a novelty is successfully launched it the market, it does not necessarily force established products out of the market. Rather, competitors of the innovative firm may respond to the innovation in a variety of different ways. They may simply reduce the price of their "old" product and make it attractive to price-conscious buyers who do not necessarily need the latest technology, they may add a number of different features to their "old" product in order to make it more competitive to the new one, they give their product a particularly smart design, which is especially attractive to certain groups of buyers or invest in the development of a more advanced product. If they know that their competitor is about to introduce a novel product, they may even try to get ahead of him with their own innovation. Depending on when, who does what, this will be reflected quite differently in market development and the competitiveness, profits and risks of the players in the market.[14]

As this example shows, in Witt's view social evolution amounts to a continuous process of individual and social learning. I adopt this view, but go one step back. I consider that the basis of learning is knowledge and put knowledge at the core of social evolution. The minor reason is that knowledge can be better captured than learning. The major reason is that the focus on knowledge provides a richer understanding of social evolution. The point I make is that knowledge not only stimulates learning and opens up new possibilities of action, but also creates new uncertainty. As I explain in chapter 6, new knowledge also challenges previous certainties. Many actors react to this not by learning, but by rejecting or ignoring this knowledge. This inhibits, for example, technological progress or the development of public awareness of the urgent need to drive sustainable development. In short: What drives social evolution is not only learning enabled by new knowledge, but also non-learning or refusal to learn triggered by new knowledge.

This problem is becoming more virulent since the middle of the last century, because since that time the production of new knowledge has become more rapid, broader and more diverse. This is due, on the one hand, to an enormous expansion of science, which is reflected, among other things, in the fact that 90% of all scientists who have ever lived are alive today. On the other hand, it is also the result of the progressive digitization of research. This has created a wealth of new possibilities for scientific research, including much better capabilities for data processing, modelling and simulation of complex cases and miniaturization of laboratories. We will discuss some of these in the chapter 3.[15]

The speed, breadth and diversity of modern knowledge production accelerates individual and collective learning because it provides a continuous stream of new knowledge. This creates new opportunities for action and, above all, opportunities to solve previously unsolved problems. This is the promise of the knowledge society for sustainable development.

But new possibilities for action also pose variations in social systems and drive their evolution. The many new possibilities for action that modern knowledge production continuously provides boost the dynamics of evolution and make transformation processes, specifically sustainable development, even less manageable and controllable than they already are. This often motivates economic, social and political actors to stick to established routines and, by this, to miss out on the opportunities offered by technological progress. It is the risk of the knowledge society for sustainable development – and the challenge for its governance.[16]

A Changing Context: Knowledge Society

The great economic importance of knowledge is certainly nothing new. Even the Phoenicians would not have risen to become the leading trading power without their superior geographical and nautical knowledge, and the Chinese economy was also built on superior knowledge. The Industrial Revolution created an economy that was systematically based on the conversion of knowledge into technology, and in which knowledge was, of course, the central factor of production. Thus knowledge has always been of crucial economic importance. So what makes the knowledge society fundamentally different from the industrial society?

Peter F. Drucker argues that the use of knowledge underwent a fundamental transformation after 1750, triggered by the speed and scope of knowledge diffusion. In the first phase of this transformation, knowledge was systematically applied to tools, products, and processes. This led to the industrial revolution. The inventions on which the industrial revolution was based, unlike earlier inventions, did not remain isolated, but formed a technology that rapidly spread to all sectors of the economy. Geographically, too, the technology spread far beyond its countries of origin. The Industrial Revolution represented nothing less than "the transformation by technology of society and civilization worldwide". After 1880, the transformation of knowledge use entered a second phase – knowledge was applied to the analysis and design of work. This phase was pioneered by the American engineer Frederick W. Taylor who created a system of management, Taylorism (named after him), which was widely applied in manufacturing. From this developed the productivity revolution, which massively improved the standard of living of broad segments of the population through higher wages, more leisure time and more health care. In the third phase of this development, which leads to the knowledge society, this changes fundamentally – knowledge becomes the central production factor. Knowledge production evolves into an activity which is distinct from the production of goods and services. Even more, it is the activity which dominates the entire production and its organization and to which all other economic activities are directed or by which they are determined. Knowledge production thus takes over the role of industrial production in industrial society. But that is not all: knowledge production is becoming independent – knowledge is produced to produce more knowledge. The knowledge society accumulates knowledge like the industrial society accumulates capital.

This implies nothing less than that the knowledge society in a developed state could become a truly dematerialized society. A dematerialized society is one which applies knowledge to produce its goods and services with a minimal use of material and energy. Dematerialization fits to the knowledge society's own logic, the logic of knowledge accumulation. Just as capital loses its value and function if it is not exploited economically, knowledge also loses its value and function if it is not exploited economically. The use and waste of natural resources certainly is a problem which offers ample opportunities for the exploitation of knowledge (and the investment of capital). If these opportunities are used well, the knowledge society will become a dematerialized society. However, this is only a probable, not an inevitable development. I will come back on this in the third chapter.

In Peter F. Drucker's view, the knowledge society is also a post-capitalist society. He justifies this on the one hand with the central role of knowledge, but on the other hand also with the fact that the capitalists lose the power of disposal over the means of production, because they no longer have the most important means of production, knowledge. Instead, it is down to the "knowledge workers" themselves, i.e. the people who create the knowledge or can use it productively. They can, in principle at least, take their knowledge with them at any time.

People who can productively apply knowledge are an important part of the knowledge worker class. The enormous knowledge machinery that was built up primarily in the industrial age and brought to a high level of efficiency with the help of modern information and communications technology is so productive that the knowledge it generates often exceeds the ability of business and society to use knowledge productively. This is particularly true when it comes to linking knowledge and technology from different disciplines. This poses the risk of a growing innovation gap, i.e., a gap between what is technically possible in terms of innovation and what actually happens.

This situation is not very dramatic but changes the innovation dynamic and market development of the capitalist economies significantly. Whereas in the industrial economy both are driven by technology, in the knowledge society successful innovation depends quite decisively on the parallel development of markets and technology. Research-intensive companies often can only recoup their high costs of research and development if they build up the market for the products parallel to product development and are on the market much earlier than their competitors. In the knowledge society, hence, economic development is not only driven by technology, but it is also increasingly pulled by the market. Market development is thus an important component of the sustainability strategy proposed in this book.

The central role of knowledge in the knowledge society leads to a new distribution problem. The problem concerns access to knowledge and education. Access to knowledge and education is decisive for the opportunities and social chances of individuals and whole families. Their knowledge determines the economic and social options for action of individuals and other actors. Even more important than knowledge is access to education – and lifelong education at that. Education imparts and renews the knowledge that individuals need to remain capable of acting in the knowledge society and to preserve their social opportunities. This is not just an abstract principle. In the coming years and decades, the digitalization of the economy will destroy a great many jobs, as we will discuss in more detail in the fourth chapter. This will not only affect unskilled jobs, but also highly skilled jobs. This will force many people to acquire new, not necessarily higher, qualifications and the knowledge required to do so. Education must not only provide them with knowledge, but above all with the motivation and ability to learn. Access to knowledge and education is also becoming an existential issue for companies, especially for small and medium-sized enterprises, as well as for other organizations. Their ability to act also depends on their knowledge and the knowledge of their employees.

Last not least, access to knowledge and education is also of great social importance. This is especially true with regard to social cohesion and the ability of societies to organize learning and creativity, to exploit the educational potential of their members and to create and maintain a strong human capital. Pointedly stated, it is an existential condition for the maintenance of a democratic, open and pluralist society. Significant inequality of access to knowledge and education in the long run changes social power structures and limits the unfolding of social diversity in social decision-making. That makes, as the German sociologist, Nico Stehr, points out, access to knowledge to a key problem of governance of Western societies.[17]

The new distribution problem of Western societies is fundamentally different from the traditional distribution problem of capitalist societies regarding income and wealth. An undesirable inequality of income and wealth can be solved in the short term, using incomes policy. The elimination of unequal access to knowledge and education, on the other hand, requires investments and changes in education which need years and even a decade or two to carry into effect. Worse still, if unequal access to knowledge and education is lasting, entrenched structures are likely to emerge. Families inherit low educational opportunities over generations. Neighborhoods, towns and cities with a large non-educated population may get poor performing schools with low standing. Such structures massively impede and delay the solution of educational problems.

As if these were not enough problems, there is another one that is particularly important in terms of governance. This is a new kind of uncertainty problem. We have already spoken above about the fact that the knowledge society, through its rapid and broad production of knowledge, is constantly opening up new possibilities for action, and is thus always in flux and difficult to predict. This situation manifests a new problem of uncertainty. In the past, uncertainty problems were defined by a lack of information and knowledge. Therefore, they were in principle solvable via more knowledge production and information processing. In the knowledge society, uncertainty is no longer a problem of a lack of knowledge, but on the contrary one of too much knowledge. Therefore, acquiring more knowledge does not solve but may rather aggravate the new problem.

The rapid and broad knowledge production of the knowledge economy is only possible through great specialization. Modern research and development is a complex social process that is organized in a strong division of labor and is almost inevitably highly specialized at the top. The result is that knowledge has become knowledges, as Peter Drucker puts it, or in simple prose that knowledge breaks down into specialized fields. While this statement is correct, it is misleading. Science and research are undeniably highly specialized, but as specialization grew, so did the understanding of the need for inter-disciplinary linkage. In the second half of the last century, inter-disciplinary research increased at universities and an applied transdisciplinary mode of knowledge production developed in the interplay between university and business research. Nowadays, important advances of science and technology are the result of linking different fields of knowledge and technology. The great advances in biotechnology, for example, would not have been possible without the linkage with information technology and microsystems engineering. At least in research, there are many specialized knowledges, but they are multiply interlinked with each other.

However, the existence of many "knowledges" creates two important practical problems. The first problem is that policymakers and administrators are often overwhelmed by the linkage of different knowledges needed to solve more complex problems and are dependent on external help. This help often comes from specialized organizations, like independent government agencies, think-tanks, lobby organizations and NGOs. This creates strong dependencies of public policy and public administration on special interests. It also promotes a strong segmentation of politics and administration. The second problem is that the many "knowledges" severely hamper development of a widely accepted understanding of the evolution of modern societies and their technological drivers. Not only does it allow self-styled gurus to spread their wild "theories," but it also permits serious scientists to flood society with a cacophony of different assessments, predictions, and explanations. The debate about climate change in the US and other countries and the Covid-19 pandemic provide illustrative examples.

This makes it clear once again that the transformation of the industrial society into a knowledge society, like every social development, has not only a sunny side, but also a dark side. On the sunny side, it opens up many opportunities for sustainable development. The enormous knowledge production provides the knowledge to decouple growth from the consumption of non-renewable natural resources at least for a long time, probably even permanently. The transformation to a knowledge society changes the role of capital and labor and thus softens structural barriers to sustainable development or perhaps even eliminates them altogether in the long run. On the dark side, however, it creates of new distributional conflicts and new insecurity, as well as a great deal of turbulence in social development overall. All this may block many of the opportunities on the sunny side and reinforce the obstacles to sustainable development in the established structures of Western society and capitalism. This underlines that governance is the key problem of sustainable development in Western societies.

The Key Problem: Governance

Governance generally means the control and regulation of processes. In the social sciences and in politics, there are different definitions and understandings of governance which I will not discuss here. In a widely shared definition which I also apply in this book, governance means the entirety of forms and devices for coordinating social action and influencing social developments. This is much more than just government. In addition to government, it also encompasses markets, organized forms of self-organization in civil society and, as a large framework, culture.[18]

In the social sciences, the concept of self-organization describes the principle that the development of social systems, unlike biological systems, is not controlled by the environment but by the systems themselves. Here, I mean something more concrete, namely that members of the civil society form organizations to solve common or other social problems. These are, for example, cooperatives for the management of water or common land, civic associations for local development and other purposes, and, last not least non-governmental organizations (NGOs). Culture here refers to the informal understandings and rules spontaneously emerging from social interactions. These rules and understandings accomplish a large part of social coordination. Nevertheless, culture is often neglected as form of governance.

The focus on governance rather than on government is particularly important with regard to sustainable development because it draws attention to the many ways of promoting sustainable development that exist outside politics and the state. Only the systematic use of all these possibilities will achieve sustainable development no matter how strong the state and no matter how powerful politics. This is what previous experience with climate policy, and indeed the climate policy of almost all countries, has taught us. The inclusion of other forms of coordination offers particularly good opportunities for the Western countries to achieve not only climate neutrality but sustainable development by the middle of this century after all. In this way, they can mobilize and bundle many social forces and thus compensate for or avoid government failure. Moreover, they may use the great creative potential of a pluralistic and open society.

A society is pluralistic when people with different ideas, lifestyles and interests as well as different ethnic and cultural backgrounds can live together reasonably peaceful and with tolerance. A society is open when this diversity is not reflected in the formation of largely segregated groups, but in which different social and cultural groups regularly interact and communicate with each other. If you look at such a society in the light of the theory of evolution outlined above, you can understand why it has a great potential for creativity. Social and cultural diversity is repeatedly reflected in the fact that people from different social and cultural groupings see things and events differently, evaluate them differently and react to them differently. In an open society, this constantly generates variations and triggers new learning processes. As we have discussed above, this always gives rise to new possibilities for action and new solutions to problems. That is the creative potential of pluralistic societies.

However, the same theory also tells us that pluralist societies have high potential for social and political conflict because any variation may create a variety of different and often inconsistent responses in society. These many responses are adopted and processed differently in politics, in markets and by companies and other organizations. This leads to very different reactions from these actors. This makes pluralistic societies difficult to govern. This goes far beyond the governance problems associated with the rapid change and uncertainty of the modern knowledge society and represents a specific and fundamental governance problem of pluralist societies.

Development of these societies is permanently influenced by a large variety of different actors with different ideologies or religious beliefs, languages, ethnicities, genders, social or regional backgrounds, and political orientations or simply with different educations, incomes, professions, jobs and lifestyles. All this is associated with an even larger variety of different interests, views and objectives because all these people act in a number of different social contexts and social settings, such as the family, a workplace, a church, party or other organizations. In all these contexts they act under different conditions and constraints. This brings their values, understandings and interests to bear in very different ways. A person who actively engages in environmental protection in her or his spare time or in her or his political party, can behave quite differently in her or his job and make conscious decisions that are environmentally harmful but bring many benefits to the company where she or he works.

In sociology, this situation is described with a term from the theater world, namely with the concept of social role. As in the theater, every social role is associated with certain behavioral requirements. The requirements of the different roles an actor plays do not always fit together. It is also like this with social roles. The fact that people in a modern society play a variety of different social roles increases the diversity of human action in a pluralist society significantly. This makes social development often into a social odyssey.[19]

On his journey back from the Trojan War to Ithaca, Odysseus (in English also named Ulysses), king of Ithaca, and the hero of Homer's ancient Greek epic poem, had to overcome many unforeseen and dangerous adventures. The journey turned out to be a great wandering. Odysseus lost all his companions and was travelling ten years until he finally reached Ithaca. Therefore, odyssey become a synonym for an epic wandering.

Social development has much in common with such a journey. There are a lot of unforeseen and unpredictable events too. But social development is much more complicated. Odysseus had a clear destination (his home island Ithaca) and a loyal crew under his command. Social development has no clear goal and the journey has no real end. Society is not a ship with single command, but rather a large fleet of sailing vessels with many different ships. The ships' captains often have their own, different interests and aims. Even if they share the target of the fleet, many of the captains believe (sometimes rightly) that they know better than the supreme command how to reach it and act accordingly. The supreme command has only limited power. Chances that the whole fleet finally reaches its planned destination are, therefore, usually quite low.

In the view of a theory that is still accepted in politics and political science known as the theory of pluralism, the social diversity of Western societies is no problem for the political institutions of Western democracies. The theory argues that the many different social interests are in political competition for political services and benefits. Through competition, they restrict each other and ensure a balance of interests which is widely accepted. This leads to a widely accepted democratic equilibrium. Pluralism theory does not assume that social interests are equal in terms of power, but it does assume that power and power resources are so broadly distributed in modern democratic societies that all interest groups mutually limit each other.[20]

There is no more idealistic way to gloss over one of the most problematic processes of modern democracies. The influence of organized interest groups is generally out of proportion to their social importance and strength. Interest groups which represent a very small proportion of the population with very special interests are often much more influential than groups representing rather general interests of larger parts of the population. Moreover, organized interest intermediation rarely balances different interests and hardly ever leads to widely accepted solutions. There are two main reasons for this: First, a highly imbalanced organizational capacity of general and special interests, and, second, a lack of competition.

Since Mancur Olson's famous book "The Logic of Collective Action" we know that the special interests of small, privileged groups in society can be organized much more efficiently than the general interests of large parts of society. Special interest groups are therefore usually much better able to mobilize their resources and networks, and more successful in the pursuit of their interests in everyday politics. Competition between interest groups is not or even cannot be organized in a comprehensive and systematic way, as is at least theoretically the case with markets. Rather, interest groups operate in everyday politics mostly without explicit competition. They are not dealing with the government as a whole, but with selected politicians and a small part of bureaucracy. They operate to a large degree in comfortable isolation.[21]

High fragmentation of organized interest intermediation does not mean that there is little conflict of interest. On the contrary, it is precisely these structures that through their mode of operation permanently generate a high degree of dissatisfaction and conflict. The assertion of special interests in segmented political and administrative structures generally leads to decisions that ignore many aspects and interrelationships of issues and, thus, violate the interests of groups that are not involved in the decision-making. Because of the fragmented structures, this only becomes noticeable to the "aggrieved" groups with a time lag, but then often provokes legal and political activities to change or reverse the relevant decision. If these activities are effective they are likely to provoke opposition from other groups. In this way, it is often difficult for government to act consistently over time.

This is illustrated by the case of German government subsidies for renewable energy. As determined in the German renewable energy act, the subsidies were fully financed by a levy on consumers' electricity bill. This has resulted in increased energy costs for households and companies. This quickly led to strong opposition by different interest groups. As a result, the act was revised but the revisions met opposition from other groups and the act was revised again – which then created new opposition. To cut a long story short: over a period of 20 years, the relevant act was revised about ten times.

The counterpart to the specialization of organized interests is the specialization of the modern bureaucracy, which makes the strong fragmentation of lobbying possible in the first place. Even though bureaucratic agencies are formally integrated into the hierarchy of the state apparatus, they lead a considerable life of their own due to their specialization. This is especially true of their communication and knowledge processing, which is generally highly selective. With the exception of a few overarching themes and activities, coordination among the agencies is rather weak and formal. Only a few countries, like New Zealand and Switzerland, have so far managed to establish a reasonably effective goal-oriented management and control of their bureaucracies.

A similar situation exists in parties and parliaments. The parties and their parliamentary groups have a certain basic ideological or programmatic orientation, but within this orientation there is usually considerable scope for groupings within the party, fractions in the parliamentary group or for individual legislators to represent special interests. The parliamentary committees, most of which are also specialized, provide favorable platforms for the deputies to do so.

In the institutional structures of modern Western democracies we, thus, find no strong and effective element of checking and balancing social interests and of reaching widely accepted political decisions. This is no surprise because these institutions are not designed for broad acceptance, but for formal legitimacy. Theoretically, they are recognized because they have come about according to rules that are recognized in society but not because of their content. This makes a big difference: decisions that are formally recognized are also respected only formally. Most social and political actors do not disregard or violate them obviously. But this does not prevent many of them from using all opportunities to circumvent the decision, to have it changed or to annul it – as we have already noted above in relation to lobbies.

For much of the history of Western democracies to date, formal legitimacy has been a major achievement over pre-democratic states. It made rule dependent on the consent of the ruled. But today, this is no longer enough. The established model of democracy in its different parliamentarian or presidential variants is coming under massive pressure from three sides at the same time.

First, the formal legitimacy that the model confers on political decisions is no longer sufficient to ensure that the decisions are actually accepted, followed and perhaps even actively supported. Apart from the fact that this leads to attempts by many actors to circumvent, change or overturn the relevant decision, there is always the danger that as a consequence of low acceptance of political decisions attitudes toward the political elites or even "the system" will deteriorate and that trust in both will be lost. This is the soil on which populist currents thrive.

Second, politically legitimized decision-makers and their administrations often get torn between the complexity of the factual matter to be regulated and the complexity of the social interests involved. This often leads them into a complexity trap. In order to do justice to as many influential interests as possible, they increasingly differentiate rules. But this also opens up more and more possibilities for interpreting the meaning of rules in connection with other rules. In the case of laws and regulations, this creates a lot of work and opportunities for courts to exert influence, and in the case of contracts between the state and a private company, for arbitration courts. What courts and arbitration tribunals decide usually does not make things any easier.

Third, important social projects, such as sustainable development or the transformation of the industrial society into a knowledge society, require the broadest possible pooling of social forces. As many relevant actors as possible must be involved with their interests in such a way that they work of their own accord toward the goal of the project. As a rule, this commitment will only exist if actors not only formally accept political decisions, but also substantially support them.

We must accept this means that the established democratic institutions of Western societies are not up to the social diversity of modern Western society, nor to its knowledge and development dynamics. They can neither cope with the many conflicts associated with pluralism nor exploit the great social learning and innovation potentials that are also linked to it. They can therefore no longer adequately cope with the factual and social complexity of social developments. They are also no longer able to meet the demands of many well-educated and committed citizens with regard to the rationality of politics and the opportunities for political participation.

The case of the Hambacher forest which we briefly discussed at the beginning of this chapter is an illustrative example. In 2015, the Paris Climate Conference decided to phase out coal by 2030 to keep global warming below 2°C. Nevertheless, the relevant authority of the German state of North Rhine-Westphalia approved further expansion of the lignite mining industry and thus also clearing of the Hambacher Forst. This resulted in the large demonstrations and counter-demonstrations mentioned at the beginning of the chapter. The state government deployed police and attempted to clear the forest. Only after an appellate court prohibited the clearing for the time being was the clearing stopped. The conflict does not end there, because lignite mining and lignite-fired power generation in the region will not end before 2038.

These are the typical back-and-forths and inconsistencies of a policy driven by different interests. Let's think about how this could have been done differently. A better way to handle the matter would be as follows: during the preparation period for the Paris Agreement, when it became clear that coal-fired power generation would have to be ended by 2030, German federal government and the governments of the affected states would have sat down with the affected companies, their workforces and suppliers, and the municipalities involved. They had worked out a plan for managing the phase-out by 2030 without major economic and social losses. The plan would have included the development of new businesses by the companies involved as well as retraining of the affected workforce. Instead, a commission was only set up in 2018 and in 2020 a law was passed that provides for high compensation payments to the affected companies but not to the workers that lose their jobs. The last coal-fired power plants are now scheduled to be shut down in 2038.

What I have described here is a case from Germany, but not a problem that is specific to Germany. Similar cases can be observed again and again in all Western democracies, especially in connection with environmental policy. It is also not just a problem of politics and policy failure, but a comprehensive governance problem. Governance of complex processes such as sustainable development or the transformation of industrial society to knowledge society cannot be the sole responsibility of government, nor can it be the sole responsibility of the market. It requires close interaction between the two and, moreover, the systematic involvement of the self-organization of civil society.

Regaining Common Grounds

In the view of the German sociologist Andreas Reckwitz the problems that we have presented in this chapter so far are not only the result of pluralism, but associated with a fundamental change in modern societies. In his book "The Society of Singularities" he argues that in modern societies the "logic of the general" has been replaced by a "logic of the particular". In simple terms, this means that social action and social structures are no longer determined by common interests and social interdependencies, but by the need of the members of society to realize themselves and by the organization of society and its economic production around this need. Singularity, in his view, is not simply a counter-current against mass society as relevant scholars have understood so far, but the society of singularity is the replacement of mass society. This also includes a structural change from mass production of functional goods to the individualized production of cultural goods, and thus from the industrial economy to a creative economy.[22]

I find this book very stimulating although I do not share its core thesis of the singularization of society. It draws attention to an important problem, namely the social consequences of a fundamental principle of Western society, the principle of individual freedom. This principle has led to individualism and the desire for self-actualization becoming important drivers of Western societies. However, individualism and the desire for self-realization are not new phenomena, nor is it new that this has always been reflected in particular products. Those who possessed the power and the material means to do so have always set themselves apart from the masses with magnificent castles, villas and other buildings, or even entire cities. One thinks, for example, of the court of the Caliph Harun-al-Raschid and of his capital city Baghdad, the extension of a small hunting lodge to the magnificent palace complex of Versailles by the French King Louis XIV or the Villa Hügel of the German industrialist Alfred Krupp and Kykuit, the villa of the American industrialist John D. Rockefeller, the first billionaire ever.

What is new is that individualism and the desire for self-realization have become a mass phenomenon. Western societies have achieved a level of prosperity that gives many, but by no means all, people the opportunity to live their individuality and realize themselves. Moreover, modern industrial mass production and the "nickel-and-dime economy" extend this opportunity to many people with modest income. Most goods that were created for the wealthier part of society to represent their singularity became and are becoming with some time lag a mass product. SUVs, designer clothes or the great vacation in distant countries are examples of this. In a few years, space flights could also become mass tourism. To put it in a nutshell: The singularity of higher-income classes trickles down to middle- and low-income classes in the form of dreams and higher desires which finally be will be serviced by the "nickel-and-dime economy".

However, as we have discussed at length in relation to the "nickel-and-dime economy", many people in Western societies and even more people in developing countries are paying a high price for this "singularity". They have to live on "nickel-and-dime" incomes or even worse on slave labor. The environment pays a no less high price. The top 10% of income earners cause more than 50% of CO_2 emissions. In this respect, singularization is a very problematic development. This is all the more true because it contains a strong moment of self-reinforcement.

The more goods with which singularity is expressed can be acquired by a broader part of society, the more people with a high need to express their singularity through material products, and who also have ample financial means to do so, have to think up something even more singular. Once it was big buildings, later luxurious cars, big yachts and private airplanes, today it must be a space flight. This in turn creates imitation effects through cheaper mass products, which further drives the process. This is associated with more and more resource consumption and environmental destruction. If Western societies would really develop to societies of singularities, they would be ecologically doomed.

Even though Western societies have not become societies of singularity, individualism and the desire for self-realization add to the problems of pluralism. They are likely to weaken common grounds. Common grounds designates the common values, understandings and rules without which even a modern society cannot function. As we will discuss in more detail in the next chapter most sociologists agree on a 150-year-old insight of the French sociologist Émile Durkheim that modern societies are no longer held together by values but by functional interdependencies. Simply speaking, this means that people depend on other people for the production of all the goods and services which they need for their livelihood. They also cannot single-handedly create the conditions which they need for a safe life.

While this is certainly true, it is both exaggerated and misleading. It is exaggerated because no society can do without some basic values that define the playing field and basic rules of the game. Just to live together and organize the production of the goods they need, they must share some basic values and understandings. People with different values cannot live together if they do not share values such as tolerance, mutual respect or individual freedom. It is misleading because people cannot functionally collaborate without common understandings of the world and of the society in which they live together. In order to organize the production of goods and services they need shared understandings of what this should be about and how the relevant decisions should be made. As I will further explain in chapter 2, sociologists call this the social construction of reality.

In the recent years and decades most Western societies have, although to a lesser or larger degree, lost common grounds. This is, as Reckwitz argues, in a large part the consequence of rising individualism and singularization. But to a probably much greater extent it is the result of much experience and information of many people with the ignoring and violating of important values, principles and understandings by many important actors. This includes many broken campaign pledges or political decisions which obviously serve the interests of some powerful groups or actors, but not the interests of the general public. It also covers recognition that important social principles such as equal opportunities or equal rights for women and men, repeatedly invoked in politics, often rarely apply in reality. Other relevant experience is that there are many small and larger problems, which politics should and could have solved long ago, but did not solve or solved only half-heartedly, such as real estate speculation and resulting housing shortage for people with lower and middle incomes in many large cities. Reports about renowned banks helping their customers to commit tax fraud or money laundering, or equally renowned automotive companies defrauding regulators and their customers with falsified emissions figures are also dysfunctional for people's trust in the validity of established values and principles. The same applies for information on many companies, even renowned ones, which offer to low-skilled workers "nickel-and-dime wages" on which they cannot live despite full-time employment. This list could probably be enlarged by most readers of this book.

Most of these events are not dramatic in terms of common grounds, but they contribute to the erosion of common grounds. This is not yet a drama in most Western societies which brings these societies to the brink of collapse. But the erosion of the common grounds is having an increasing impact, albeit to varying degrees, on the ability of Western societies to make decisions and to act. This is manifested in cleavages and polarization which render solution of social and political conflicts difficult. It is also manifested in populist movements and autocratic governments, which question or even endanger the democratic system. Last not least, it is manifested in development of parallel societies with little common grounds.

The loss of common grounds is, for the most part, emerging from a long spontaneous process and the recovering of the common grounds is likely to take a long process too. The process of recovery, however, must not completely be left to spontaneous development. Like sustainable development, it can be advanced by decentralized activity which follows Durkheim's insight on the relevance of functional interdependence for social cohesion. This approach recognizes the fact that even though Western societies are diverse and lack to a smaller or larger degree common grounds, they inevitably share many problems which they cannot solve alone. In other words: There are many cases in which people for their own good are dependent on effective collective decision-making. This provides a good gateway to bring people functionally together and to reintegrate socially diverse and individualistic societies step-by-step.

The Institutional Solution: A Deliberative Switch

In my view, the best, probably even the only way for Western societies to reach sustainable development and to master the transformation of the industrial society into a knowledge society is a deliberative switch. By a deliberative switch I mean the introduction of a strong component of deliberation into the established institutions of Western societies. The concept of deliberation describes social and political institutions and a political culture that are systematically geared to achieving broad acceptance of political decisions despite diverging interests. They can be designed in a way which allows populations to reach broad acceptance without compromising the system's ability to innovate. This is important because sustainable development requires much and often radical innovation.[23]

The guiding principle of deliberation is a rational, open and thorough debate on common problems. Available options for action should be discussed openly and reasonably in order to reach a common understanding and a widely accepted final decision or even consensus. This may sound utopian and unrealistic, but it works even in very difficult situations: Jürg Steiner, former Professor of Political Science at the University of North Carolina at Chapel Hill, together with three colleagues, has successfully conducted such discussions. These were talks between ex-guerrillas and ex-paramilitaries in Colombia, Serbs and Bosnians in Srebrenica (Bosnia-Herzegovina) and between poor inhabitants of Brazilian favelas (slums) and police officers in which an understanding between hitherto hostile groups was sought and found. Although they took place under completely different conditions, the talks that Steiner and his colleagues conducted are a model for talks on long-term, reliable activities for sustainable development.[24]

Deliberation is not a new concept; it has existed since the 1980s. The term originates from the American political scientist Joseph Bessette. The most important theoretical foundations are assigned to the German philosopher and sociologist Jürgen Habermas and the American philosopher John Rawls. Since the 1980s and 1990s, an increasing number of scholars have contributed to the theory of deliberative democracy as an alternative to the traditional theory of democracy. Similar ideas are also found in the Harvard Negotiation Project which works on the theory and practice of solution-oriented negotiation techniques.[25]

There is also considerable deliberative practice. On the level of pre-decisional discourse and of decision-making in small bodies, like the juries in the

American court system or in some parliamentary committees, such practices even have existed before the concepts of deliberation and deliberative democracy have been introduced in political science and other disciplines of social science. Switzerland has introduced a kind of deliberative format by combining the referendum with an elaborate consultation process (the "Vernehmlassung") back in 1874. The consultation was mandatory required by law and now it is even regulated by the constitution. The rule is that government or parliament must invite cantons and the municipalities as well as parties and interest associations to give their opinion on drafts of constitutional amendments, new laws and other decisions of major importance. Even actors who are not invited, including ordinary citizens, may submit an opinion. The Federal Council or a parliamentary commission must consider and weight these and draw up a proposal that meets with the broadest possible approval. This procedure is closely related to Switzerland's direct democracy, especially the referendum. It is intended to ensure that laws and other rules passed by government and parliament also meet with approval in the referendum. In this respect, the referendum is a test of the ability of government and parliament to adequately implement the interests of the Swiss population, and the "Vernehmlassung" is the procedure for exercising this ability.

While the "Vernehmlassung" still is a governmental act and leaves it to government and its bureaucracy to determine what is the solution that fits the interest of Swiss people best, most of the deliberative procedures applied involve the people in form of a randomly selected group of citizens directly. It is the task of these groups to work out a proposal which is representative for society at large.

There are different formats of deliberative procedures, including deliberative polls. A deliberative poll combines surveys with deliberation. The first step of a deliberative poll is a representative survey on a certain issue. In the second step, a small representative sample of respondents is asked to develop a proposal for assessing or resolving the issue on the basis. Before they meet in a usually one-day event to develop their proposal, they receive detailed information about the issue. In the course of the event, they discuss their assessment or proposal with politicians and experts, who then develop a position paper or a proposal for a decision. In the third step, the participants of the initial survey are asked for their opinion about the paper or proposal.

The most widely used format of deliberation are mini-publics. This is the format on which the proposal of deliberative governance in this book relies. Mini-publics exist in a variety of different forms which I will briefly explain further down. They all are based on the principle that a smaller or larger group of randomly selected citizens is commissioned with working out a consensually agreed proposal for the solution of an important political or public problem. An indispensable part of this principle is that the group gets thoroughly briefed at the beginning of its proceedings and is advised by a group of recognized experts. Moreover, the group may also listen to a group of relevant stakeholders. Stakeholders are actors that are affected by or can affect the solution of the problem concerned.

Since the 1990s mini-publics are quite frequently used to involve citizens and other stakeholders in urban development and city planning. A group of citizens and other stakeholders which may include several hundred people are not only consulted, but are given the opportunity to engage with plans in forums and work groups and to jointly develop a position statement. The detailed discussion and the development of a joint opinion distinguish deliberative practices from conventional forms of citizen participation in public planning and development projects.[26]

Mini-publics are not only organized by cities and other local actors, but also by state and national governments and other national actors. Examples are the British Columbian and the Ontarian citizen assemblies on electoral reforms convened in 2004 and 2006 respectively, the convention on the constitution which Irish government established in 2012 and the citizen assembly which the Irish government established in 2016 to discuss some nationally important issues including abortion, the G1000 citizen assemblies in Belgium and the Netherlands discussing different issues of great public interest, the French citizen assembly on climate operating in 2019 and 2020 and the Danish consensus conferences on technology held since 1998. These conferences have been mandated by government or cities, but I can well imagine that such conferences can also be successfully conducted by other actors, including business companies or NGOs, to work out concrete conflicts about sustainable development, such as phasing out coal. In the following chapters I will provide a number of examples and suggestions for applications of deliberative procedures by a variety of different social actors.

As I already mentioned there are different forms of mini-publics. A rather simple form is the citizen jury. This is a form of mini-public where a small group of citizens are randomly selected to deliberate on a given policy issue and provide recommendations to the organizing entity. The jury is usually given a specific question to answer or a problem of a clearly defined scope. A citizen jury could, for example, be assigned to public agencies to evaluate the draft of a law or regulation, or of a budget. The latter has been done in Australian cities.

A more elaborate procedure is the consensus conference. In this case recommendations or collective decisions are not made by a jury alone, which in this case is called a panel, but also includes a larger audience of randomly selected citizens which may actively participate in the proceedings. Following the basic principle of mini-publics the members of the panel are randomly selected and receive comprehensive information before they meet. The audience too receives comprehensive information but probably a lower amount. At the beginning of their proceedings, the panel deliberates on a common and precise understanding of the problem which it has to address. Moreover, they commonly decide which questions should be discussed with experts and stakeholders. Afterwards, these questions are discussed in hearings with experts and stakeholders in front of the audience. From a certain point in time the audience is more actively participating by asking questions or by short comments. Consensus conferences were created in the United States in the 1960s, and were initially used to resolve issues around emerging biomedical technologies. In recent years, consensus conferences have been further developed by the Danish Board of Technology Foundation. Meanwhile consensus conferences are used in many other countries, including Australia, Austria, Ireland, Norway and the United Kingdom. They have dealt with a wide variety of issues including biotechnology, health, abortion, electoral reform, nuclear waste and climate change.

A similar form to the consensus conference is the consensus forum. It differs from a consensus conference by the number of active participants and by the proceedings. The consensus forum is usually a one-day activity in which some 80 to 130 participants are directly involved in preparing a proposal. They work in small groups and each discusses certain aspects of the overall problem. At the end, the proposals of the different working groups are brought together in a joint paper that is adopted in the plenary session of the forum.

An elaborated form of the consensus conference and the consensus forum is the citizen's assembly. It works like a consensus conference, but over a much longer time and in several sessions. Like the consensus forum it also works partially in work groups. Citizen assemblies are usually installed to work out elaborate proposals on a complex theme. Citizens' assemblies have been used, for example, in France, the UK, Spain and Germany to advise government on climate change.[27]

Deliberative procedures increase the governance capacity of Western societies to a degree which reasonably may be called revolutionary. Yet, they are not a panacea – nor should they be. They can also be overused. After all, their impact also depends on public attention to these processes and their proposed solutions. An inflationary use of deliberative procedures therefore damages their effect. This is especially true for politics. Yet, the problem of overuse of mini-publics can be solved by a mini-public too.

The German community in Belgium, which, together with the French and Flemish communities and the parallel regions, is one of the "member states" of the somewhat complicated Belgian federal system, introduced some years ago in an interesting variant of a citizen assembly, which is called the citizen council. The council's main responsibility is to control the use of mini-publics by the government of the community. It consists of 24 randomly selected citizens who rotate over 18 months. Every 6 months, one third of the members is replaced. The council itself does not carry out any deliberative procedures, but can appoint mini-publics to a limited extent to deal with problems that it considers particularly important. The proposals of these mini-publics must be discussed in parliament and in the government. The council monitors these debates. Through rotation, many citizens have the opportunity to be members of the council over the years. This is an element of social learning worth emulating.

Mini-publics are, by their very nature, temporarily installed organizations. Deliberative principles may also be used as an element of permanent organizations, like business companies or public agencies. I will discuss examples of this in following chapters. Here, I want to discuss a case which is particularly interesting with respect to sustainable development and efficient governance. The case involves cooperatives, in particular the Emscher cooperative. The Emscher cooperative is the wastewater management association of the Ruhr district, Germany's largest former coal and steel district. It currently manages one of the world's largest environmental projects and a technical masterpiece. The aim of the project is the renaturalization of the river Emscher with all its tributaries, together more than 150 kilometers long. In the more than 150 year-long mining era in the Ruhr district, many sewers could not be laid underground because the ground kept subsiding due to coal mining. Therefore, a small river, the Emscher, and its tributaries were converted into surface sewers. Since the beginning of the 1990s, the Emscher cooperative has worked to transform the entire river system of the Emscher with all its tributaries in a state which is as natural as possible in an urban area. The project has an investment volume of over 5.5 billion Euros and a time frame of 30 years. The technical masterpiece of the project is 51-kilometer long sewage channel. The major technical difficulty was to provide the channel with a sufficient gradient in the almost flat land of the Ruhr district. The technical, innovative way in which the Emscher cooperative solved the problem made it interesting for experts worldwide. Notably, it is also the only big public project in Germany in recent years and even decades that has managed to stay on its schedule and on its budget.

The basis of the high performance of the Emscher cooperative is the inclusion of all stakeholders, such as cities and counties, the mining company and other companies with much wastewater and unions, as members of the cooperative and a strongly consensus-oriented management. The management always includes the relevant stakeholders in all major decisions and attempts to reach consensus. This grants the project wide support.[28]

The Emscher cooperative could serve as a model for public agencies which are less bureaucratic and more tuned to the common good. This model could be applied in many areas, such as urban and regional planning, regional development, public transportation, education, housing and environmental protection. These are areas with a variety of different stakeholders, different or even diverging interests and a high potential for conflict. They are also areas which are important for everyday life of many citizens. In the Emscher cooperative, deliberative decision-making was a management style rather than an institution. In principle, however, deliberative decision-making in cooperatives could also be introduced as an institution. A simple way to do so is to make the regular member assembly itself a deliberative body. A more difficult but probably better way would be to establish a citizens' council modeled on the citizen council of the German community in Belgium as an advisory body for management and the members' assembly of cooperatives.

In this book, the theoretical and practical knowledge outlined above will be used to design a set of deliberative institutions which in principle may be implemented within the established political systems of Western democracies. The aim is to switch these systems to deliberation without calling for a fundamental change. The assumption is that such a switch is sufficient to resolve all the major problems of current structures which hinder Western societies to reach sustainable development until the middle of this century.

Although a deliberative switch may resolve the problems of current structures it will not be an operation that can be easily performed. Rather it will generate more or less strong resistance as significant reforms of existing structures usually do. Established structures are particularly beneficial for certain actors, many others have become habituated with them. Moreover, deliberative practices limit the power of the representatives of the established system who however have to agree on introduction of deliberative principles. So why should they agree on that?

There are two answers to this question. The first is that the complexity of sustainable development and its problems will create increasing incentives for politicians and other political actors, including major interest groups, to form broader alliances. A prime example of such a situation is the massive economic turmoil in the 1960s and 1970s that gave rise to neo-corporatist practices in European countries. But in the case of sustainable development this response may come too late. The other answer is that politicians will have no choice, because many actors, like cities, NGOs or companies, institutional investors and coalitions of such actors will decentrally start a lot of deliberative activity to solve problems and conflicts of sustainable development. This could lead to a situation where sustainable development is no longer a matter of politics and government, but one of a society that drives politics and government. As I will explain in the last chapter, this is currently merely a hope, but a hope that is by no means unrealistic.

The Deliberative Way: Threefold Sustainability

Deliberative governance is one of the two pillars on which the strategy for sustainable development builds up that I propose in this book. The other one is threefold sustainability. These two pillars are linked to each other by strong synergies. The concept of threefold sustainability, which I will discuss at length in the following chapter, asserts that development of societies cannot become sustainable if sustainability only relates to environment. Rather, economic and social development must be included as well. Social development must either become sustainable in environmental terms as well as in economic and social terms or it will not become sustainable at all.

This is the implication of two facts which we have discussed at length in this chapter. The first fact is that a large proportion of the conflicts associated with environmentally sustainable development are caused by negative economic impacts of this development. This is especially true in capitalist societies. The second fact is that the resolution of these conflicts requires a high capacity of political and social institutions to reach widely accepted solutions to the conflicts. This is bound to certain social conditions which the concept of threefold sustainability subsumes under social cohesion.

What is important here is that the concept of threefold sustainability not only calls for equally considering the environmental, economic and social dimensions of sustainable development, but does so in an integrative form. In other words it claims that the three dimensions should not be considered successively, but as interrelated aspects of any problem of sustainable development. A typical example of such an approach, is, as we briefly addressed earlier in this chapter, decoupling growth from the use of unrenewable resources by innovations which reduce resource use and increase growth.

In recent years, technological progress has not only been a driver of growth but also of decoupling growth from resource consumption. Decoupling growth and resource consumption is now within the realm of possibility. This possibility is a cornerstone of the sustainability strategy proposed in this book. It assumes that it will not be possible to eliminate the growth constraints of capitalism in the near future. These are (still) far too firmly anchored in the technical, economic, social, cultural and political structures of capitalist societies. The strategy therefore relies on decoupling growth from the consumption of natural resources as quickly and for as long as possible.

It will not work with a moderate increase in resource productivity, but requires an increase of at least a factor of 10. In plain language, this means that Western societies and other major consumers of natural resources may only use one tenth of the natural resources they use today to satisfy their needs. This may take two or three decades, but even then it is an ambitious goal. To achieve this ambitious goal, technology as the most important driver of growth in capitalist societies will be exploited. As will be shown in chapter 3, digitization, biotechnology and microsystems engineering – and especially the interconnection of these technologies – offer enormous potential for drastically reducing the consumption of non-renewable natural resources. Technologically, it seems to be within the realm of possibility that this approach will ultimately lead to a complete decoupling of growth and the consumption of natural resources.[29]

In evolutionary terms, threefold sustainability means that environmental, economic and social developments are interlinked as co-evolving developments. Simply speaking, co-evolution means that environmental, economic and social developments systematically influence each other. This means, for example, the following: Economic growth that is not decoupled from the consumption of natural resources not only destroys the natural foundations of humanity, but also slows itself down beforehand because it will face increasing planetary boundaries (natural limits to growth). But also: more sustainable development that is achieved at the expense of economic growth will fail in the long run because of the conflicts it creates. And: Environmental and economic developments that damage each other make a society incapable of acting in the long run. I will describe this in more detail in the following chapter.[30]

At a first glance, calling for threefold sustainability may seem to make problems of sustainable development more complex. But this is deceptive, because in solving almost all environmental problems of sustainable development, the associated economic and social effects are always in play. Superficially, they are not part of the defined problem, but they are an inevitable part of the solution. They always lead to conflicts of greater or lesser magnitude. However, this is exactly what deliberative procedures can avoid. This is one side of the synergy between deliberative procedures and the concept of threefold sustainability.

By their very nature, deliberative procedures cannot ignore the economic and social dimensions in solving environmental sustainability problems. These dimensions inevitably come into play simply because of the representative composition of the members of juries, consensus conferences, consensus forums and citizen assemblies. These dimensions are part of the social reality of sustainable development and therefore also manifest themselves in different understandings of the participants in deliberative procedures. Deliberative procedures can therefore only arrive at consensual proposals if they take all three dimensions of sustainability into account. That is certainly difficult.

However, these difficulties can be overcome with the help of the concept of threefold sustainability. This concept shows systematic connections between the three dimensions. These interrelationships are open and can be made both positive and negative. For example, the three dimensions can be positively linked through the use of innovative technologies to increase resource productivity. The "nickel-and-dime economy", on the other hand, links them negatively. This knowledge can be used to solve sustainability problems. This is the other side of the synergy between deliberative procedures and the concept of threefold sustainability.

Notes

1 In the notes and references in this book, I will always quote available English editions of books and articles although I may have used myself the original version. – There is a vast body of literature on climate change, for example Emanuel Kerry (2018). What We Know about Climate Change. Cambridge, Mass.: MIT Press; Joseph Romm (2016). Climate Change: What Everyone Needs to Know. Oxford and New York: Oxford University Press. Moreover, there are many organizations providing facts and evaluation of climate change, such as Intergovernmental Panel on Climate Change https://www.ipcc.ch, NASA https://climate.nasa.gov, Brookings Institution https://www.brookings.edu/research/ten-facts-about-the-economics-of-climate-change-and-climate-policy or the Earth Day Movement https://www.earthday.org, Natural Resources Defense Council https://www.nrdc.org and the Environmental Defense Fund https://www.edf.org.

2 These conflicts can often be observed in relation to climate change. See Anthony Giddens (2011). The Politics of Climate Change. Cambridge UK and Malden MA: Polity Press.

3   My understanding of institutions and of their role is based on modern institutional analysis in economics and in sociology. See for example Mary C. Brinton, Victor Nee eds. (2001). The New Institutionalism in Sociology. Stanford: Stanford University Press. W. Richard Scott (2013). Institutions and Organizations: Ideas, Interests, and Identities. Los Angeles and London: Sage. Ronald L. Jepperson, John W. Meyer (2021) Institutional Theory: The Cultural Construction of Oganizations, States, and Identities. Cambridge UK and New York: Cambridge University Press. Stefan Voigt (2019). Institutional Economics: An Introduction. Cambridge: Cambridge University Press. Oliver Williamson (1990). The Economic Institutions of Capitalism. New York and London: Free Press.

4   A comprehensive analysis of institutional conditions of governance of common goods is provided in Elinor Ostrom (2015). Governing the Commons: The Evolution of Institutions for Collective Action. Cambridge, UK: Cambridge University Press. See also Elinor Ostrom, Roy Garner, Jimmy Walker (1994). Rules, Games, and Common Pool Resources. Ann Arbor: University of Michigan Press.

5   Ulrich Beck (1992). Risk Society: Towards A New Modernity. London: Sage.

6   For a comprehensive and empirically well-founded analysis of inequality in Europe and the United States see Thomas Piketty (2017). Capital in the Twenty-First Century. Cambridge, MA: Harvard University Press. The perilous side of inequality is described in Joseph E. Stiglitz (2012). The Price of Inequality. How today's Divided Society Endangers Our Future. New York: W.W. Norton. See also Joseph E. Stiglitz (2015). The Great Divide. London: Penguin Books. – The bibliographical information for the book of Barbara Ehrenreich is: Barbara Ehrenreich (2010). Nickel & Dimed: Undercover in Low-wage USA. London: Granta Publications. I look at the same phenomena from the opposite angle and analyze what "nickel and dime" does to the economy and sustainable development.

7   The book of Barbara Ehrenreich which is cited in footnote 6 provides an impressive illustration of this situation.

8   This problem and its relevance for social organization and collective action is described in Mancur Olson (1965). The Logic of Collective Action. Public Goods and the Theory of Groups. Cambridge MA: Harvard University Press. For a broad introduction see Russell Hardin (1982). Collective Action. London and New York: Routledge. Dylan Kissane, Alexandru Volacu eds. (2015). Modern Dilemmas: Understanding Collective Action in the 21st Century. Stuttgart: Ibidem.

9   For an introduction to the sociology of Herbert Spencer, see John Offer (2010). Herbert Spencer and Social Theory. New York: Palgrave Macmillan.

10 There is a vast literature on social movements, for example Stefan Berger, Holger Nehring eds. (2017). The History of Social Movements in Global Perspective: A Survey. London: Palgrave Macmillan; Donatella Della Porta, Mario Diani (2010). Social Movements: An Introduction. Malden: Blackwell; Jeff Goodwin, James M. Jasper eds. (2014). The Social Movements Reader: Cases and Concepts. Malden: Blackwell.

11 For an introduction into Luhmann's theory see Niklas Luhmann (2012). Introduction to Systems Theory. Cambridge UK and Malden, MA: Polity Press. For a more in depth presentation see Niklas Luhmann (2012). Theory of Society. Vol. 1. Stanford: Stanford University Press. For the theory of Witt see Ulrich Witt (2003). The Evolving Economy: Essays on the Evolutionary Approach to Economics. Aldershot: Edward Elgar. Ulrich Witt (2016). Rethinking Economic Evolution: Essays on Economic Change and its Theory. Cheltenham: Edward Elgar. A pioneering work in evolutionary economics which is particularly interesting in our context is Douglass C. North (2005). Understanding the Process of Economic Change. Princeton: Princeton University Press. A stimulating application of evolutionary economics on economic modernization is offered in Johann Peter Murmann (2003). Knowledge

and Competitive Advantage. The Coevolution of Firms, Technology, and National Institutions. Cambridge UK: Cambridge University Press. There quite a number of introductions to economic theory of evolution, see for example Kurt Dopfer, Jason Potts (2008). The General Theory of Economic Evolution. London and New York: Routledge. Geoffrey M. Hodgson (1999). Evolution and Institutions. On Evolutionary Economics and the Evolution of Economics. Cheltenham UK: Edward Elgar. Richard R. Nelson, Sidney G. Winter (1982). An Evolutionary Theory of Economic Change. Cambridge, MA: Harvard University Press.

12 For the report to the Club of Rome see: Donella H. Meadows, Dennis L. Meadows, Jørgen Randers, William W. Behrens III (1972). The Limits to Growth: A Report for the Club of Rome's Project on the Predicament of Mankind. New York: Universe Books.

13 The concept of a knowledge society has been introduced by Peter F. Drucker (1993). Post-Capitalist Society. New York: Harper Collins, quotation from page 20.

14 The process of creative destruction is explained in Joseph A. Schumpeter (2008). Capitalism, Socialism, and Democracy. New York: Harper Perennial (Third Edition).

15 Source of the figure on scientists: https://futureoflife.org/2015/11/05/90-of-all-the-scientists-that-ever-lived-are-alive-today/

16 An elaborate analysis of this condition is provided by Nico Stehr (2001). Fragility of Modern Societies: Knowledge and Risk in the Information Age. London: Sage.

17 See Nico Stehr (2015). Information, Power, and Democracy: Liberty is a Daughter of Knowledge. Cambridge UK: Cambridge University Press. Nico Stehr (2016). The Governance of Knowledge. London and New York: Routledge. Nico Stehr (2017). Knowledge and Democracy: A 21st Century Perspective. London and New York: Routledge.

18 For different understandings and theories of governance see Christopher Ansell, Jacob Torfing eds. (2017). Handbook of Theories of Governance. Cheltenham UK and Northampton, MA: Edward Elgar.

19 An illustrative description of the structure of modern societies is provided by the articles in Stuart Hall, David Held, Don Hubert, Kenneth Thompson eds. (1996). Modernity: An Introduction to Modern Societies. Malden, MA: Blackwell.

20 The pluralist theory of democracy was established by Robert A. Dahl. See Robert A. Dahl (1977). Polyarchy: Participation and Opposition. New Haven: Yale University Press. Robert A. Dahl (2005). Who Governs: Democracy and Power in an American City. New Haven: Yale University Press. Robert A. Dahl (2006). An Introduction to Democratic Theory. Chicago: University of Chicago Press.

21 Olson Mancur, Jr. (1965). The Logic of Collective Action: Public Goods and the Theory of Groups. Cambridge, MA: Harvard University Press.

22 See Andreas Reckwitz (2020). The Society of Singularities. Cambridge UK: Polity Press.

23 For the general principles of deliberative democracy see André Bächtinger, John S. Dryzek, Jane Mansbridge, Mark E. Warren eds. (2018). The Oxford Handbook of Deliberative Democracy. Oxford: Oxford University Press. John S. Dryzek (2000). Deliberative Democracy and Beyond: Liberals, Critics, Contestations. Oxford and New York: Oxford University Press. Jan Elster (2008). Deliberative Democracy. Cambridge UK and New York: Cambridge University Press. James S. Fishkin (2011). When the People Speak: Deliberative Democracy and Public Consultation. Oxford: Oxford University Press. John Parkinson, Jane Mansbridge eds. (2013). Deliberative Systems: Deliberative Democracy at the Large Scale. Cambridge UK: Cambridge University Press. Jürg Steiner, André Bächtinger, Markus Spörndly, Marco R. Steenbergen (2004). Deliberative Politics in Action: Analysing Parliamentary Discourse. Cambridge UK: Cambridge University Press.

24 Jürg Steiner, Maria C. Jaramillo, Rousiley C.M. Maia, Simona Mameli (2017). Deliberation across Deeply Divided Societies: Transformative Moments. Cambridge UK: Cambridge University Press.

25 For a short history of the concept of deliberative democracy see: Antonio Floridia (2018). "The Origins of the Deliberative Turn", in André Bächtinger, John S. Dryzek, Jane Mansbridge, Mark E. Warren eds. (2018). The Oxford Handbook of Deliberative Democracy. Oxford: Oxford University Press. The Harvard Negotiation Project is described in Roger Fisher, William Ury (2012). Getting to Yes: Negotiating an Agreement Without Giving In. London: Random House Business Books.

26 Many examples of practical applications of deliberative principles can be found in André Bächtinger, John S. Dryzek, Jane Mansbridge, Mark E. Warren eds. (2018). The Oxford Handbook of Deliberative Democracy. Oxford: Oxford University Press. And John Gastil, Peter Levine eds. (2005). The Deliberative Democracy Handbook. Strategies for Effective Civic Engagement in the Twenty-first Century. San Francisco: Jossey-Bass.

27 For more information on deliberative procedures the following links may be useful https://healthydemocracy.org, https://www.newdemocracy.com.au, https://www.democracy-international.org, https://delibdemjournal.org/

28 I am referring here and in the following para to a study by Uli Paetzel and myself on the Emscher cooperative that has not yet been published.

29 I refer here to the Factor 10 concept of Friedrich Schmidt-Bleek. See Friedrich Schmidt-Bleek (2008). The Earth: Natural Resources and Human Intervention. London: Haus Publishing. Friedrich Schmidt-Bleek (1998). Das MIPS-Konzept. Weniger Naturverbrauch – mehr Lebensqualität durch Faktor 10. Munich: Droemer. Franz Lehner, Friedrich Schmidt-Bleek (1999). Die Wachstumsmaschine. Der ökonomische Charme der Ökologie. Munich: Droemer.

30 As I described in the preface, the concept of threefold sustainability which is applied in this book has been developed by a group of scholars in a study for the German industrialist and member of the Club of Rome, Klaus Steilmann. See Franz Lehner, Anthony Charles, Stephan Bieri, Yannis Paleocrassas and Nicholas Ashford, Willy Bierter, Roberto Camagni, Anthony Courakis, Wolf D. Hartmann, Friedrich Schmidt-Bleek, Friedrich Schneider (2001). The Steilmann Report. The Wealth of People: An Intelligent Economy for the 21st Century. Bochum: Brainduct.

2 Sustainability

A Threefold Challenge

In the sustainability strategy proposed in this book, the concept of threefold sustainability plays a key role. It offers a new approach to the common good. In this approach the common good only exists as social construct of reality. It emerges as a widely shared understanding from everyday social interactions in a society. In this view, a collective good is a collective good as long as people's experience and communication in everyday life shows the commonality.

For our further discussions, I introduce here a more precise definition of threefold sustainability. I define threefold sustainability as the ability of a society to secure and improve in the long term firstly, its natural basis of life by a high level of resource productivity, secondly, a fair standard of living of the vast majority of the population, and thirdly its social cohesion, that is its ability to make and maintain widely accepted collective decisions.[1]

The first, environmental part of this definition emphasizes that environmental sustainability does not primarily mean nature, but the natural basis of human life. Sustainability is therefore not something that good people do for nature, but something that people do for people and humanity. This is reflected in the widely accepted definition of sustainability of the World Commission on Environment and Development, established by the United Nations in 1983 and known after its chairmanship as the Brundtland Commission. In its final report, the commission defines sustainable development as "development that meets the needs of the present without compromising the ability of future generations to meet their own needs". In the report the commission also says: "In essence, sustainable development is a process of change in which the exploitation of resources, the direction of investments, the orientation of technological development, and institutional change are all in harmony and enhance both current and future potential to meet human needs and aspirations".[2]

The second, economic part of the definition reflects the entrenchment of sustainable development in the structures of capitalist societies. This leaves hardly any chances for sustainable development at the expense of the living standard of large parts of the population. Capitalist societies must therefore implement sustainability strategies that are compatible with the established

DOI: 10.4324/9781003261421-2

lifestyles of Western societies and also leave enough room for developing countries to satisfy their needs in the same way as Western countries. However, this can only be achieved if economic growth can be decoupled from the consumption of non-renewable resources. This makes resource productivity the central environmental adjusting screw of sustainable development.

The third, social part of the definition points at the governance problem resulting from the pluralist structures of Western societies. We discussed this problem in the first chapter in some detail. In relation to sustainable development, this problem is critical. The many small and large conflicts that are always associated with sustainable development can only be permanently resolved or contained if their solutions are widely accepted. Solutions where this is not the case almost always generate new conflicts, because the defeated actors often try to change or undermine these solutions. Therefore, societies that are unable to regularly find widely accepted solutions to the conflicts of sustainable development have little chance of achieving sustainable development.

An important link between the three dimensions of sustainability is created by radical innovations. However, this is a somewhat ambivalent link. Radical innovations to solve environmental sustainability problems mostly create new growth and new markets and employment opportunities in the innovative companies and industries. But at the same time jobs are often lost in companies and industries whose products are forced out of the market by the innovative products. In order to avoid sustainable development having many losers, compensation must be created for this.

One message that runs throughout the book is that the governments of Western countries cannot create sustainable development on their own. This is true even if governments were much more consistent and competent in pursuing sustainable development. Sustainable development is a very complex process that can only get off the ground properly and stay off the ground if it is driven simultaneously in many places and at many levels of society. This requires functioning markets, many innovative companies and a lot of social self-organization. This in turn requires an activating government which creates a good framework for markets and a supportive environment for innovative companies and social self-organization.

A New Approach to the Common Good

In the first chapter I explained that environment and sustainable development are practically not a common good. Goods are not common goods because they are in the abstract interest of all people, but only because they are produced and reproduced as a common good in the everyday life of society. Common goods may exist abstractly or be defined legally, but for them to be accepted and treated as common goods, people need to understand them as common goods in their everyday lives. The commonality of the good must be self-evident to them. Nature would therefore be a real common good if all people in a society had the same or at least a very similar understanding of nature and also acted according to this understanding. Similarly, sustainable development would only be a real common good if people in a society could agree with a very large majority on a concrete understanding of sustainable development with clear goals and clear principles of behavior and acted accordingly. In the best case, this understanding would be so strong that it would also largely prevent free-riding.

With this argument I am referring to a concept that in sociology is called the social construction of reality. According to this concept, people base their social interactions actions on socially constructed understandings of their social and natural environment which they accept as correct by them and their social environment and which thus are considered "objective". In other words, these concepts represent for them facts of everyday life that can be relied upon because they are also considered facts by their social environment.[3]

The understanding of environment and sustainability as common goods has probably not yet been properly established in the process of social construction. Until the middle of the last century, a very different understanding of nature and the environment prevailed, not only in Western societies. The environment was understood above all as a resource which people could make use of. Moreover, nature was partly seen as a hostile environment that people had to tame. This understanding has been established over many generations and is still alive in Western societies – not only among climate deniers and people with similarly extreme attitudes, but in the everyday actions and lifestyles of most people. Much of our lifestyle for generations has not been in accordance with the environment and neither are our infrastructures or other means to support our lifestyle. The social diversity of modern Western societies renders emergence of a common understanding of nature and sustainable development in everyday life difficult.

This is in effect an institutional problem. Current institutions of Western societies encourage a competitive pursuit of social interests. This applies to the actions of political parties, organized interest groups and bureaucracies, as well as to the activities of environmentalists. Environmental protection and sustainable development have not been a major topic of political debate for a long time, but when they gained prominence, most political parties in most Western countries sought to distinguish themselves from each other rather than negotiate a common political program for the environment and sustainability. Political debates remained fairly general. In effect, this has left concrete environmental policy largely to the activities of well-organized interest groups and their counterparts in the bureaucracy. These mostly operate in highly segmented structures in which overarching problems are neglected. When conflicts do arise, they are resolved competitively. Each interest group tries to assert its special interests. Joint solutions are the exception, not the rule. On the part of the bureaucracy, this is supported by wrangling over competencies and power games.

This is the tragedy of competitive democracy: the more weight an issue gains on the political agenda, the more the parties demarcate themselves from one another, the less willing they are to cooperate, and the more the issue is left to special interests. Environmentalists are partly participating in this game and operate via their allies in politics and administration. Others find their purpose in demonstrations and in putting pressure on politics and business via well-orchestrated protest actions. A great willingness to engage in joint activities between politics, business and civil society is rarely found, and if so, it tends to be at the local level. As a result, sustainable development emerged mostly as a permanent zero-sum game instead of a common good. In game theory, a zero-sum game refers to conflicts in which the gains and losses of the participants balance each other out. This describes in other words the situation that I identified in the first chapter as the most important cause of the failure of sustainability policy and of many other activities for sustainable development.

If this is to change and environment and sustainability are to truly become a common good, then the everyday experiences of citizens and other actors must change accordingly. They need to experience on a day-to-day basis that all members of society benefit more or less equally from activities for sustainable development and that everybody has a reasonably fair share in the costs and risks of these activities. If this experience persists over time, then environment and sustainability emerge as clear and actionable social constructs and common goods. Then the basis for the joint resolution of conflicts over sustainable development also grows.

An illustrative case is the ability of business to deal rationally with sustainability problems and to seek innovative economic solutions. Today, a growing number of companies is in the process of making their products and production processes environmentally sustainable. This should, however, not obscure the fact that the largest parts of the Western economies still represent many non-sustainable structures of the past. Many companies remain stuck in established routines and ingrained ways of thinking. This is not least due to the fact that these patterns of thought are repeatedly reaffirmed in social debates and minor and major conflicts about sustainable development. Many managers, entrepreneurs, trade union leaders and employees, as well as their counterparts from the environmental side, are still strongly caught up in the conventional zero-sum game. This encourages stubborn insistence on one's own views and positions much more than collective learning. This situation will change only to the extent that both sides are confronted with positive evidence and experience of reconciling business and environmental sustainability. These changes will be slow for many years, but may over time adopt momentum. The more companies successfully switch to sustainable development, the more the process of change will accelerate. Market competition on the one hand and social communication on the other will ensure this.[4]

In big politics it is even worse. There, the major political parties would have to agree with the major business, labor, and environmental associations on a common program for sustainable development and a suitable narrative for communicating that program broadly. The program would have to describe in reasonably concrete terms how and in which time frame sustainable development will be reached. The narrative would have to explain in a language that can be understood by the general public the concept of sustainable development underlying the program, the scientific basis and practical consequences of the program as well as the costs and financing of the program. In contrast to these requirements, most programs for sustainable development in politics and business remain nebulous.

This approach will be time consuming, but it is promising. There is an interesting role model for such an approach. In the 1970s a number of Western European countries, including Germany, Ireland, the Netherlands, Belgium, and the Nordic countries engaged in concertation of their economic and labor market policies with the umbrella organizations of business and labor. This model which was called neo-corporatism, has been successful in terms of low inflation and low unemployment, but has not been able to hold up against the rising tide of neoliberalism. A prime success factor of the neo-corporatist model was that it drastically reduced power of special interests.

Concertation of economic policy for sustainable development could be an important pillar of a policy to achieve sustainable development by the middle of this century. Yet, it cannot be the sole pillar. This is due to the fact alone that in the vast majority of Western democracies it will take a long time before the major parties, contrary to the logic of party competition, can bring themselves to agree on a joint program for sustainable development that is actually viable. That may be more time than is good for sustainable development. But sustainable development is anyway not a task that big politics can shoulder alone. Rather, it must involve society as broadly as possible and, therefore, must also be advanced through cities, markets and the self-organization of civil society. Only the interplay of these forces and big politics can produce the stream of everyday experience that eventually leads to the social construction of a widely accepted understanding of environment and sustainable development. This process must gain such a strong momentum that nature and sustainable development are truly understood and treated as a common good, and not as a collective good. Otherwise, nothing will change the fact that sustainable development is hampered by many small and large conflicts and by much free-riding.

Nowadays, there are deliberative alternatives to the neo-corporatist model. In the previous chapter, I mentioned that some countries, including France, the UK, Spain and Germany and the European Union, have used citizens' assemblies or consensus conferences to develop a national or European strategy respectively to combat climate change. This was done in quite different ways. In Germany the citizens' assembly, which in Germany is called "bürgerrat" (citizens' council) was organized by an NGO which was specifically established to organize this kind of activity. The assembly had no official mission and its report was formally a position paper of a private organization. Shortly before the federal election in 2021 the elaborate report was handed over to the major political parties and parliament. The French citizens' assembly on the other hand was installed by President Macron and the French government and had an official mission to work out an elaborate proposal for French climate law. Government promised that the proposal of the assembly would be carefully discussed by government and parliament. In the end this promise was only partly kept and government watered down much of the proposal's more ambitious and politically disputed recommendations. This could probably have been avoided if the climate law was subject to a referendum.[5]

What happened in France with the citizens' assembly is not a particularly French problem, but corresponds to a typical behavior of the governments of most Western democracies. In somewhat simplified terms, most democratic governments first react to a problem that is considered important in society with grand plans and promises, but these are quickly watered down in day-to-day political life. Incidentally, this also applies to the world climate conferences.

To explain this further I return to the distinction between common goods and collective goods briefly mentioned in the first chapter. Unlike the use of language in other disciplines, economists make a clear distinction between a common good and a collective good. Both type of goods are non-excludable which means that they may be consumed by any member of society or community in which the good is available. In contrast to a collective good, a common good is rivalrous. Rivalrousness means that the consumption of the good by one actor reduces or limits consumption by other actors. In the economic sense, nature is a common good, whereas sustainable development is a collective good. Nature is a common good because a large part of natural resources are finite and consumption of natural resources, thus, is mostly rivalrous. In everyday life, however, the connection between one's own actions and the finiteness of natural resources is only recognizable in the abstract. Therefore, in effect, nature is treated as a collective good. Sustainable development, in contrast, is on its own indeed a collective good in the sense of the economic definition. It is not rivalrous: if your city reaches sustainable development you will profit from it whether or not you contributed to it. Yet, broken down to concrete measures for sustainable development, this collective good is not even a real collective good, because many actors benefit from the concrete measure, but many others primarily have to bear its costs and risks.

In principle, this is exactly what regularly happens in the politics of democratic countries when it comes to important problems such as sustainable development or social justice. These problems are declared to be a national concern and thus a common good in political Sunday speeches, but in everyday political life they are quickly treated as a collective good. This allows all sorts of interest groups to recognize the fundamental importance of the problem and the need for effective action, but to ensure that their own special interests are not significantly affected when it comes to the concrete design of the measures. After all, the rationale for this is that, while not entirely environmentally friendly, it makes little difference to sustainable development.

The case of the French citizens' assembly on climate offers some more general insights. A positive one is that citizens' assemblies and other mini-publics are well suited to reach consensual or at least widely consensual solutions to a complex problem which are comprehensive, elaborate, detailed and competent. A negative insight is that under current institutional conditions of Western societies even a proposal which really represents the general interest of society is likely to fail at the strong influence of well-organized special interests. A conclusion from this insight is that citizens of Western societies would be ill-advised to leave the sustainable development of their society solely or primarily to politics and government. In order to really achieve sustainable development in a reasonable time frame of some two or three decades, it must be driven by decentralized and bottom-up activity by markets and innovative companies, by cities, and last not least by NGOs and other forms of self-organization of civil society. To make that really happen, many people and other actors have to understand that sustainable development is not really a collective good because any actor that does not participate in the production of the collective good of sustainable development is wasting finite natural resources and hampers the common good.[6]

The Threefold Challenge

I defined threefold sustainability at the beginning of this chapter as the ability of a society to simultaneously secure its natural basis of life, a fair standard of living of the vast majority of its population, and its social cohesion. The ecological and economic components of this definition are tailored to Western capitalist societies and their structural conditions out of which sustainable development must occur. In line with our argument that sustainable development of capitalist societies, at least in the foreseeable future, is only possible by decoupling economic growth from the consumption of non-renewable natural resources, we concretize these two components by the factors of resource productivity and economic growth. We have already discussed this in detail in the first chapter.

The social component of the definition, on the other hand, reflects the basic problem of sustainable development, namely the fact that this development must always take place from within existing, unsustainable social structures and is therefore inevitably associated with many minor and major conflicts. Since these conflicts are a major obstacle to sustainable development, their prevention or permanent resolution must be a central concern of any sustainability strategy. This means that decoupling of growth from resource use must be done through political decisions and other forms of social decision that are widely accepted in the society (or the social system in question). If this is not the case every resolution of a conflict generates new conflicts. We therefore define social cohesion specifically as the ability of a society to make widely accepted decisions and other social decisions. Behind this definition is the evolutionary insight that societies are continuously reconstituted from the social interactions of their members. Social cohesion of a society must therefore be confirmed again and again by everyday social decisions.

This is also true in relation to sustainable development. Societies can only maintain their ability to make widely accepted social decisions on sustainable development by making such decisions regularly. This capacity is not a given property of societies. We have discussed this in the first chapter in relation to the pluralist Western societies, but other types of societies have comparable problems.

The need to regularly reach social decisions that are widely accepted in society may appear to rather narrowly limit the possible range of solutions. However, this does not have to be so. Often, restrictions can be avoided by extending decision-making and the implementation of decisions over a longer time span or incorporating them into a more complex solution procedure. We discussed an example of this kind of procedure in the first chapter as an alternative to the actual Hambacher Forst policy. Such a procedure becomes particularly important with respect to resource productivity. As I will explain in chapter 3, the best measure to increase resource productivity is a special kind of resource tax. This tax would not only drive resource productivity, but also foster innovation and growth. Yet, the tax would also increase prices of many goods significantly and by this endanger living standards of lower- and middle-income people. This would inevitably feed conflict on the distribution of benefits, costs and risks of sustainable development. In order to avoid this, the introduction of the resource tax could be embedded in a general tax reform which relieves income from work and entrepreneurial activity. This could also contribute to employment security which in the context of digitalization of the economy may become an important issue of sustainability. We will further discuss this in chapter 4.

The relationships just outlined point to the fact that the environmental, economic and social components of sustainable development are not separate but coevolutionary developments. They also let us see that the interrelationships between environmental, economic and social development are not straightforward. Rather, they are influenced by intervening factors, such as the tax regime. A crucially important intervening factor is social inequality. We have already noted in the first chapter that social inequality massively affects the perception of sustainable development as a common good, and that it creates significant problems in relation to both sustainability and social cohesion. Beyond that, social inequality strongly reinforces the growth constraints of capitalism.[7]

In 1954, the American social psychologist Leon Festinger published an article that tells us why it is unrealistic. The title of the essay was "A Theory of Social Comparison Processes". Festinger argued in the article that human beings evaluate their abilities, living conditions and other aspects of their lives by comparison with people in their social environment if they do not have objective information. Social comparison includes the people who are in social reach of the comparing person. In open, Western societies this also includes people from higher income groups. This means that many people in Western societies base their ideas and expectations of a fair standard of living on the standard of living that people in somewhat higher income groups have. So they will try to adjust their standard of living and lifestyle "upwards".

As we discussed in the first chapter, this works quite well in today's nickel-and-dime economy – but at the expense of the environment. It is very unlikely that these people will give up the standard of living they have struggled to achieve for the sake of the environment as long as many people above them are living better. This is true not only for people who earn little, but also for many in middle-income and higher-income groups because they as well have people above them who live better. To put it more generally: The high social inequality in Western societies induces a strong upwards drive of aspirations for large parts of the population which impedes far-reaching changes of lifestyle in favor of environment. The standard of living of Western societies does the same to the aspirations of people in poorer countries.[8]

Such intervening factors can be found still more. They manifest the fact that sustainable development is embedded in a complex social system with a complex natural environment. This fact must be faced by any sustainability strategy that is to have a chance of success. This does not mean, however, that this strategy should be as complex as the social system and its environment. On the contrary, it will probably only be successful if it succeeds in processing the complexity of the system and its environment with the simplest possible means and structures.

Following this insight, I define the environmental dimension of sustainability solely in terms of resource productivity and do not consider the various environmental problems, such as climate change, water scarcity, species extinction and world hunger, individually and concretely. The underlying assumption is most of these problems can be solved by drastically improving resource productivity. I proceed similarly, as explained in the first chapter, with the economic dimension, which I define in terms of a fair standard of living of the vast majority of the population. At least for the foreseeable future this condition can hardly be met without growth. Finally, I define the social dimension as social cohesion and focus it on the ability to make widely recognized decisions or social decisions. I do not address values, cleavages and other factors influencing this ability, but consider it as an institutional problem – a problem of adapting institutions to social conditions.

The Environmental Dimension: Resource Productivity

For some decades, climate change has become the prime issue of sustainable development. In relation to environment this is certainly an important concern of humanity. Climate neutrality, however, does not mean sustainable development. It is quite possible that humanity reaches climate neutrality, but still falls short of sustainable development – even in environmental terms. An illustrative case is electro mobiles.

Today, electric vehicles are considered to become the individual mobility solution of the future. This may be true at least according a recent study of the German Ministry for Environment. This study shows that over their life cycle electric vehicles consume less energy and emit less CO_2 and other greenhouse gases than cars with gasoline or diesel engines. But even electric vehicles are not climate neutral. They are not yet so in their operation, but with a declining proportion of non-renewable energy in the electricity mix used to charge their batteries, they will perform better. A bigger problem is the raw materials which are needed for the production of cars and batteries and the way in which these materials are obtained. Two of these materials, namely cobalt and lithium, are scarce and known reserves may not last beyond 2050. Extraction of these and other materials used for electro mobiles, including copper, is associated with huge material flows and massive interventions into ecosystems. For the extraction of lithium in Latin America large quantities of groundwater are pumped out which dry up entire areas and thus also destroy the living conditions of the indigenous population. In Africa, cobalt mining is associated with child labor and other poor working conditions. In a nutshell: Even if electric vehicles may be climate neutral, they probably are not sustainable. This is not to say that electromobility should be abandoned, but merely that it makes sense to leave alternatives open.[9]

In this context we should consider the rebound effect of electromobility. The rebound effect; sometimes also called the boomerang effect. The rebound effect describes a situation in which efficiency improvements lead to cheaper costs and therefore to more consumption. Such an effect can also be observed with electromobility, specifically with bicycles and pedal scooters. The electrification of bicycles and pedal scooters has created opportunities or incentives for many people to increase their use of bicycles and pedal scooters. This likely replaces the use of automobiles in many cases, but in many cases also walking. Moreover, since electric bikes are much cheaper than cars or motorcycles, they may also induce more mobility. This may increase use of copper and other scarce raw materials which is anything but a step towards sustainability.

This situation and similar problems concerning the use of copper for machines and equipment for renewable energy draws our attention to the extraction and consumption of natural resources. A long-standing concern in this respect is the amount of resources which future generations will find available to serve their needs. Again, this is an important aspect of sustainable development, but the problem goes far beyond that. It lies, as the German ecologist Friedrich Schmidt-Bleek explains, above all in the large flows of materials that we move every day to obtain the resources required to meet our needs. In order to understand the relevance of this point, one should know that "the amounts of solid substances and water which we actually use (to generate energy, to produce goods and services, to construct infrastructures and buildings, use for drinking, cleaning, irrigation of fields and generating hydropower) constitute only a fraction of the mountains of materials left behind, for example as mining waste with no market value". Schmidt-Bleek refers to the mass of material that is moved to create a product and its raw materials but is not ultimately incorporated into the product as the product's ecological rucksack.[10]

How large this rucksack is can be illustrated by a few examples. In order to use lignite as an energy source, forests must first be cut down and fields cleared, and a lot of soil and water must be moved away. In German lignite mining areas, even entire villages have been torn down and rebuilt elsewhere. After the field is prepared in this way, the lignite is mined and transported over a shorter or longer distance to a power plant. The transport requires some kind of equipment, which also contains material and which itself also consumes energy. The same applies to the power plant that generates the electricity. So there is a lot of natural material in the production of the kilowatt hour of electricity that leaves the power plant at the end.

With a complex product, such as a machine tool or a car, it is all much more complicated. Ores and coal are mined in various places around the world. For this purpose, opencast mines or other mines are set up for which a lot of material has to be extracted from the ground and a lot of water has to be pumped. The ores and coal extracted from the ground are transported to places where they are smelted into iron, copper and other metals. The iron is used to make steel, which requires coke, which is extracted from coal. This process always produces residual materials and waste that have to be reprocessed or disposed of. Steel, copper and other materials are used to make many small and large components for the machine. This also repeatedly produces waste that has to be reprocessed or disposed of. Many parts of the final product are produced by suppliers at different locations and assembled again at different locations to form more complex parts, such as motors or control systems, while at other locations the computer programs for controlling machine tools or cars are developed. In the end, the whole is assembled into the final product at one or more locations. The whole process involves huge transportation distances and energy consumption.

A famous example of transportation has been produced by Stefanie Böge in her diploma thesis. She investigated the transport chain in the production of a strawberry yogurt that ended up being sold in a Stuttgart supermarket. Strawberries from Poland, bacteria from northern Germany, milk and sugar from southern Germany, jars, lids, labels, packaging and other materials from different places traveled a total of over 9,000 kilometers. For modern industrial products, transportation chains are much more complex than for a yoghurt because almost all manufacturing companies rely for their supply on global sourcing.[11]

Every product which we produce and consume thus carries an ecological rucksack which is by far heavier than its own weight. As Friedrich Schmidt-Bleek mentions, the floor of his office would collapse if the ecological ruck-sack of his computer would be filled in the office, and that the gold wedding ring of a couple weighs ecologically more than the family car with which they drive their children to school. Every kilogram of industrial product carries on average a rucksack of 30 kg. Plastic has a relatively low rucksack of 5 kg per kilogram, copper one of 500 kg and gold one of more than 500,000 kg. Mobile phones which weigh some 100 or 200 g carry a rucksack of about 75 kg, 3.5 kg of which are used to gain the 10 g copper in the phone. Even services, like an insurance or bank loan, have a big rucksack which relates, for example to the computer systems with which loans or insurances are calculated and administrated.[12]

It does not take much imagination to realize how much we interfere with the earth's ecosystems by using natural resources. The use of natural resources along the entire value chain from the cradle to the cradle, i.e. from the extrac-tion of raw materials to the recycling or disposal of residual materials and waste, is always associated with burdens for the environment in the form of degradation of soil, pollution of air and water, climate change, water scarcity and destruction of biodiversity. This exceeds the carrying capacity of the earth and causes ecosystems to change permanently. This supports Friedrich Schmidt-Bleek's argument that the material flows which men induce and their ecological impacts are the key problem of sustainable development.[13]

The rather obvious conclusion that Schmidt-Bleek draws from this insight is that environmental sustainability can only be achieved by drastically reducing the overall consumption of resources. To achieve this, environ-mental protection must start at the beginning of the production chain and massively reduce the consumption of natural materials already there. If this is not to be at the expense of living standards and global economic growth, the goods and services needed or desired must be produced with far fewer natural resources and, above all, with far smaller ecological rucksacks than is currently the case. We will discuss this in more detail in the next chapter.

Resource productivity is a particularly pertinent approach to threefold sustainability. It offers an understanding or a concept which can be used to greatly reduce the complexity of sustainability policy and avoid the com-plexity trap. It also offers a concept that can be integrated into the operation of industry and the economy as a whole. Last but not least, it offers a con-cept that may be positively linked with living standards and social cohesion.

Resource productivity reduces the complexity of environmental problems significantly for three reasons. First it offers an approach which does not necessitate addressing these problems individually, unlike the end of pipe approach. This is particularly important because these problems are multifariously interlinked and the interlinkages are not fully known and controlled. Second, resource productivity can be driven by a few rather general instruments which may be applied on all relevant resources. Third, resource productivity does not need to be controlled for all or most natural resources and for all or most products in order to be effective in terms of sustainable development. Rather, it is sufficient to control a relatively small number of strategically relevant resources and products. I will explain this in the next chapter.

Driving resource productivity fits well into the logic of the capitalist economy and the profit striving of its enterprises. Due to this motive, companies in capitalist economies attempt to minimize use of scarce and costly resources – if competition adequately works. They will try to use resources as productively as possible and they will also invest in productivity. If natural resources, hence, are scarce and have a realistic price tag, companies will have an incentive to invest in resource productivity. The challenge for environmental policy is to impose on strategically selected resources price tags which include rucksacks. This provides companies with opportunities to increase resource productivity not only by the design of their products but also of their production systems. This will be explained in the next chapter as well.

A crucial aspect of resource productivity is the positive link between environmental sustainability on one side and living standard and cohesion on the other which it may create. This is the key condition for avoiding or resolving the many economic and social conflicts associated with the development of environmental sustainability. It does not arise automatically, but must be established institutionally.[14]

The Economic Dimension: Living Standard

In 1988, Congress and the President of the United States established the Competitiveness Policy Council as an independent advisory body to advise them on policies to promote competitiveness of the US economy. The Council offered a remarkable definition of competitiveness which related the competitiveness of an economy to the maintenance and increase of the living standard of a society. Some years later, the European Commission applied a similar concept. This was remarkable because the definition put the focus on the standard of living of the general population and not on the relative strength of the economy compared to other economies, as was often the case at the time.[15]

The Competitiveness Policy Council and the European Union apply a concept of living standard which includes not only material wealth, but also factors like health, education, employment and housing. With this understanding of living standard as reference point, resource productivity describes how much living standard for the whole population is produced with a given input of natural resources.[16]

The choice of standard of living as the economic dimension of sustainability is likely to be acceptable even for many committed environmentalists, especially since standard of living can be easily interpreted in terms of quality of life. Yet with respect to real development, such an interpretation only makes sense if it emerges in the everyday interactions of Western societies. It must in other words become a social construct rather than a claim of environmentalists. As long as the social construction of living standard in the Western societies is as it is, and as long as Western societies' existing living standard is the dream of people in poorer countries, sustainable development which is also economically and socially sustainable, can only be reached with growth and the decoupling of growth and resource consumption.

In the evolutionary view underlying this book it cannot be taken for granted that decoupling growth and resource consumption is a permanent solution of capitalist societies' sustainability problems. Whether this will be the case or not depends on a variety of factors, such as technological development and Western societies coping with social inequality. Insofar, it may be that the British scientist Tim Jackson is right when he calls decoupling a myth and argues that humanity will inevitably reach planetary limits. But for the time being, decoupling is the only way to postpone these limits as far as possible in order to give Western societies the time they need to achieve sustainable development in some way or another.

How much time this is can be seen if one thinks through a well-founded vision of an economy without growth. Tim Jackson describes such a vision in his book "Prosperity without Growth: Foundations for the Economy of Tomorrow". His vision is built on the recognition that while prosperity has an indispensable material component, it is far from being reducible to that. At the same time, however, he shows the extent to which people in Western societies and elsewhere are trapped in an iron cage of consumerism. He argues that material goods play a major role in our lives not only as a means of satisfying material needs, but also "as a powerful 'language of goods' that we use to communicate with each other – not just about status, but also about identity, social affiliation and even – through giving and receiving gifts for example – about our feelings for each other, our hopes for our family, and our dreams of the good life". This sentence encapsulates how much our material consumption is anchored in our lives and how far the way is to another, much less material understanding of prosperity.[17]

This is not only a question of individual learning, but much more one of the social construction of a fundamentally new social understanding. A major component of this understanding is, in Tim Jackson's vision, a new understanding of work, which is not just a means of subsistence but an indispensable basis of social cohesion. Moreover, the vision also includes development of a new economic understanding that, for example, understands investment as an expression of our commitment to the future and new governance structures that drive or better lead the new society forward. Such understandings may well emerge as Western societies move far along the path to sustainability. But if these understandings are the prerequisite for Western societies to develop sustainably, neither will happen. This is already ensured by the great social inequality of Western societies.

High inequality is a major threat to sustainable development. It inhibits emergence of the understandings Tim Jackson calls for not less than the decoupling of growth and resource consumption. This manifested in the "nickel-and-dime economy" which is probably the worst result of the rising social inequality of the past decades. Workers with nickel-and-dime wages are hardly capable to understand work in the sense of Jackson. They are also neither willing nor able to pay the higher prices for goods that would inevitably result from an effective resource tax. Also stuck are entrepreneurs and managers who act under the double pressure of the harsh price competition of the nickel-and-dime economy and of the shareholders' value doctrine. Moreover, governments which are incapable of an effective income policy and other measures to significantly reduce inequality, are likely to attempt to maintain even modest growth rates at any environmental price in the hope that some of the growth will also benefit lower- and middle-income groups and prevent them from being further left behind by the development of prosperity.

In most Western societies both inequality of income and of wealth have reached a high level. This is illustrated by data from French economist Thomas Piketty. After the First World War, or more precisely between 1915 and 1948, income inequality in Western countries fell, but since the 1970s it has been rising rapidly again. This is due in particular to the decoupling of the compensation of executives of large companies from other incomes. There is a similar trend in wealth, which is due in particular to the weak economic growth that has persisted for years. It is worth noting that the concentration of wealth is much higher than the concentration of income. The 10% of the population with the highest labor incomes account for 25 to 30% of total labor income. The 10% with the highest wealth, on the other hand, have a share of over 50% of total wealth. This is remarkable because wealth can be converted into economic and political power much more than income. Indeed, concentrated wealth has created a concentration of economic power which is dangerous both for democracy and the market.[18]

Behind Thomas Piketty's data, we find a growing low wage sector in most Western societies, social deprivation of the middle class, strong inequalities in living style, but also in economic and political power, and in educational opportunities. The growing low wage sector and inequalities in living style gave, as we discussed in chapter 1, birth to the emergence of a nickel-and-dime economy in most of Western society. Social deprivation of the middle classes adds to this. Social deprivation means that social groups perceive or fear that their income, wealth, living standard or social chances, and the educational opportunities and social chances of their kids decline in relation to that of other groups. Social deprivation of middle class is a major source of political dissatisfaction in Western societies.

Growth is necessary to create a balance here. With increasing inequality and social deprivation, governments and business in most Western societies are coming under increasing pressure to reduce inequality and to increase lower and middle incomes. The middle class in particular is often decisive in elections in most Western countries. This forces parties and governments to increase the incomes of the middle class in particular through tax cuts and other income policy measures. It also fixes them on economic growth. Economic growth allows a certain degree of redistribution without massive distributional conflicts. Income increases for lower and middle incomes can be financed from growing tax revenues and corporate profits without significantly affecting higher incomes and wealth. In most Western countries, a more far-reaching redistribution is likely to fail at the economic and political power of the privileged classes. As we will discuss in chapter 5, the reduction in inequality that is possible within this setting is unlikely to be enough for sustainable development.

In the coming years, the governments of Western societies will be confronted not only with great problems of their own inequality, but with the even greater problems of even greater inequality between rich and poor countries. For some years now, these are no longer problems that Western societies can look at from a distance, but problems that directly affect them in the form of growing flows of migration. This increasingly affects and even threatens their political stability and prosperity.

In the poor countries are most people who do not enjoy the material security, food, water and energy supplies, education, health, transport and employment and working conditions that most people in Western societies can take for granted. The relatively few people that can afford it adopt a lifestyle that copies the Western lifestyle. For many of the people who cannot afford this, Western lifestyle is what they aspire or at least dream of. An increasing number of people are no longer waiting for development of their own countries but try to migrate to richer countries, Western countries in particular.

Already migration creates heavy conflicts and cleavages in Western societies. Already Western countries, the United States and the European Union in particular, are hardly able to stop migration even though the means they use for this purpose become increasingly drastic. If living conditions for many people, in particular for younger people, in the poor countries are not rapidly improved, but rather worsened, migration will also increase and so will the problems of Western societies. Rapid improvement of living conditions in the poorer countries and creation of decent livelihoods for their people needs much growth and this growth must become sustainable within a few decades. This is reflected in the United Nations' sustainable development goal 8 which calls for sustainable economic growth.[19]

The poor countries do not only need growth for themselves but are for their own development dependent on growth in Western countries and other richer countries. They depend on the transformation of Western economies from "high volume to high value" which will, as Robert B. Reich argued some twenty years ago, create a fairer global division of labor and better development opportunities for developing countries. This transformation is, as I will argue in the fourth chapter, hardly possible without significant growth. Western countries also need growth in order to be willing and capable of investing much more in development assistance, fair trade and in the reduction of global inequality. Without growth, significant investments of Western countries in the global reduction of inequality are likely to create, in Western countries, distributive conflict which makes a reasonable developmental policy fail.[20]

The argument presented in this part provides a good rationale for the choice of standard of living as the economic dimension of sustainability, and the orientation of this concept towards the capitalist system and its growth model and lifestyle makes sense. However, it also makes clear that it is not just the average standard of living in society that matters, but that of the very largest part of the population. This makes the reduction of inequality a central problem of sustainable development. This is not a problem that can be solved by growth alone, but one that requires a change in the distribution logic which Thomas Piketty describes for the first decades of the twenty-first century. The solution of this problem will be decisive for the social cohesion of Western societies and their ability to achieve sustainable development.

The Social Dimension: Cohesion

The capacity of a society to establish and maintain widely accepted understandings and rules without recourse to coercion is of crucial importance for a society's ability to reach sustainable development. It determines a society's ability to permanently accommodate the many conflicts that are always associated with sustainable development. Moreover, it defines the extent to which the ability to settle conflict depends on government regulation and power. Social actors with a shared understanding of the importance of sustainable development and the right way to achieve it are generally more willing to seek solutions to their conflicts on their own than those who lack this understanding. Resolving their conflicts is easier because they do not have to agree on fundamental questions of goals and means, but only on the distribution of benefits, costs and risks. Social actors who share a widely accepted understanding will also be more willing to voluntarily take effective action toward sustainable development than those who lack this understanding. They are also more likely to act on their own in the spirit of laws and rules which are relevant for sustainable development and are less likely to try to circumvent these laws and rules. Laws and rules can therefore be kept more general and do not have to consider every possible behavior in detail. A high degree of cohesion thus also protects against the complexity trap. Last not least, a widely shared understanding of the importance of sustainable development and the right way to achieve it constitutes a strong incentive for politicians and business leaders to engage in effective activities to promote sustainable development.

From an economic perspective, a widely shared understanding of the importance of sustainable development and the right way to achieve it is particularly interesting because it enhances effective market solutions for sustainable development. As the French economist and Nobel laureate Jean Tirole in contrast to neo-liberal economists demonstrates in his book "Economics for the Common Good" markets alone cannot reach the common good. Rather, achievement of the common good requires the interplay of state and market. The most important activity of government in this context is to set an effective framework of the market that is geared at the attainment of the common good. But in the highly diversified Western societies, government is hardly capable of enacting a regulatory framework for the market which is effective in terms of sustainable development without a widely shared understanding of sustainable development. But precisely in these societies it is highly desirable to govern sustainable development as much as possible by a well-regulated market. If markets are well regulated activity for sustainable development will spontaneously emerge out of market transactions without causing much conflict.[21]

Take energy as an example. If energy is highly taxed and, therefore, rather expensive, customers will attempt to buy energy efficient devices at a reasonable price. If competition works there will always be some producers that will attempt to offer as soon as possible such devices. Energy efficiency will become an important competitive advantage for companies. There will be strong incentives for most or even all companies in the concerned industry to develop energy efficient devices. In this case, there need not be many losers in the industry. Most importantly, there will be no large cohesive groups of losers. One or two companies may miss out on this development and therefore slump or even go bankrupt, but other companies will benefit. Jobs will probably be lost in the former, but additional jobs may be created in the latter. Some shareholders will lose wealth, but others will gain. The tax will not create a comparative disadvantage for domestic companies on domestic markets because it affects foreign companies equally. The exception from this rule are companies in energy intensive industries with strong international competition. For these companies, a rule could be found that offers them a temporary opportunity to secure their international competitiveness despite higher energy taxes by innovating for high energy efficiency in their production. Such innovation is the replacement of coal by hydrogen in the production of steel on which some steelmakers currently work.

In the case just described we need not expect heavy political and social conflict on sustainable development. Rather, reasonably regulated market transactions may create a win–win condition which enhances social construction of sustainable development as a common good. However, this presupposes that, in parallel with the introduction of energy tax, lower and middle incomes in particular are relieved of income tax to such an extent that they do not suffer any real loss of income as a result of the introduction of an energy tax. This will not impair the effect of the energy tax on energy consumption.

A quite different situation exists in the case of CO_2-certificates on energy production. An efficient regime of CO2-certificates which leads year by year to a higher price of the certificates creates massive incentives for power companies to switch to renewable energy. This process is, as we discussed in the first chapter at the example of lignite open cast mining, likely to create losers and provoke heavy economic and social conflict. Exemption rules, as in the first case, are not sufficient to avoid conflict. Rather, the actors concerned must develop together with government a longer-term exit and transition strategy. The strategy must enable the energy companies to write off their investments in conventional energy, build up activities in new energy and other new business areas, and retrain their personnel. This also creates a win–win condition which enhances social construction of sustainable development as a common good.

In the first case, the role of government is confined to create an adequate and reliable framework of the market, in the second case, government must get involved with all stakeholders in the long-term management of a transformation process. Both cases require, as we will further discuss in the following chapters, high cohesion. In modern Western societies it is, however, difficult to reach high cohesion.

Some 150 years ago, one of the classics of sociology, the French sociologist Émile Durkheim claimed that modern societies are no longer held together by common values and norms, but by functional interdependence, especially the division of labor. People in a modern society are involved in a multi-layered network of work and contractual relationships. As a result, they are interdependent and cooperate with each other in many ways. Durkheim calls this organic solidarity because social cohesion arises from social structures. This concept is based on postulate that people are by their nature social beings who subordinate their individual interests to common goals of groups in which they live. On this last point, I do not follow Durkheim. As the definition of cohesion which I use in this book indicates, I consider the extent to which individuals are willing to work for common goals and goods as a variable feature of societies and their culture.[22]

Durkheim's concept of social cohesion was quite controversial in his time. The German sociologist Ferdinand Tönnies, for example, argued against Durkheim that even in modern societies there are two forms of cohesion which he calls "Gemeinschaft" (community) and "Gesellschaft" (society). The former is based on common values and norms and predominantly exists in rural and small-town milieus as well as in agriculture and handicrafts, and in religious groups. The latter is based on functional interdependence and prevails in large cities that are economically supported by industry and commerce. These two forms have been at the core of the conflicts associated with transformation of agrarian society to industrial societies. Before I continue on this case, let me clarify some terminological matter in order to avoid confusion of readers from different disciplines using different terminology.[23]

In sociology, values are understandings of the meaning, purpose and fundamental principles of society whereas norms are concrete rules on human behavior which are based on values. Modern institutional approaches in economics and sociology speak of understandings and rules rather than of values and norms. This is not only a matter of wording. Rather, the assumption is that in everyday life values and norms are inseparably intermingled in understandings and rules. Understandings are general, broad narrative or pictorial conceptions of the world that can have an empirical or scientific but also a normative basis. For example, an understanding of democracy can refer to how democracy functions in reality or how it should function normatively. In both cases, it includes some values, for example, as a measuring rod for functionality or basic principles of the concept, and some norms defining the operation of democracy. Rules, on the other hand, are concrete instructions for behavior that can be based on political or organizational decisions, social agreement, religious or other moral prescriptions, scientific insights, or practical experience. Rules always have some values as justification.

In institutional approaches, understandings and rules are labeled as institutions whereas in a more traditional and still widely accepted terminology institutions are reputable organizations and agencies, such as parliament, the European Commission, the World Bank, the pope or the protestant church, which issue, convey, adjust, maintain, monitor or enforce understandings and rules. The institutionalist view is that it is understandings and rules through which these organizations govern behavior. I use in this book the term institutions both for rules and understandings and for the organizations and agencies that are in charge of them because in everyday life both are inseparably linked. The credibility of an understanding on the creation of the world depends on the source of the understanding. Most people may accept the scientific theory of evolution, but many religious people, particularly in the United States, adhere to the Christian doctrine of creation.

This brings us back to Ferdinand Tönnies' two forms of cohesion. These forms are not merely of historical relevance, but both are active in modern societies. While "society" is the dominant form of cohesion in Western societies, there are still many rural, small-town and religious milieus where "community" is dominant. This seems to be particularly true for the United States where in a number of states and counties "community" plays a strong, even dominant political role. The parallel existence of the two forms may create massive cleavages and conflicts and a serious problem of cohesion because they may be associated with incompatible criteria for the acceptance of political decisions or other social decisions. We will discuss this in chapter 5.

Although in modern Western societies social cohesion no longer depends on shared values and norms, but on functional interdependence it nevertheless requires a minimal level of consensus on basic understandings and rules about the fundamental principles of the society in question, for example freedom, social justice or tolerance, and the way in which these principles are to be implemented, for example through social market economy, direct democracy or an open culture. In modern Western societies, a minimal level of consensus on understandings and rules presupposes a minimal level of justice: Basic social conditions must be widely perceived as fair and social institutions considered to safeguard reasonably fair representation of different interests in political decision-making and civil society.

In terms of Durkheim, we may express this more materialistically: A minimal level of justice means that people perceive their various functional interdependencies as being by and large as beneficial for them. Their functional interdependencies must provide them with a reasonably good livelihood, a reasonable level of social and physical security, and a reasonable chance for self-realization.

If societies fail to provide a minimal level of justice for all people, smaller or larger groups in society and their political representatives will challenge some or all of the basic understandings and rules. They will distrust the institutions from which these understandings and rules originate, or which uphold them. They will also tend to fundamentally reject decisions and decisions made according to these understandings and rules. The events following the 2020 US presidential election and the defeat of Donald Trump or the activities of German "Querdenker" (contrarians) in the Covid-19 pandemic are illustrative examples.[24]

What I have just described as a minimum level of justice is not an easy condition, but one that is rather difficult to fulfill, especially in modern Western societies. Justice is not merely an abstract principle, but a social construct which emerges from the day-to-day interactions and communications of society. It is, hence, shaped by experiences and communications of various social actors. We have already discussed in chapter 1 that modern Western societies are highly diversified and that this is reflected in a multitude of different, often contradictory and competing social interests which are represented by thousands of interest organizations. In this situation, any political decision or other collective decision is likely to produce considerable dissatisfaction which may add up to feelings of injustice if some social groups perceive that they get more often than other groups dissatisfactory outcomes from their social interactions. This leads to a conclusion which may sound like circular reasoning.

A society is the more likely to produce dissatisfactory outcomes for some groups the less it is capable to reach widely accepted decisions – that is the lower its cohesion is. In other words: Cohesion comes from cohesion. This is, however, not circular reasoning but manifests the insight of the theory of social evolution that societies or other social systems develop from within. In academic terminology, social systems are self-organizing and self-referential. Practically this means that as long as certain rules, e.g. principles of justices, are reinforced in the day-to-day operations of the system, the principles remain valid or even may be further developed. However, if in a significant number of decisions, the principles are not applied they become obsolete and eventually lose their validity.

The cohesion of modern societies is a very dynamic process. Society as a whole, but also its larger and smaller parts, are constantly changing because hitherto widely shared understandings and rules are questioned. Established understandings and rules may no longer be followed in parts of society or are even countered by alternative understandings and rules. If such changes are either widely accepted or widely rejected in formal or in spontaneous social decisions over time, cohesion of society is reinforced. If, however, changes are accepted by parts of society and rejected by others, cohesion may suffer. Society may split. As we will further discuss in chapter 5, this may develop an explosive force that hardly permits sustainable development.

A Key Issue: Radical Innovation

In the first chapter, I explained that technological progress and its huge potentials for dematerialization is a corner stone of my approach to threefold sustainability. More precisely, I am confident that technological progress will make radical innovations possible now and even more so in the coming years. With that production and consumption can be dematerialized within two to three decades to such an extent that humanity as a whole can satisfy its needs within planetary boundaries. In the year 2009 Johan Rockström and Will Steffen together with 26 other environmental scientists published a concept of planetary boundaries which defined "the non-negotiable planetary conditions that humanity needs to respect in order to avoid the risk of deleterious or even catastrophic environmental change of continental or even global scales". The concept includes nine different boundaries, namely climate change, ocean acidification, stratospheric ozone depletion, atmospheric aerosol loading, global phosphorus and nitrogen cycles, global freshwater use, land use change (conversion to cropland), biodiversity loss and chemical pollution. Several of these boundaries, including climate and biodiversity, are already hurt or endangered. This indicates that sustainable development may require a lot of radical innovation.[25]

In the relevant research, a distinction is made between radical and incremental innovations although the boundaries are sometimes quite blurred. Most of the innovations that we can observe every day in the economy are incremental innovations. Incremental innovations introduce improved products in existing markets. The basics are familiar technologies. Innovating companies essentially know the demand and competition on these markets. The innovation is matched to the known demand structures and customer relationships. The automobile industry is a typical example for incremental innovations. Over some 100 years, automobiles have been continuously improved. They became faster, more comfortable and secure, and electronically equipped, but in essence the product and its function have remained the same. This applies to e-mobility too although for the automobile industry it brings far-reaching changes. Companies regularly engaged in incremental innovation are often closely networked with their most important customers and involve major customers in their innovation processes. At Airbus and Boeing, for example, important customers are involved as lead customers in the development of new models or the further development of existing models.

Radical innovations, on the other hand, are innovations based on new knowledge and technology that introduce new products which either change an existing market or even a whole industry fundamentally or create a new market. They are associated with great uncertainty and significant risks for the respective companies, but also with great economic opportunities. The potential customers and markets for radical innovations, as well as their impact on existing markets and customer relationships, are at best only partially known and can only be assessed to a limited extent. Prominent examples are the internet and 3-D printing. The internet has created many new economic opportunities such as streaming services or apps for smartphones. It has already changed the retail sector fundamentally and with that the centers of many European cities. It is changing the finance industry and may within a few years even put an end to established forms of banking. 3-D printing is likely to fundamentally change industrial structures in one way or another within a decade.

Radical innovations are also referred to as disruptive because they tear companies out of their previous economic entanglements and force them to build new economic networks. Established business models become obsolete and companies, even large and previously strong companies, disappear from the market or retreat into niche markets. A prominent example is Kodak. Until the turn of the millennium, Kodak was a major player in the photographic industry. It also started early to look at digital photography, but they did so hesitantly and with too little investment. When digital photography became established, it was soon integrated into mobile phones and Kodak quickly disappeared from the market. Today, it is a specialist for digital print systems.

Incremental innovation is not disruptive, but nevertheless may create considerable losses in terms of profits and jobs. An example for this is more environmentally friendly packaging, which many customers are certainly in favor of and for which many customers are also willing to pay a little more. If individual companies do this for individual products, this innovation is unlikely to have a dramatic impact on growth and living standards, even if companies have to accept slightly higher costs and customers slightly higher prices. But once most companies package their products in an environmentally friendly way, there may be significant shifts between manufacturers of different packaging materials and providers of different packaging services. Companies that fail to convert their packaging products to renewable or recycled raw materials cost-effectively, or fail to do so in time, may well be forced out of the market. Companies whose products are made from renewable or recycled raw materials which are not recyclable themselves or which do not have efficient recycling logistics also risk deleterious effects.

The same applies to companies whose packaging design is not very con-ducive to sustainability. This list could be extended, but the cases mentioned are enough to make it clear that the switch to sustainable packaging will have a significant number of losers. At the same time, many innovative companies will be among the winners. Overall, this may result in considerable losses of profits and employment.

How big the losses from incremental innovation may be is shown by a study on the employment effects of the automotive industry's shift to e-mobility. E-mobility is likely to cost many jobs in the automobile industry because electrical cars, especially their engines, are much simpler in design and require less work. For Germany alone, an expert panel predicts a loss of more than 400,000 jobs; 80,000 of those in the construction of the engine. Similar developments may emerge in other industries. Overall this may lead to massive job losses in the coming years and decades. We will discuss this in more detail in chapter 6.[26]

For radical innovation, the case is more varied. Radical innovation creates, as a rule, new products and new markets. This leads to new growth and employment. Radical innovation to increase resource productivity can therefore generate new growth and new employment in new promising markets, thus linking sustainability with growth and living standards. Inso-far, radical innovation may be a silver bullet for threefold sustainability. The emphasis, however, is on may be. Radical innovation to increase resource productivity is just as disruptive as other radical innovation. It can just as well lead to massive employment losses and corresponding losses of living standards in parts of the population. Radical innovation to increase resource productivity can at the same time generate structures that promote wasteful use of natural resources.

Information technology, for example, is on the one hand the indispensable basis for the enormous progress in biotechnology which in turn is the basis for huge increases in resource productivity in the pharmaceutical industry and the health care system, in materials technology, and in agriculture. Examples include medicines that are precisely tailored to individual patients, materials made entirely from renewable resources and with a low ecological rucksack, or the many possibilities of urban agriculture. On the other hand, the same applications of information technology enable far-reaching automation and miniaturization of research and development, and of production in pharma-ceutical and chemical industries. This may result in massive job losses in these industries which will affect well-educated as well as unskilled workers. But at the same time it may create many new jobs in the same industries. Radical innovation is, much more than incremental innovation, the driver of Schumpeter's process of creative destruction. In this process, many workers may lose their jobs and not easily find a new job in the ascending business because their current skills do not match the requirements of the new jobs.

In terms of sustainable development, a key problem of radical innovation is that it is likely to initially generate winners and losers. This seems to prevent exactly what the approach of this book actually expects from radical innovation: It is supposed to be a vehicle to strongly advance environmental sustainability while avoiding or resolving the economic and social conflicts associated with it. But as a strong driver of creative destruction radical innovation may on the contrary be a main source of these conflicts. Indeed, radical innovation has a high potential for economic and social conflict, but it also has a high potential to resolve these conflicts. In essence this means that radical innovation is not by its very nature the silver bullet we want it to be but must be made into one.

Theoretically this may be considered a problem of governance which may be described simply, but which is difficult to solve. The problem is to institution-ally regulate behavior of relevant actors in a way which restricts undesirable outcomes of innovation without dampening innovation dynamics. The solu-tion of this and similar problems requires a well-designed mix of well-regulated markets, self-organization of civil society and activating government in the governance of sustainable development. This mix may be first designed as a general model, but then must be tailored to concrete problems.

The general model could be designed by a citizens' assembly which further develops the successful model of the Danish Board of Technology's consensus conferences on technology assessment. In terms of the economy as a whole, this model could probably only be a master plan, because the problem is strongly shaped by the specific conditions of the individual sectors of the economy. More concrete models would have to be developed for individual sectors. Even these models often may be too abstract for practical application. In many cases, practical solutions can probably only be developed in relation to more narrowly defined sectors of the economy or even to specific companies. This too could by accomplished by consensus conferences.

These citizens' assemblies and consensus conferences must find solutions that are not only widely accepted in the population, but also by the relevant interest groups. Otherwise, they risk the fate of the proposals of the French Citizens' Assembly on climate change.

The Deliberative Way: Activating Government

Economic and political debates on governance in Western societies are often reduced to the question of market versus government. In her book "Governing the Commons", Nobel laureate Elinor Ostrom suggests an alternative form of governance, namely self-organization by stakeholders. The theme of the book is development of institutions for managing common property. Among the cases which she studies are common land in the Swiss Alps and Japan, and water resources in Spain, the Philippines and California. In all these cases relevant stakeholders successfully established by agreement institutions to prevent overuse of the common resource or unfair practices.[27]

The institutional structures which Ostrom analyzes are partly venerable; they have existed for many centuries. Yet in modern diversified societies with their rapid production of knowledge they gain new topicality. They offer a device for decentralized problem resolution which includes all relevant stakeholders. The Emscher cooperative which I discussed in the previous chapter is an example of this. As we discussed in that case, cooperatives are an organizational form which can be widely applied. Moreover, cooperatives may systematically incorporate deliberative procedures in their planning and decision-making and become deliberative cooperatives.

Deliberative cooperatives are a particularly suitable organizational form for decentralized activities to promote threefold sustainability because they include all relevant stakeholders and bring together their diverse interests in deliberative decision-making. This gears them to substantially effective and socially acceptable decisions. As I cannot emphasize enough, decentralized, deliberative-oriented activities are essential for achieving sustainable development of Western societies.

Organizing such activities in the form of cooperatives generally only makes sense if the activities are long-term or permanent. Short-term and singular activities are usually organized as projects with limited scope. Such projects, however, may apply the principles of deliberative cooperatives in an analogous way.

Wide application of deliberative cooperatives in particular, and similarly organized projects, bears a great potential for avoiding losers in radical innovations and sustainable development. The general idea is that actors who are affected by a problem or otherwise have an interest in its solution join forces to solve this problem cooperatively. In the first chapter we briefly mentioned the case of phasing-out of conventional energy. In this case, power companies, workers, unions, educational facilities, environmentalist and government agencies could form an alliance to design and implement a phasing-out project which would allow energy companies to write off their investments in conventional power plants and other facilities, to invest in facilities for renewable energy and to develop new business areas, such as new digital services in energy supply, and last not least retrain their employees so that their skills match requirements of the future activities of the companies or the demand of employers in ascendant industries and businesses. Since the members of the alliance may still be caught in a long history of competitive pursuit of their interests and of many related conflicts, they may be well advised to commission a consensus conference with the working out of a concrete design for the project. This would bring in a lot of external knowledge in the project and could provide public support.

Decentralized activities offer a versatile toolbox for a government that wants to advance sustainable development, but often faces narrow political boundaries in doing so. Governments can use this toolbox without having to initiate or even organize the activities. Rather, they could confine themselves to an activating and loosely coordinating role. In the academic literature, the concept of an activating, enabling or empowering state is primarily applied to social policy and issues like welfare and inclusion. Here, I apply the concept and its basic idea more generally. I define the activating state as a state that relies not only on hierarchy, state regulation and public administration to solve social problems, but also on social self-organization. To this end, it must create a framework that enables decentralized actors to solve societal problems decentrally and on their own responsibility without compromising the overarching common good.[28]

In relation to society as a whole, decentralized self-organization is a spontaneous process whose outcome for society as a whole is a priori open. Thus, in our concrete context, it can make a positive contribution to threefold sustainability, but it can also be the opposite. Stakeholders in a decentralized project of self-organization are a priori designing this project in way which best fits their interests. They cannot or can only partially assess the impact of their project on other projects and on overall development – and even if they could, they might decide to behave with respect to the overall development as free-riders.

This is a similar kind of problem which Jean Tirole analyzes with respect to markets and the common good. But the problem cannot be solved in the same way, namely by government regulation. Regulation of social self-organization would be an unacceptable intervention into one of the basic rights in democratic societies, to wit the right of association. No less bad, it would also be a dysfunctional intervention, because social self-organization gains its strengths from its openness, its diversity, its creativity and its flexibility. Government regulation would hence largely destroy self-organization as toolbox for solving common problems. Even where regulation of social self-organization is legal, it should be kept as minimal as possible. This is the essence of activating government.

Activating government does not use negative incentives, such as law or penalty taxes, to control behavior of social actors, but rather positive incentives. These may be monetary incentives, such as subsidies or tax reductions, and non-monetary incentives, like quality seals, honors or privileges. The use of positive incentives fundamentally expands the government's options for action in managing social developments. Because they are generally binding, negative incentives are suitable for limiting the behavioral options of social actors and for standardizing social action. Positive incentives, on the other hand, create opportunities to activate a wide range of different possibilities for achieving a common goal and to align many actors with different possibilities and potentials for action to such goals.

Notes

1 In this book, I apply the term of social or collective decision not only to purposive decisions but also to spontaneously emerging agreements. In other books, the term is reserved for purposive decisions whereas spontaneous decisions are referred to as social choices.

2 See World Commission on Environment and Development (1987). Our Common Future. Oxford: Oxford University Press. The quotations are from pages 43 and 46.
3 Readers who would like to learn more about the social construction of reality should read the pioneering work of Peter L. Berger, Thomas Luckmann (1991). The Social Construction of Reality: A Treatise in the Sociology of Knowledge. London: Penguin Random House. (Originally published in 1966). See also Vivien Burr (2015). Social Constructionism. London and New York: Routledge.
4 There is a wide body of literature which describes what business can do and already do on sustainable development. See for example: Peter Fisk (2010). People, Planet, Profit: How to Embrace Sustainability for Innovation and Business Growth. London, Philadelphia and New Delhi: Kogan Page. Kate Raworth (2018). Doughnut Economics: Seven Ways to Think Like a 21st-century Economist. London: Random House Business Books. Klaus Schwab with Peter Vanham (2021). Stakeholder Capitalism: A Global Economy that Works for Progress, People and Planet. Hoboken NJ: John Wiley. Joseph E. Stiglitz (2020). People, Power, and Profits: Progressive Capitalism for an Age of Discontent. New York: Penguin.
5 For an English version of the "Bürgerrats" final report see https://buergerra t-klima.de/neuigkeiten/buergerrat-klima-publishs-english-version-of-final-results.
   For a short description of the proceedings of the French citizens' assembly and an analysis of its impact see https://www.dw.com/en/frances-citizen-climate-assem bly-a-failed-experiment/a-56528234.
6 For stimulating discussion of opportunities to reach the common good see Philip Kotler (2019). Advancing the Common Good: Strategies for Business, Government, and Nonprofits. Santa Barbara: Praeger.
7 Cf. Jens Jetzkowitz (2019). Co-Evolution of Nature and Society: Foundations for Interdisciplinary Sustainability Studies. Cham: Palgrave Macmillan. Marcello Basili, Maurizio Franzini, Alessandro Vercelli eds. (2012). Environment, Inequality and Collective Action. London and New York: Routledge.
8 See Leon Festinger (1954). 'A Theory of Social Comparison Processes' in: Human Relations, 7, 117–140. Festinger's theory has been further developed meanwhile. Cf. Jerry Suls, Ladd Wheeler eds. (2000). Handbook of Social Comparison: Theory and Research. Heidelberg: Springer Nature.
9 For the Study of the German Ministry of the Environment see: https://www.bmu. de/publikation/wie-umweltfreundlich-sind-elektroautos.
10 See Friedrich Schmidt-Bleek (2009). The Earth: Natural Resources and Human Intervention. London: Haus Publishing. Quotation from page 14.
11 Stefanie Böge (1992). Die Auswirkungen des Strassengüterverkehrs auf den Raum. Die Erfassung und Bewertung von Transportvorgängen in einem Produktlebenszyklus. Diplomathesis, University of Dortmund.
12 See Friedrich Schmidt-Bleek (2009). The Earth: Natural Resources and Human Intervention. London: Haus Publishing, pp. 20–24.
13 See William McDonough, Michael Braungart (2003). Cradle to Cradle: Remaking the Way We Make Things. New York: Macmillan USA.
14 The process of creative destruction is described in chapter 7 of Joseph A. Schumpeter (1942). Capitalism, Socialism and Democracy. New York: Harper. The most recent edition is published in 2008 by Harper Perennial Modern Thought (New York).
15 Cf. Competitiveness Policy Council (1992). Building a Competitive America: First Annual Report to the President and Congress. Washington. European Commission (1998). The Competitiveness of European Industry. Luxembourg: Office for Official Publications of the European Communities.
16 The wider concept of living standard is for example described in Eurostat (2018). Living Conditions in Europe. 2018 edition. Luxembourg: Publications Office of the European Union.

17 See Tim Jackson (2017). Prosperity without Growth: Foundations for the Economy of Tomorrow. London and New York: Routledge. Quote from page 114.
18 Cf. Thomas Piketty (2017). Capital in the Twenty-first Century. Cambridge, MA: Belknap Press of Harvard University Press.
19 The UN's sustainable development goals are described and discussed in Jeffrey D. Sachs (2015). The Age of Sustainable Development. New York: Columbia University Press. A short description of SDG 8 may be found on page 487.
20 Robert B. Reich (1991). The Work of Nations. New York: Alfred A. Knopf.
21 Cf. Jean Tirole (2017). Economics for the Common Good. Princeton: Princeton University Press.
22 Steven Lukes ed. (2013). Durkheim: The Division of Labour in Society. Basingstoke: Palgrave Macmillan.
23 Ferdinand Tönnies (2020). Community and Society. Augusta, GA: Mockingbird Press.
24 For operational reasons, I use here a simple minimalist definition of justice. For a more elaborate concept see Harry Brighouse, Ingrid Robeyns eds. (2010). Measuring Justice: Primary Goods and Capabilities. Cambridge UK: Cambridge University Press.
25 The study of Rockström and others is published in Ecology and Society 14, 32, quotation from page 2 of the internet version of the paper. See https://www.stockholmresilience.org/download/18.8615c78125078c8d3380002197/ES-2009-3180.pdf - For a comprehensive description of current problems of sustainable development and of the planetary boundaries see Jeffrey D. Sachs (2015). The Age of Sustainable Development. New York: Columbia University Press.
26 Cf. https://www.handelsblatt.com/politik/deutschland/autoindustrie-umstellung-auf-e-mobilitaet-gefaehrdet-410-000-arbeitsplaetze/25405230.html
27 Elinor Ostrom (2015). Governing the Commons: The Evolution of Institutions for Collective Action. Cambridge UK: Cambridge University Press.
28 A broad overview of the established approach to the activating state is offered by Robert Weissberg (1999). The Politics of Empowerment. Westport, CT: Praeger. For a more general view see Angus Stewart (2000). Theories of Power and Domination: The Politics of Empowerment in Late Modernity. London and Thousand Oaks: Sage.

3 The Economic Charm of Ecology

Political, social and academic debates on sustainable development have focused for years on climate change. While I agree that climate change is a pressing problem, I think the focus is too narrow and misleading. It continues to eclipse other important environmental issues on the political, economic and civil society agendas and it may lead to solutions that serve climate protection but are undesirable from a sustainability point of view. In contrast: The approach proposed here can also be applied to the goal of climate neutrality without compromising this goal or sustainable development.

As I explained in chapter 1, the approach of this book is based on the Factor 10 concept. The guiding principle of the concept is to satisfy human needs with the lowest possible consumption of non-renewable resources. This does not only include resources that go into the products, but also the "ecological rucksack" of products, that is all resources that do not go into the product itself, but are only consumed to produce the resources that go into the product. I also include the ecological footprint which measures the amount of biologically active land which is necessary to serve people's needs for their way of life. This measure tells us how much Western countries need to increase their resource productivity in order to get by with the nature at their disposal. It also tells us how much rich countries are living environmentally at the expense of poor countries.[1]

Considering ecological rucksacks and footprint highlights how ambitious sustainable development is. If we do not want to impose sustainable development in a massive conflict with established economic conditions and lifestyles, then we have to heavily dematerialize the products which we consume. This alone is a really challenging goal. But if this also has to take into account ecological rucksacks and footprints, we have to engage in far-reaching reshaping of the social systems in which we live. This includes the transformation of Western economies from high volume to high value, shaping the digital economy and remodeling production systems, implementing a fair international division of labor, and last not least redesigning cities and agglomerations.

This is a challenging, but feasible task. It requires a great deal of technical, organizational and social innovation, as well as investment in research and development and in human capital. There is already much knowledge

DOI: 10.4324/9781003261421-3

available for many small and large steps towards the ambitious goal. But these must be initiated as quickly as possible. There is also enough time. The time target for many countries to achieve climate neutrality is 2050. Achieving sustainable development will hardly be faster. The approach of this book also sets the year 2050 as a deadline by which Western countries must have succeeded in moving onto a sustainable path of development. Even the 2050 target is only realistic if the available time is used well. This in turn requires flexible, adaptive structures in government, business and civil society. In the modern knowledge society, a lot can happen in just under three decades, and above all a lot of unexpected or even "unthinkable" things can happen.

One of the important challenges here is to avoid a highly complex set of regulations, an inflated bureaucracy and entrenched structures. Climate policies of many countries show worrying traits of such a development. In contrast, the Factor-10 concept can be applied in a way that reduces complexity, promotes bureaucracy dismantling and avoids entrenched structures. The way is to focus it on a few strategically selected resources and products. These are particularly resources and products which play an important role in industrial production and carry big rucksacks, but are not extremely scarce. Focusing on a few strategically selected resources and products enables government to achieve great effects with a reasonable effort and reasonable costs for business and other actors. It allows the design of relevant policy in a way which includes imports. A tough sustainability policy in the Western countries does, thus, not constitute a competitive disadvantage for these countries' industry and does not create an incentive to move production to countries with low environmental standards.[2]

The best instrument to drive resource productivity is dynamic, but reliable taxation supplemented by some dynamic, but reliable standards. Dynamic but reliable taxes and standards increase at regular intervals over a longer period of time in a transparent manner. Companies and other players must be able to adjust early and reliably to higher taxes or standards. This procedure creates massive incentives for innovation and ensures that economic and social players have a reliable framework for longer-term cooperation and projects. The precondition is that legislators and the bureaucracy are capable of acting reliably in the long term. This is a difficult precondition.

Effective resource taxes, however, have an ugly downside: They drive prices of goods andd may thus severely affect the standard of living of a large part of the population. This would advance the kind of distributive conflict which is so detrimental to sustainable development. The solution to this problem is a significant tax cut for lower and medium income groups and SMEs. The related tax loss should be compensated by the income from resource tax. As a desirable side effect, this could reduce labor costs significantly while resource costs increase accordingly.

The Factor 10 concept unfolds its effectiveness for threefold sustainability all the more, the better the enormous knowledge production of the modern knowledge society is used. Today's huge knowledge production provides a broad knowledge base for far-reaching dematerialization of products, production and distribution. This includes, for example, an increasing number of materials which are produced from renewable resources or "waste" materials. It also includes new production technologies which may be used to increase resource productivity of industrial production. But these opportunities are often badly used because the regulatory framework of markets and other public policies often provide poor incentives for innovation and challenging sustainability projects. Moreover, innovation systems of companies, regions and national economies are often badly designed.

Cities are key actors both with respect to sustainability problems and the solution of these problems. Cities are on one side the places where problems of sustainability and the costs of these problems are concentrated. On the other side, cities are the places where much of the knowledge and creativity needed to solve these problems are concentrated. Moreover, sustainability is becoming an important factor for the attractiveness and competitiveness of cities. This leads to increasing competition, but also mutual learning concerning sustainable development among cities across the world. This is building up to a great process of collective learning on sustainable development. Probably more than national governments, cities will turn out in the coming years as the drivers of sustainable development. Together with private actors and their self-organization or market activities they will bring in a creative element of ordered "chaos" in sustainable development. Most national governments, but also the European Commission and international organizations will fall far short of sustainable development without much decentralized activity.

Resource Productivity or Climate Neutrality?

I argue at the beginning of this chapter that the focus on climate neutrality is pushing other important environmental issues, hunger, deforestation, biodiversity, soil erosion, overfishing, plastic waste, water scarcity and overpopulation into the background. This will probably provoke some readers to ask whether my focus on resource productivity is more far-reaching. This question is not unjustified, because at least superficially, my approach is at the core about a single goal, namely to expand or even overcome the planetary boundaries of economic growth. Yet, this single goal is positively related to the elimination of hunger and of deforestation, and the solution of other important environmental issues. The elimination of hunger is hardly possible without sustainable growth. Deforestation on the other hand drastically narrows the planetary boundaries and thus limits sustainable growth.[3]

It is even less likely that the principal goal of my approach, threefold sustainability, can be reached without solving these problems. That is in the nature of things. Social systems and their natural environment are closely coupled. The natural environment is itself a highly complex system which consists of different ecosystems, for example marine ecosystems or alpine ecosystems. Ecosystems describe how in a certain place animals and plants mutually depend on each other and interact with each other and with their physical environment. They describe how animals and plants are interlinked in food chains and how they compete for food, space and energy.[4]

Theoretically speaking, social systems and ecosystems form co-evolving systems. They mutually adapt to each other in their evolution. Changes in a social system generate changes in ecosystems and vice versa. Climate change is a good example of this. It is nature's reaction to our way of life and production, and it is now forcing changes in this way of life and production. Other interventions of human activities in nature also lead to reactions of nature, which we perceive as environmental problems. If these problems remain unsolved, they will sooner or later generate or force massive economic, political and social changes.

An illustrative case is plastic waste in the ocean. Every year, several million tons of plastic waste are dumped worldwide. This harms several hundred species of animals that live in the sea or on the coasts. Important habitats, such as coral reefs, are also damaged. If one also considers that the oceans are being exploited by large, often heavily subsidized fishing fleets of industrial countries to the limits of fish stocks and beyond, it does not take much fantasy to envisage that long before the middle of this century the oceans may be exhausted as an important source of food for mankind, as some scientists predict. It may not be possible today to estimate how great the risk of depletion of the oceans is, but the very existence of a significant risk should prompt governments of this world to commit themselves to combating plastic waste in the oceans and their overfishing as much as to fighting climate change. Degradation or loss of marine ecosystems will have massive impacts on human wellbeing as well as on other ecosystems. Some of these effects we may not even know now or not be aware of. This is particularly true because there may be immediate or distant interactions with other problems.[5]

An example: Degradation or loss of marine ecosystems will hit many developing countries particularly hard, as they will lose a source of food and an important trade. This is likely to significantly aggravate problems of food supply, poverty, hunger and health in Africa. The same holds for the EU's trade policy on Africa. The EU Commission wants to conclude a free trade agreement with Africa which is criticized in the EU parliament because it massively affects African agriculture through the export of subsidized food from the EU. This too exacerbates the major hunger problems in these countries. In the end, even Europe pays a high price. Part of this price is that trade relations with Africa, and with that political relations, are not sustainable. This may worsen Europe's economic and social relations for years and even decades. The probably larger part are growing flows of poverty refugees.

The real price is not the cost of the refugees, but what the refugee flows are doing to Europe, especially the European Union. The European Union is deeply divided over how to deal with refugees. This has developed into a general cohesion problem for the Union. Moreover, deep political divisions have emerged in most member states. This is manifested as strong right-wing populism in societies, authoritarian tendencies and a growing polarization which complicate or even prevent a long-term and reliable sustainability policy.

Climate neutrality, to reiterate, is a very major goal for humanity. But the one-sided fixation on this goal leads to neglecting other major problems of our interaction with nature and the multi-layered connections between these problems. At present, we can hardly foresee the consequences of this neglect. But all we know about the evolution of systems, be they natural or social systems, is that this involves many risks. The unthinking intervention in certain parts of a system produces a variety of "side effects" that can hardly be foreseen. It is, hence, quite possible that the one-sided focus on climate neutrality produces adverse effects on the climate.[6]

The best way to intervene meaningfully in a system as complex as our environment will be a simple, manageable way. However, this way must correspond to the complexity of the system. Friedrich Schmidt-Bleek has identified such a path with the Factor 10 concept. The way is to intervene as little as possible in nature. Since we are already far from innocence, this actually means to drastically reduce these interventions. This is the meaning of resource productivity and the Factor 10 concept.

This way is also economically and politically simple and manageable. The state does not have to prescribe concrete solutions for sustainable development to the economy and society. It can largely limit itself to enact effective incentives to drive resource productivity. Concrete measures to increase resource productivity are left to economic and social creativity. In this way, the state does not run the risk of prescribing the future on the basis of today's knowledge.

The importance of this can be seen in the example of electromobility which we already discussed in chapter 2. We also briefly noted there that some of the materials needed for electric cars are in extremely short supply and will also run out. Currently several companies and laboratories are working on innovative solutions to the problems, e.g. alternative materials for batteries and engines or lower-energy production processes. Should these solutions fail to materialize, or fail to materialize on time, or should there be massive problems in the supply of scarce raw materials, e.g., due to unrest in a supplier country or a trade conflict, Western societies or perhaps even the entire world would find themselves in a situation with no clear way out. Almost everywhere, governments are relying exclusively on electromobility as a climate-neutral solution for private motorized transport. They have set a clear path from which it is hard to come back down. This has created entrenched structures that increasingly exclude other solutions. When many countries and most car producers have fully switched to e-mobility, neither the realization of its lack of sustainability nor extreme scarcity and high prices for certain raw materials are likely to bring a short-term shift away from electromobility. The costs for this would be prohibitive and alternatives would probably not be available in the short term. What is more likely, at least in the short and mid-term is a sharp increase in the cost of electric cars. This could make investment in development of alternatives profitable. But even then change may produce heavy economic and social problems.

I outline this scenario only to highlight how problematic it is if governments determine a specific technological solution to a problem. This creates strong incentives for companies to rely on this solution and to abandon research and development on alternative solutions. As a result, the relevant industry loses its ability to adapt to unexpected future developments. This would not be a problem if the relevant developments were clear and could be predicted with a high degree of probability. However, this condition is unrealistic in the modern knowledge society. To understand this, one only has to consider what changes information technology and biotechnology alone have brought about in the last two or three decades. These include social media, the internet of things, additive manufacturing, gene therapy, biomaterials or mRNA vaccines. Given the speed and scope of current knowledge production, the near future is likely to bring even more and perhaps more far-reaching changes. These may include new fuels or new methods to produce hydrogen. The determination of technological solutions by governments is therefore a very risky approach that should not be a model for further sustainability strategies.

The one-sided focus on climate neutrality and the definition of electro-mobility as a major solution are dangerous weaknesses of sustainability policy in many countries. Yet there is a reason for the respective political decisions. The reason is complexity. Climate policy alone is not only factually complex, but above all politically complex. Politically, it involves a large number of different interest groups, specialized policies and bureaucracies. This is associated with a large number of competing interests and corresponding conflicts. In the economy, there are competing interests between innovative companies that expect to gain economic advantages and a better international competitive position by playing an active role in environmental and climate protection and companies that are either weak in innovation or do not have economically viable innovation opportunities. Depending on the industry in question, the trade unions are probably involved on one side and on the other. We could think this through even further and include, for example, ministries of agriculture, health, labor or justice with their specific viewpoints and interests. If we want to refine the whole thing a bit more, we also look at different interests and conflicts within each ministry. When you consider all of this, it's almost a miracle if climate policy even functions to some degree. This is probably mainly due to the fact that climate problems are felt by a broader public and in many sectors of the economy, and that climate change has arrived on the international stage.

The environmental politicians in parliaments and departments of the environment, as well as the environmental associations, are trying to push through laws and regulations that, according to all knowledge, are necessary to achieve climate neutrality in their respective countries by 2050. They are probably also supported by the ministries of foreign affairs, which represent the countries in international climate activities. Economic policymakers and the ministries of economics as well as business associations also want to achieve climate neutrality in principle. But all the many actors involved in environmental policy share one concern, namely that laws and regulations on climate protection do not place too great a burden on them or on their clients. This makes a comprehensive environmental policy extremely difficult. It is much less difficult to reach agreement on a more narrowly defined environmental policy, namely climate policy, and to focus this policy strongly on a few issues and solutions, such as electromobility.

A similar picture with different constellations of politicians, administrations and interest groups could be described with respect to the other important environmental problems. If we put all these pictures together to form an overall picture of a comprehensive environmental policy, then we see a situation which is nothing but a big mess.

The approach which is proposed in this book offers a way out of this situation because it allows the integration of a range of different environmental policies in a strategy which does not require a lot of special legislation and subsidies. The approach can deal with the material complexity of sustainable development without requiring a complex set of tools. While material complexity can hardly be reduced in a meaningful way at the current level of knowledge about ecosystems and the interrelationships of environmental problems, it can be managed with a relatively simple set of tools. This reduces political and social complexity of environmental protection and sustainability significantly. It is true that a comprehensive sustainability policy touches on a large number of societal interests, much larger than the number of interests affected by specific policies on individual environmental problems. Crucially, however, these many interests need only agree on the broad outlines of a relatively simple set of instruments, such as a tax and a few standards. These instruments can then be adapted to sectoral specifics in a decentralized manner.

This approach can easily be applied if environmental problems can be translated into a resource problem. This is not always possible, but more often than one may expect. Rather obvious cases are overfishing or water scarcity. Fish stocks and water are resources in the usual sense of the word. In a different way, climate change is also a good case. CO_2 may be defined as resource which is needed for the production of goods but does not go into these products. It is, hence, part of their rucksack. A similar practice can be followed with waste, in particular plastic waste, fertilizer or soil. The approach may even be applicable to deforestation or biodiversity. I will discuss this in more detail further down in this chapter.

The simplicity of the proposed approach is a crucial success factor. Activities to promote sustainability are, as a rule, themselves interventions in nature. In other words, they create variations in ecosystems, to which these often react with changes. These in turn often generate economic, social and political changes which change the conditions for action of sustainability policy and of sustainability strategies of private actors. The more different measures are used to promote sustainability, the more diverse this process and the more complicated and unmanageable it becomes.

A major conclusion from the argument in this part is that sustainable development not only requires major changes of the behavior of many individual actors, but the integration of these changes into the overarching network of social interactions. Much more prosaically put, what is needed for sustainability (and also for climate neutrality) are new structures, such as new production systems, new distribution and logistics structures. It also requires a new international division of labor in which developing countries are no longer used as the richer countries' factory for cheap mass production of technologically simple goods.

It does not really help sustainability much if a respectable number of companies learn that increasing resource productivity or decreasing CO_2 may be economically profitable if this remains one of many nice examples of a still rather small minority of companies, but leaves the structures that advance unsustainable activities of many companies unchanged. The importance of this conclusion is highlighted by two key problems of sustainable development, namely big rucksacks and big footprints.

Factor 10, Rucksacks and Footprints

Big rucksacks manifest the fact that sustainable development is not only a matter of products, but of systems of production and distribution which expand far beyond the society in which a product is produced or consumed. Big footprints point to the fact that ways of production and life in Western and other more wealthy countries create huge negative effects for the livelihoods of future generations in these countries but even more for the livelihoods of present and future generations in poorer countries.

Ecological rucksacks are built up from the very beginning to the very end throughout the value chain including consumption. The load starts with the extraction of raw materials and their preparation, it continues with the use of energy and materials through different production stages, which often include subcontracting of parts and their preliminary stages, and ends with the disposal of waste and the recycling of products and materials. In between, there is a lot of transportation. Resource productivity thus must be considered from cradle to cradle, that is from the extraction of raw material to waste processing and recycling.

The importance of including resource consumption from the beginning and all the way to the end was shown by a feature on the American TV channel CNN on July 10, 2021, entitled: "How marginalized communities in the South are paying the price for green energy in Europe". The story tells of people in the southern United States who suffer enormous noise and dust pollution because forests in their immediate vicinity are cut down using industrial methods and all the wood is processed into pellets. The pellets are exported to the EU, where they fetch good prices as a renewable energy source. The report is certainly right when it states that this is anything but environmentally sound. However, there is a method to this nonsense: with its corresponding regulation, the EU is following a procedural proposal by scientists at the UN according to which emissions from the burning of biomass should, for the sake of simplicity, be accounted for where the wood is felled. This is intended to avoid multiple calculations. If the emissions are added to the resultant energy's ecological rucksack in the European Union, energy from the pellets from the south of the United States is neither sustainable nor climate friendly.

This example also indicates that use of natural resources must be related to the benefit that is achieved with it. Trees that are cut down and made into pellets may fetch a higher price than trees whose wood is used to build houses or furniture, or which absorb CO_2 as forests, but their benefit in terms of satisfying human needs is much less. This is what we may learn from the way in which Friedrich Schmidt-Bleek looks at resource productivity. In his Factor 10 concept resource productivity is not considered directly in relation to products, but to the services or utility that these products provide for the respective consumers. This is the MIPS concept. MIPS means material input per unit of service (utility). In this view, we would not look at electric vehicles, but at the mobility service they generate. More practically, we look at resource consumption (including its rucksack) per passenger kilometer. Most importantly, we would consider resource consumption, including all rucksacks, over the entire life cycle of the product and its function, including disposal or recycling of the discarded product. This is the appropriate way to define resource consumption to meet our need for mobility or any other need. Automobility requires not only vehicles, but also roads, parking lots, service facilities, and more. All this must be included in the rucksack of passenger kilometers and of cars.[7]

If we apply the MIPS concept, we easily realize that the resource consumption which is necessary to meet the needs of Western and other richer societies is integrated into a complex network of relations, mostly with global dimensions. At first glance, it seems that this network can only be influenced by international agreements and cooperation. This is a popular argument of lobbyists against national policies. However, this argument is false and the potential source of a costly error. It is false because most of the resources are consumed by a few countries which also are responsible for the vast majority of environmental problems. These are the Western countries, China, Russia, India and Arab countries. Most developing countries consume only a disproportionally low share of the world's resources and many of the environmental problems they create reflect the unequal trade relations of these countries with the richer countries. Rucksacks too are in effect mostly the product of the richer countries' production and consumption and can be reduced by them. The richer countries, therefore, must and can solve the sustainability problems of this earth largely on their own. This is even truer with regard to the ecological footprint which simply describes the fact that the richer countries live at the expense of the poorer ones.

To put it in a nutshell, for environmental reasons as well as for reasons of global justice, the richer countries have to find ways to drastically reduce their resource consumption and to massively increase their resource productivity. They must do this largely by national means and strategies. Rucksacks must play a central role in this. By reducing rucksacks, resource productivity can in principle be increased without fewer goods and services being available.

Meeting this challenging task within the next two or three decades requires three interrelated measures in Western societies: firstly, a demater- ialization of goods and services through an ecological redesign, secondly, a dematerialization of production and consumption through a reorganization of production systems and value chains, and of the international division of labor, thirdly, a dematerialization of material consumption through the development of new material and energy technologies, urban agriculture and new ways of reusing residual materials and waste. The first two points we discuss in this part, the third one is dealt with further down in this chapter.[8]

Ecodesign is a systematic approach to product design that aims to reduce resource and energy consumption and environmental impacts over the entire life cycle of products. This includes the use of renewable resources and residual materials as well as increasing the lifetime, reuse or recycling of products and improving the functionality of products. The approach is broadly applicable to virtually all products and services in a modern econ- omy, including buildings, vehicles, machinery and equipment, furniture and clothing, packaging, and even food. It is an effective device to avoid big rucksacks and big footprints in the first place. An original example of eco- design is compostable tableware made from wheat bran, coffee waste, or tree leaves and bark. I will not go into that here, but if you search the internet, you'll find many more examples and ideas.

A great and lasting reduction of rucksacks and footprints is impossible without addressing the production systems within which they are generated. A good example of this is the globalization of supply chains in the automotive industry. In the 1980s and 1990s, automotive industries around the world took their cues from the Japanese model of lean manufacturing. This production model had helped the Japanese automotive industry achieve higher productiv- ity and quality, giving it considerable competitive advantages internationally. An important element of this model was close involvement of the supplier industry in both development and production. It was therefore linked as clo- sely as possible to the automotive plants. This also enabled "just-in-time" supply, which at the time was hailed as an important organizational innovation. An important element of this system was avoidance of material waste, i.e. effi- cient use of resources. As early as the 1990s, however, an opposing trend began to take hold, namely global sourcing. The global procurement of supplier parts brought many companies price advantages above all, but also access to new technological solutions, a reduction in dependencies and other benefits. The price advantages arose from low wages, but often also from lower labor and environmental standards. But low labor and environmental standards are, as rule, also associated with big rucksacks. Big rucksacks also are generated by the long transport distances and the elaborate logistic systems of global sourcing.

In recent times there are signs of a renewed trend towards more localized procurement. Although this is not primarily for environmental, but for organizational and financial reasons, it could improve resource productivity again. It would be an important first step, but more far-reaching changes of production systems are needed for sustainable development, especially for reducing rucksacks and footprints. Western economies must move away from their established production system, which is dominated by large corporations and which could become even more dominated by these corporations as digitalization progresses. This system is now already heavily geared towards mass production. If the internet of things is primarily determined by the large corporations and their global production, this effect will be even stronger. In addition, the global supply chains that promote large rucksacks and footprints are more likely to be reinforced instead of retracted.

What also makes the large corporations problematic, especially from a sustainability point of view, is their economic and political power. We addressed in the first chapter the power of the large retailers, who by dictating their price force farmers to use massive amounts of fertilizers and pesticides. Another example is big oil companies which are responsible for environmental destruction and poor working conditions in Nigeria and other countries. The political power of large corporations is no less problematic. Time and again, it helps them to prevent, circumvent or weaken stricter environmental protection rules. In many countries, energy companies have delayed or prevented the switch to renewable energies and got involved far too late. The automotive industry in the USA, Germany and other countries also continued to resist sustainable mobility when it had long been clear what damage automobiles with internal combustion engines were doing to the climate. Such examples prove the correctness of a statement by Harvard professor Karl W. Deutsch, one of the leading political scientists of his time:

> To have power means not to have to give in, and to force the environment or the other person to do so. Power in this narrow sense is the priority of output over intake, the ability to talk instead of listen. In a sense, it is the ability to afford not to learn.

This is an ability that has become an anachronism in the modern knowledge society.[9]

Large corporations will continue to play a role in the future, but they should no longer dominate the economy and its structures. They also should not dominate politics and economic policy. The dominant role should be played by small and medium-sized enterprises, cooperatives and creative self-employed people which are embedded in networks of innovation and financing. These are the enterprises which have little or no power, and therefore must assure their competitiveness by creativity and innovativeness. They are, thus, a crucial source of the ability to learn and innovate that the economy must achieve and secure in the long term in order to meet the challenges of sustainable development and the modern knowledge society.

A thought-provoking impulse is provided by the scenario which Jeremy Rifkin describes in his book "The Zero Marginal Cost Society: The Internet of Things, the Collaborative Commons, and the Eclipse of Capitalism". The scenario describes an economy which is shaped by innovative self-employed people and cooperatives and large numbers of prosumers which work together in networks, joint workplaces, open innovation systems and other collaborative forms including a new financial system. Although it is a bit too idealistic and too simplistic I find this scenario appealing in terms of threefold sustainability.

A central role in Rifkin's scenario is played by the development of a zero marginal cost society. As the name says, a zero marginal costs society is a society in which marginal costs for most goods are near zero. In prose this means that once fixed costs (for infrastructure, machinery and equipment, research and development, management and administration) are covered, each additional unit of a product can be produced nearly free of costs. The result is an economy of abundance. Rifkin's argument makes some sense in relation to digital goods, for example music, movies or e-books which may be streamed or downloaded. Streaming or downloading itself does not involve significant costs. Nevertheless, there may exist direct production costs, such as royalties for composers or authors. In the digital economy, there will be rapid technological development in the coming years and decades. This will require massive investments in research and development, new technology, and public and operational infrastructures, which will keep driving up fixed costs. The same applies to the sustainable renewal of the economy. Therefore, even with marginal costs close to zero, prices will hardly be so low that one can speak of a zero marginal cost society and an abundant economy. The prediction of the zero marginal cost society and its abundance is, in my view, at least much exaggerated and only rudimentarily realistic.

I hope that I am right about the latter, because if the forecast actually came true, it would be quite a disaster for sustainable development. If almost all goods would be available in abundance, most people would consume all they want and as much they want. The result would be an increase in consumption which would go beyond all limits because costs or prices of goods would no longer restrict consumption. This is a good example of the rebound effect. As I explained in chapter 2, this effect describes the case that increasing energy efficiency and resource productivity does not reduce but rather increases energy or resource consumption. This poses the great danger that resource consumption, especially by rich societies, will exceed planetary boundaries in spite of great increases of resource productivity. This danger is all the greater because if the costs and prices of goods are low, financial control instruments, such as a resource tax, would also become less effective. To avoid this, financial instruments would have to increase costs for consumers to such an extent that the zero marginal cost society would fall by the wayside. Rifkin is aware that this may be a problem but his solution to the problem is that people will learn to consume the environment in a reasonable way – an extremely optimistic solution.

However, it does not take a zero marginal cost society to produce economic structures that are similar to those which Rifkin describes. The internet, 3-D printing, new or revitalized forms of organization, changing attitudes in the population, particularly among young people, the weakness of established structures and other factors create favorable conditions for the development of those kinds of structures. But the new structures will by no means emerge with the inevitability that Rifkin suggests. Given the problems with commons outlined in the first and second chapters, they will also not be as dominated by collaborative commons as Rifkin predicts. What can be established is an economy with many innovative SMEs and self-employed people that are on one side integrated in supraregional and often global innovation and financing networks, but on the other one in localized and customized production systems. Cooperatives will also play an important role in these new structures as carriers of collaborative projects and public functions. We will discuss this in more detail in the following chapters.

The Driving Force: A Dynamic Resource Tax

An important insight of our discussion of the governance problem of sustainable development is that in the modern knowledge society hierarchical coordination by government or in big companies is rendered difficult by rapid change of knowledge and social situations, and high uncertainty. The implication of this is that spontaneous or decentralized coordination by markets, culture and social self-organization has gained greater significance. But this also means that the regulation of markets has gained new topicality. We discussed in the last chapter that markets need a regulatory framework to reach the common good. By the same token, markets need a regulatory framework that drives threefold sustainable development and which matches the conditions and opportunities of the modern knowledge society.

As we have discussed earlier in this book, modern knowledge society provides on one side a rapid and broad flow of knowledge which always opens up new possibilities for action and enables new solutions to problems. On the other side, this is associated with high uncertainty which hardly allows to predict what kind of solution for a certain problem may be at hand in the medium or long run. A regulatory framework that prescribes specific technical or organizational solutions is therefore not appropriate. This solution could become obsolete in a short time because new knowledge provides other and better solutions. The specification of a certain solution can thus lead to massive misinvestment, but also to R&D deficits with regard to alternative solutions. The situation is similar with rules that specify certain targets. These may also become obsolete as a result of new knowledge and new technology. However, it would be completely nonsensical to constantly adapt predefined solutions and targets to new knowledge and new possibilities, because this would make the regulatory framework obsolete and turn it into a danger for ecological and economic development. It would create regulatory chaos and thus make rational and foresighted economic action, long-termed projects on radical innovation or change management, difficult if not impossible.

The Japanese government has found an interesting solution to this dilemma. In 1999 it introduced its "Top Runner Program". This program sets standards on energy efficiency for different product groups for a number of years on the basis of the most efficient product on the market. Products that meet this standard are awarded a Top Runner label whereas those that do not meet the standard are labelled differently. In addition, the best solution is defined as a standard that all products in the group must achieve by a certain date. This drives competition among companies and creates a strong incentive to develop the most efficient product on the market. But it also does not set standards which are unrealistic.[10]

In principle, this solution can be applied to other resources and product groups. However, it has one major disadvantage: it is only indirectly reflected in the price of products and may not have a strong impact on consumer behavior and producer profit. A more efficient solution would be to combine a top runner approach with a resource tax. Instead of a label, top runners would be given significant tax reductions. Products on the slow end, on the other hand, could be subject to a penalty in the form of higher tax rates. This could achieve significant price differentiation between products with higher and lower resource productivity. Different sectors of the economy could be treated differently depending on their technological and organizational capabilities to reduce the consumption of resources.

A resource tax is the most effective and simplest management tool for government to drive resource efficiency. It has a direct impact on prices and ensures that market logic creates massive incentives for resource efficiency and corresponding investment in innovation. However, the tax has to be designed properly. Two conditions are essential: a dynamic design of the tax and a long and reliable time horizon. Dynamic design means that the basic tax rate, but also the tax incentives or the penalty tax are periodically increased. This would mean that products with a lower tax rate than the average for the respective product group would not be able to survive on the market in the long term if they fall much behind their top runner position. At the same time, early investments in innovations, especially radical innovations, would become worthwhile. Companies whose products are far superior to the average of the product group in terms of resource efficiency can thus secure a considerable competitive advantage over a longer period. However, innovations, especially radical innovations, require time and a certain investment security. The resource tax and, above all, the procedure must therefore be reliable over a longer period of time, extending far beyond a legislative period.

This cannot be secured for a resource tax scheme which is introduced by a relatively small majority in parliament. Rather, such a scheme is likely to be watered down or even abandoned if parties come to power which opposed the decision to introduce the scheme. What is needed, hence, is resource tax scheme which is supported by most parties and interest groups. Preferably, the tax scheme should also have large public support. A good way to accomplish this is the commissioning of a citizens' assembly.

Another important design criterion for the tax is the inclusion of the utility of a product. In concrete terms, this means that the resource tax should not consider resource efficiency but resource productivity. Resource efficiency means that a certain product is manufactured with the least possible use of resources. Resource productivity relates the use of resources to the total utility of the product. In the case of a PC, therefore, performance and service life would be taken as the reference values. In other words this means that the basis of the resource tax should not be resource consumption, but MIPS. Calculation of MIPS values is not simple and depends on reliable and valid data and adequate methods. This is not an implementation problem: the necessary data and methods as well as computer programs for determining MIPS values are to a large extent already available or can be made available in short time. The problem is one of reliability, validity and trustworthiness. Therefore, the database as well as methods and computer programs should not be developed and maintained by government agencies, but by renowned and independent scientific institutions. These institutions should also determine top runners and slow ends. To keep the tax as simple possible, product groups with generally low MIPS values should be exempted from the tax. For the same reason, the top runners for each product group involved should be determined in an open competition for a given period of time, e.g. for four years.

A MIPS-based resource tax can be established by national governments or the European Union without creating a competitive disadvantage for domestic companies. Like a sales tax or value added tax, the resource tax would be applied to all products sold on the concerned market.

An effective resource tax may help to solve most, but not all environmental problems. It must be complemented by standards and bans. Deforestation can be countered by taxing timber heavily as a resource if not reforested, but this does not protect virgin forests and other forests that are important to the climate or the lives of indigenous populations. Such forests can only be protected by not allowing import and sale of wood from such forests or food from deforested areas. Food problems in large parts of Africa too cannot be solved with a resource tax. A major reason of these problems is the import of subsidized food products from the European Union, which destroys local agriculture. The European Union could therefore make an important contribution to solving the problem by not subsidizing food exports and by making its free trade agreements with Africa different and fairer. The latter would also be a way to combat deforestation of rainforest or other destruction of land for the production of beef for Europe. Other important problems that cannot be addressed through a resource tax are animal welfare, biodiversity, health, food quality or labor. These issues have in common that very specific qualities or minimum qualities must be achieved and maintained. This can only be ensured by specifying clearly defined mandatory standards or minimum standards. As far as qualities are concerned which are variable or which can only be achieved in a longer transition process, the top runner procedure can also be applied. Here, too, government can work with tax incentives, alternatively to or in conjunction with a periodic raising of standards according to the Japanese model.

In the opening part of this chapter, I pointed out that a resource tax has serious drawbacks. If effective, it will result in significant price increases. That is the desired effect. It motivates consumers to purchase goods and services that have high resource productivity. For producers, it creates massive incentives to change products and production processes so that they have the lowest possible material intensity. The undesired effect is that significant price increases of many goods would inevitably lower the standard of living of large parts of the population, particularly in low- and middle-income groups. This would in effect also increase social inequality.

As a solution to this problem I proposed at beginning of the chapter a significant tax cut for lower- and medium-income groups and SMEs. With respect to lower- and medium-income groups we are obviously talking about income tax. There is, however, a problem involved with this solution. Low-income groups often pay little or no taxes. They hence would gain little or nothing from this solution. Consequently, an effective resource tax would massively affect their living standard and drive many of them into poverty. The only other tax this group pays is value-added tax. At first glance, a sharp reduction in VAT on everyday goods and an equally sharp increase on all other goods could appear to be the solution. Quite apart from the fact that this would not secure the standard of living of lower income groups because they also need other goods, such as furniture, kitchen equipment or even cars, it would be an environmentally wrong solution because it would cancel the price effect of the resource tax.

For the lower income groups, therefore, compensation must be created through income policy measures. An interesting proposal for a compensation for lacking purchasing power of low- income groups has been made already many years ago by Nobel Laureate Milton Friedman, one of the fathers of contemporary neoliberalism. His proposal is a negative income tax: people with income below a certain threshold would receive a subsidy by the tax office that would raise their income to that threshold. The threshold defines a minimal standard of living. The rationale behind his proposal was to allow all people in society to satisfy their needs through market transactions and avoid the need for social welfare payments. We will discuss this in more detail in chapter 5.

The Environmental Promise of the Knowledge Society

I argued in the first chapter that the developed knowledge society could become a truly dematerialized society through its own logic of knowledge accumulation. I also argued that this is not an inevitable development, but it a promising one. It is worth taking the environmental promise of the knowledge society seriously and making use of it. It is the promise of great technical and organizational possibilities for dematerializing Western societies and decoupling their growth and prosperity from their consumption of non-renewable natural resources.

The technical possibilities are to a considerable extent already available, but to a much larger extent will be developed in the near future. They allow not only a relative but an absolute dematerialization. I define relative dematerialization as a more productive use of available natural resources. This also includes their recycling or replacement by less problematic non-renewable resources. Examples of relative dematerialization include less and simpler packaging, better insulated buildings, replacement of non-biodegradable resources with degradable, energy-saving equipment, shorter logistics routes, replacement of sand by recycled building materials, of cotton by wool or of coal by natural gas, and greater use of recycled paper, glass or plastic, the saving of copper by using copper alloy cables, the production of materials or the generation of energy from waste and residual materials, the introduction of stricter speed limits and, last but not least, the creation of good local transport services that significantly reduce the share of private motorized transport in mobility. In probably no society, the many possibilities of relative dematerialization are largely used yet.

The use of natural resources along the entire value chain is always associated with burdens on the environment. It often permanently alters ecosystems and already exceeds the regenerative capacity of the earth. Relative dematerialization, thus, is important and should be advanced quickly. This is all the more true as the demand for natural raw materials has doubled in just a few decades. This cannot be sustained economically for much longer, because resources such as lithium, which has been irreplaceable for information technology up to now, have become very scarce. Environmentally, this is increasingly leading to catastrophes.

As important relative dematerialization is, without absolute dematerialization it is not possible to decouple growth and prosperity from the consumption of non-renewable natural resources and thus to achieve sustainable development. I define absolute dematerialization as the complete replacement of non-renewable resources by renewable ones. Of particular importance here are "artificial" raw materials or materials that are industrially produced in laboratories or factories. I write the word "artificial" in quotation marks because these materials also have a natural basis. They are produced by bacteria, microbes, animals and plants or are made from renewable resources. There are many examples of such products, particularly from biotechnology, that already exist today or are in development.

A large proportion of these products are used in medicine. These include medicines for previously incurable diseases, drugs that are specifically tailored to diseased organs or to specific patient characteristics, artificially produced skin for patients who require skin transplantation, and tissue that can be printed. The latter is to be used for the 3-D printing of artificially produced organs. However, this development is still in its infancy.

From the point of view of dematerialization, a particularly interesting field of biotechnology is the production of biodegradable materials by microorganisms and plants. Microorganisms are microscopic living organisms, especially algae and bacteria. Microorganisms and plants, which are often genetically improved, are used or are intended to be used as biological factories for the production of many substances. In particular, they are intended to replace plastics and other materials that are still made from petroleum with materials made from plants, such as corn, wood or dandelions, from microorganisms, from animals and even from greenhouse gases.

From an environmental point of view, plastics play a major role in this process. Their use and their disposal at the end of the life of the products generated with them is one of the biggest environmental and health problems today. There are research and development projects working on using bacteria to eliminate the already existing plastic waste in drinking water, the sea and on land. The problem is that bacteria have to be genetically modified for this purpose. Therefore, they cannot or not yet be used in open waters and on open land, but only in sewage treatment plants and other closed areas. A forward-looking solution to this problem is the development of bioplastics that are fully recyclable or readily biodegradable. Such materials already exist, but they cannot be produced on an industrial scale, or only at very high cost. That is why they are still a niche product. But there are several projects in process that could soon change this.

A particularly interesting natural material is spider silk, i.e. the silk from which spiders build their thin but extremely tear-resistant webs. The tensile strength and the elasticity of spider silk can compete with high-tech fibers such as Kevlar and carbon, as well as with steel. This makes it very attractive to the medical, aerospace, automotive, building and textile industries. Therefore, several research groups and companies are working on the artificial production of spider silk.

Even some things that seemed impossible a short time ago can become reality. At the University of California at Riverside, scientists led by Juan Pablo Giraldo are researching mRNA vaccines that can be produced in edible plants and eaten with them. Giraldo and his interdisciplinary team work at the interfaces between biology and nanotechnology. For the project, they are using chloroplasts as factories for the vaccine. Chloroplasts are the small organs that in cells of plants and green algae convert sunlight into energy and produce carbohydrates and other substances that plants need to grow. Specially designed nanoparticles will be used to introduce genetic material into the chloroplasts that will stimulate them to produce mRNA vaccine.

A final example is the replacement of sand. Sand is a versatile natural resource that has been scarce for a long time. We are not talking about desert sand, of which there is plenty, but which cannot yet be used for the purposes for which sand is needed. It is about the sand that is currently or was long ago created by rivers. Mankind has been using much more of this sand than earth can supply for a long time. Therefore, there are a number of projects, especially in relation to the construction sector, looking for alternatives for sand. For example, building blocks made from mushrooms but also from desert sand are being developed and tested.

The great successes and the rapid pace of progress in biotechnology, as in the pharmaceutical and chemical industries, are in large part a consequence of automation, digitalization and, increasingly, the application of microsystems technology for miniaturization of research and development and production. Miniaturization in particular will drastically change biotechnical or chemical laboratories and factories in the coming years. We are familiar with this development from information technology where the miniaturization of electronic components has made it possible to reduce entire computer centers to a small computer. In biotechnology and chemistry, laboratories and production facilities are to be accommodated on one chip or a combination of chips. This is a much more difficult task than miniaturizing electronics but a task that is likely to be reached within a few years. If, or better said, when this will be the case it will drastically change research, development and production in biotechnology and chemistry. Analyses and production processes will be greatly accelerated, which will make some research and development possible in the first place. The use of materials will be reduced and the control of processes improved.

As we briefly touched on in chapter 2, this may come at a high price in the form of massive job losses. Miniaturized and automated systems require far fewer personnel than traditional laboratories and factories. Personnel is needed primarily for the invention, design, evaluation and control of research and development, and production processes, the planning and design of experiments, and for the maintenance of equipment. Many jobs will therefore be lost in laboratories and factories. However, miniaturized systems can also create new business areas and new jobs. For example, they enable a strong decentralization of processes. Instead of having to send substances to large laboratories for tests and wait days for the results, for example, they can be analyzed immediately on site in a "chip lab".

What this means can be imagined with the example of the Covid-19 pandemic. If chip labs had been widely available in the days of Covid-19, the pandemic would probably have proceeded very differently and, above all, with much less economic and social damage. People could have been tested every few days at their place of work, school, nursing home, before shopping in the city, at event venues, and on other occasions. This would have allowed consistent tracking of infections and rapid containment of the pandemic. Lockdowns would have been unnecessary. This would have saved much human suffering and much economic and social damage. It would also have created new economic opportunities and new jobs.

However, a pandemic is not needed to create new economic opportunities and new jobs from automation and miniaturization. Creative people with ideas for new materials or new products could much more easily start a biotechnical or chemical company with the necessary laboratories and factories to realize their idea. Their financial risks would be reduced by drastically shortened development times. Many new ideas for bio-technical or chemical products could be quickly implemented economically. In many cases, this could be combined with 3-D printing. In biotechnology and chemistry, a strong mid-sized economy could develop that is integrated into strong international innovation networks. This represents a huge economic potential and a huge employment potential considering the many possible applications of biotechnology. It also represents a huge potential for dematerialization.

An exciting but for many environmentalists and others very provocative example of relative dematerialization is the development of a new type of nuclear power plant currently being developed by companies such as Terra-Power and Nuscale with millions and millions of venture capital. These plants are supposed to be reactors that are extremely safe compared to conventional nuclear power plants, as well as much smaller and therefore much less expensive. Some can also be operated with nuclear waste from previous power plants, giving them fuel for hundreds of years. The plants can be used not only for electricity production, their heat can also be used for the production of hydrogen or heat. If these plants deliver what their developers promise, they would enable extensive decentralization of the energy supply. This could significantly reduce and simplify power grids. This, in turn, would reduce the ecological rucksack of electricity by saving material and reducing transmission losses. Therefore, these projects should be given a chance and not hastily dismissed as unrealistic or dangerous.

To reiterate, the promises of the knowledge society outlined here represent developments that are possible but far from inevitable. What will actually happen depends on how politics, business and civil society respond to the technological possibilities described above. It depends, first of all, on whether they succeed in closing the innovation gap mentioned in the first chapter. This in turn depends, especially in Western societies, on how the actual or feared risks of new technologies, especially biotechnology, genetic engineering and nuclear power, are dealt with. Consensus conferences on technology assessment according to the model of the Danish Board of Technology could help to find solutions which are both consensual and innovative.

A Key Actor: The City

Cities are key actors of sustainable development. On the one hand, they are the places where many sustainability problems are rooted, but on the other hand, they are also the places where most of the knowledge, creativity and innovative milieus required to solve these problems are located. Currently, more than 50% of the world's population live in cities, and by the middle of this century this figure will be 70 to 80%. In Western countries, especially in Western Europe, this is already the case. But cities also already consume about 80% of the world's energy and over 70% of the world's total natural resources. Most importantly, they consume many times their land area for their supply, with many large cities in Western Europe and the US consuming well over a hundred times more.[11]

Many cities have understood these problems and the need for action. These include Copenhagen, Zurich, Los Angeles, London, Berlin, Vienna, Milan, Paris, Amsterdam, Helsinki, Vancouver, San Francisco and many others. They have recognized sustainability as a major factor in their quality of life and their competitiveness in the battle for creative personnel and innovative companies. These are the drivers of competition, but also of collective learning that are driving sustainable development in Western countries.[12]

Competition between cities is a major, probably even indispensable success factor for the sustainable development of Western societies. It drives development, mobilizes economic and civil society forces, and ensures that successful sustainable development measures are quickly adopted by other cities. But this positive effect quickly reaches its limits where cities operate under very unstable conditions. This applies to financial and infrastructural conditions, building fabric and other material conditions as well as to social and cultural conditions. It makes sense for cities to be able to live out their uniqueness and specific identity to the extent that the majority of their population wants them to, but they also need to have the opportunity to do so. To put it more clearly, there must be something like equality of opportunity between cities. Otherwise, the relationship between cities is threatened by an absurd, almost perverse version of Schumpeter's process of creative destruction: what is created in some cities in terms of sustainable development is destroyed in other cities because they are left behind by a lack of opportunities. As a result, these cities are threatened with material problems, such as comparatively poor living conditions and population losses, especially losses of young and qualified people, but also social and cultural segregation. This leads to social divisions that no longer allow sustainability as a common good. Even if it does not come to that, the conflicts associated with segregation and division inhibit the sustainable development of the whole country. This problem can only be solved by an activating policy for cities that really activates and does not merely distribute money.

For their sustainable development, cities must deal with three sets of issues: First, with their supply and disposal systems and the area they can use for this, second, with their way of life and the area they can use for this as living space, and third, with the social milieus that shape their city and its capabilities for sustainable development. These complexes of issues are closely interrelated. On the one hand, this creates a high degree of complexity of cities' sustainability problem, and on the other, considerable synergies.

Since cities, especially in Western societies and other rich countries, have far too large an environmental footprint, they must solve their supply and disposal problems mostly on their own soil in order to reach sustainable development. This may seem quite impossible because cities do not own enough land. Since cities in Western countries and elsewhere can no longer live at the expense of other countries and their land and water, they must make the seemingly impossible possible. This is anything but impossible. It needs a kind of agricultural revolution, but while most revolutions are difficult to accomplish, this revolution is particularly feasible.

In 2010, the American microbiologist and environmentalist Dickson Despommier published a book entitled "The Vertical Farm: Feeding the World in the 21st Century." In this book, he promoted the idea of cities that take on the functions of a natural ecosystem, producing most of their own food and recycling all or most of their waste. The revolution consists of the replacement of traditional soil-based agriculture with so-called urban agriculture. This should be done in vertical farms in which agricultural areas are stacked on top of each other, so to speak. Combined with energy recovery from waste and low-pollution effluents, this type of agricultural production allows any city to mimic a well-functioning ecosystem with high bioproductivity and low waste.

In Dickson Despommier's view soil-based agriculture, established for centuries, has failed: "Without irrigation and lots of additives (e.g. agrochemicals, modern farm machinery) farming could not go indefinitely in the same place. It's simply not an ecological option". It does not even allow for the biodiversity that a truly environmental approach to land would require, because that would reduce agricultural yields too much. That is no longer possible today because the growth of the earth's population has pushed agricultural landscapes to their limits and beyond. In his view, soil-based agriculture is no longer a sustainable solution. It is hard to ignore this insight. At the very least, it makes sense to replace soil-based agriculture with vertical farming to the extent to which is necessary to allow soil-based agriculture to be practiced in an environmentally sound manner and the environmental footprint of each country to be reduced to an appropriate level. This applies not only to Western countries and other richer countries, but also to poorer countries.[13]

I have experienced time and again that people are reserved or even rejective to the idea of vertical farming without soil. They have classified the food produced in this way as artificial and second-class compared to "natural" food. This is understandable, but wrong. In vertical farms, plants grow in conditions that match their natural conditions and without the use of pesticides, herbicides or fertilizers. I have tasted gherkins and tomatoes in a vertical farm that reminded me of the gherkins and tomatoes from my grandfather's garden. That is much better than the gherkins and tomatoes produced by non-organic farming on soil. This is not surprising, considering that the soils of farms, even of organic farms are quite polluted by acid rain.

Vertical farming produces food of high quality with a minimum of natural resources, land and interference with nature and systematically recycles its waste. There are two basic processes involved, hydroponic and aeroponic cultivation. In hydroponic processes, the plants grow in substrates such as clay granules or rock wool, and are supplied with nutrients by drip irrigation. There are also variants in which the plants grow directly in the nutrient solution. In aeroponic methods, the plant roots hang freely in the air and are sprayed with the nutrient solution. The nutrient solution, lighting and temperature are precisely adjusted to the conditions of the plants. Vertical farming is much more productive than soil-based agriculture, even than soil-based agriculture in greenhouses. This is especially due to the fact that it can produce year-round and has no weather-related crop failures. Compared to soil-based agriculture, it has a 70–95% lower water requirement. Its logistics routes can be greatly shortened. Modern computerized distribution systems allow just-in-time delivery so that vegetables, lettuces and fruits reach the market fresh and in an optimal state of ripeness.

The weak points of vertical farming are the high energy demand and the high investments. The high energy demand is mainly due to lighting and air conditioning. However, better and better systems are being offered for this purpose, so that the problem should soon be solved. The high investment costs are a structural problem that can and must be solved. They harbor the danger that vertical farming will be dominated by a few large companies. This not only creates undesirable economic dependencies, but also promotes large-scale distribution concepts with greater ecological rucksacks and losses in quality. A solution to this problem lies in a cooperative organization of vertical farming which also could include traditional farmers.

Even the most problematic foodstuff from an environmental point of view, meat, can soon be produced in an urban environment. However, this no longer has anything to do with agriculture. The meat will be produced biotechnologically directly in the laboratory without animals. It is basically the same type of process as that used to produce human tissue and human organs outside the body. This meat, referred to as clean meat, is nonetheless real meat and is intended to look and taste like it. It is made into cutlets, steaks and other pieces of meat by 3-D printing. This still requires some development, but it is already underway. Other animal products, especially milk, can also be produced using biotechnological processes.

Despite all the technical possibilities of urban agriculture, it should not be overlooked that soil-based agriculture is not only a production system, but also a major cultural asset of mankind. In near-natural forms, it is also a major element of landscape quality. The Swiss Alps, for example, would lose much of their scenic quality and tourist appeal without traditional livestock farming. Therefore, soil-based agriculture should not be completely replaced by urban agriculture, but returned to an environmentally sustainable scale to become part of a complementary and mutually supportive urban–rural relationship.

The second set of issues includes settlement structure and mobility as key problems. The settlement structure is a problem that highlights the time dimension of sustainable development. There are many beautiful books, magazines and websites with quite great futuristic pictures of the city of the future. The problem with many of these images is that they are new buildings on large open spaces. The problem of western cities, especially European cities, is that they have a long history of developed cityscapes with a large, good and sometimes historically valuable building stock and developed infrastructures, but little open space. So they have to develop their future mostly from these structures. There is a bit of irony here in that a significant amount of traditional fabric and established structures have already been removed once as part of a fundamental reorientation and urban planning based on that. I am referring to the Charter of Athens which was discussed at an international architectural congress in 1933 and published by the Swiss architect Le Corbusier in Paris in 1943. This charter, which had a strong influence on urban development, especially after the Second World War, called for a clear functional division of cities between the areas of housing, work and leisure.

Today, this charter is already outdated. The Charter of European Planning published in Barcelona in 2013 calls for abandoning the division of functions and for a spatial reintegration of functions. The idea is a city of short distances and closer social coexistence. As far as residential forms are concerned, the New Urbanism that emerged in the USA in the 1990s is also following this path. On the one hand, cities are to be densified, but on the other hand they are to be provided with much more landscape and green spaces as an integral part of the city and its buildings. The spatial reintegration of functions and the creation of landscape and greenery should also take place via the vertical. Buildings are to become increasingly hybrid, for example, serving simultaneously as residential buildings and workplaces, and on the roofs as parks or energy plants. Landscapes are to be created as vertical gardens on the exterior or interior walls of buildings. All of this already exists, but not to the extent and quality that the city of the future needs.

As part of functional reintegration, industrial production should be brought back to the city. This is certainly possible for information technology and biotechnology companies, but with modern technical means could also be made possible for other industries. Reindustrialization of cities is desirable because tertiarization is increasingly turning out to be a wooden rather than a royal road. This is especially true for the modern knowledge society. As I will explain in chapter 6, it is above all industry rather than services that provides many impulses for modern knowledge production. It is also industry that leads a large part of new knowledge and technology to economic use.

Therefore, it makes sense to involve industry much more strongly and directly in the creative milieus and innovation processes in cities.

The problem with the changes mentioned here is that more functions, especially urban agriculture and industrial production, and more green space must be realized with the same amount of land, probably even with less. In most Western countries (and in other countries as well), the growth of cities' land area can no longer continue, but must rather decrease. Sealing of land has long since reached an extent that is already too big from the point of view of climate and the management of climate consequences, especially floods, not to speak of biodiversity. This implies that more area must be developed and linked to a meaningful and livable habitat in the vertical. A funny example of this is a waste incineration plant in Copenhagen, the world's leader in climate neutrality of cities. This plant has been built over with a hill on which also a ski slope runs. The heat generated by the incineration process is used to cool the slope.

Functional restructuring is a difficult and lengthy process that also has its limits. Modern large cities can only be functionally integrated to a limited extent in such a way that people consistently have short distances between where they live and where they work. In many cases, it will be more feasible to reduce the frequency of trips between home and work through modern digital forms of work with home offices and other forms of "homework". Nonetheless, functional reintegration will help make the urban landscape more decentralized and colorful, and better balance spatial living conditions. This may also help to counter segregation.

In the long run, large cities cannot achieve sustainability without a dense, comfortable and fast public transportation network. With such a system, the city of Zurich has managed to reduce the share of cars and motorcycles in inner-city mobility to 20%. Other cities, such as Berlin, Vienna, Milan, Paris or Tokyo, also achieve high values, but in many cities in Europe and the USA the share of cars is 80% and more. A particularly interesting example is Los Angeles. Until the 1970s, Los Angeles was still a city with very modest mass transit, a city that was almost entirely automobile. Within about 40 years, LA has built a diverse mass transit system that does not often find its equal. The network includes not only trains and buses, as is the case in many places, but also small call buses, a vanpool, bicycles, ride-sharing arrangements, and the use of express lanes for vehicles with multiple occupants. Even better pedestrian and bicycle access to Metro stations is being addressed by Metro LA Many buses and trains run at short intervals for most of the day, and in the next few years many lines are expected to run at intervals of 10 minutes or less for much of the day. Ninety-nine percent of passengers are expected to reach a bus stop within one quarter of a mile (about 400 m). London is following a similar path.

A dense, comfortable and fast public transportation network is also an often-underestimated condition for the social milieu that shapes cities' capabilities for innovation and for sustainable development. This is the third issue of sustainable development cities have to deal with. The term social milieu is used to describe a social environment with certain characteristics that strongly influences the behavior and interactions of the actors in its sphere of influence. Social milieus promote or inhibit certain developments in the space in which they are effective. We are particularly interested here in urban milieus that promote problem awareness and creative solutions for sustainable development. In regional research, such milieus are generally referred to as innovative or creative milieus. They develop in particular from knowledge-intensive contact networks of regional or local actors, especially universities and other research institutions on the one hand and entrepreneurs and start-ups on the other, as well as from common ideas and interests of the actors and their identification with "their" city or region. In some cities, for example in Barcelona, Berlin or London, creative milieus have developed gradually out of economic and social life and the attractiveness of the place; in other places, they have been specifically triggered by the creation of attractive localities. This is true, for example, of Silicon Valley, which was launched by Frederick Terman and Stanford University through the creation of the Stanford Research Park. Following this model, such parks were also created in other places with sometimes much, sometimes little success.

Creative milieus thrive above all on the fact that they are always able to attract or retain young creative people. The new knowledge that is repeatedly brought into cities in the minds of these people is the fuel of urban creativity. For most of these people, urban quality is a major factor that attracts them to the city or binds them to it. For these people in particular, this quality also includes environmental quality and sustainability of the development. A dense, comfortable and fast public transportation network is not only an important element of this quality, but also a visible symbol of the city's capability to meet the challenges of sustainable development.[14]

The Deliberative Way: An Ordered Chaos

The example of cities shows that sustainable development is a multifaceted and multi-layered process in which many different problems are solved by many different actors with many different interests in many different ways. This is a gigantic process of transformation management and an equally gigantic collective learning process. This process can, as we discussed before, not be controlled hierarchically and organized centrally. With hierarchical control and central organization, far too much information and far too many learning opportunities would be lost. Collective learning in social evolutionary processes arises from variations. It therefore arises from the fact that many social actors understand many things differently and act differently. This situation constitutes the great creative potential of pluralistic society. In more general terms, this means that the collective ability to learn arises from diversity. This applies to the individual as well as to social groups and entire societies.

In relation to individuals, psychologists speak of cognitive complexity. They use this concept to describe the ability or inability of people to grasp and structure complex situations. Simply put, the greater an individual's cognitive complexity, the more intellectually complex his or her grasp is of the world. An individual's cognitive complexity depends, among other things, on how varied the information and experiences are that he or she was confronted with in their life to date, especially in childhood and adolescence. Cognitive complexity, in turn, shapes the intellectual performance of individuals, particularly their ability to comprehend complex situations. Cognitive complexity thus builds evolutionarily on itself – the more complex an individual's cognitive structures already are, the better it can expand its cognitive complexity. It is a similar story with collective learning. The more diverse a group or a society is, the more it is potentially able to take different interests into account in its decisions, to adapt to new situations or to generate new ideas, new knowledge and new solutions to problems.

Against this background, the diversity of the process is a major, even indispensable factor for the success of sustainable development. It ensures that the social learning capacity necessary for sustainable development is achieved and maintained. It not only ensures that new solutions to problems are discovered again and again, but also creates creative milieus in ever new parts of society from which such solutions spring again and again. This is what makes the great potential of Western societies for the path to sustainable development. This path is opened up by the broad involvement of cities, markets and civil society's self-organization in the process.[15]

However, this broad involvement also marks the difficulties of this path. It brings a strong element of chaos to the process of sustainable development and it makes the process difficult to manage and even less controllable. Even what happens in markets with a clear, precise and functionally well-aligned regulatory framework can only be determined to a limited extent. The many sustainability activities of an increasing number of cities are even less manageable and controllable. The development becomes almost unmanageable and uncontrollable when many social actors participate in projects of social self-organization.

Chaos has a creative charm, but it can also lead to undesirable circumstances or events. In our concrete case, it can lead to sustainable development being missed or gambled away. The chaos of our way to sustainable development therefore requires a certain control and order. Social evolution can only be influenced and controlled by restricting social action. The more social action is restricted, the less it leads to variations and fewer different reactions to the variations become possible. But this also means that less learning is possible.

The state can certainly restrict the social actions of the actors relevant in our context by means of regulation and activating policies in such a way that undesirable consequences of the actors' actions for sustainable development are largely avoided. It must also do this, but in doing so, it must be careful not to restrict society's ability to learn and the economy's ability to innovate too much. The less the government has to intervene and the more it can limit itself to enabling rather than controlling, the less danger there is of this.

The need for government intervention depends heavily on the often-neglected form of governance that we already talked about in the first chapter, namely culture. In concrete terms, it is primarily a question of the extent to which it is possible, through social construction, to establish viable common understandings of sustainability and the actions that are necessary or useful for achieving sustainability. This is what mini-publics are particularly good at. They do not restrict behavior through rules and other guidelines, but bring together different understandings and interests in a consensual decision. This does not restrict social diversity, but preserves it as a driver of creativity and social learning. The fruitful chaos is not eliminated, but only somewhat ordered.

Notes

1 On the ecological footprint se Mathis Wackernagel, Bert Beyers (2019). Ecological Footprint: Managing Our Biocapacity Budget. Gabriola Island BC: New Society Publishers. Mathis Wackernagel, William Rees (1996). Our Ecological Footprint: Reducing Human Impact on the Earth. Gabriola Island BC: New Society Publishers.
2 An encouraging description of a feasible strategy of dematerialization is offered by Andrew McAfee (2019). More for Less: The Surprising Story of How We Learned to Prosper Using Fewer Resources – and What Happens Next. New York: Simon & Schuster.
3 A comprehensive picture of sustainability problems and their interrelations is provided by Donald G. Reid (2020). A New World System: From Chaos to Sustainability. London and New York: Routledge. See also Jeffrey D. Sachs (2015). The Age of Sustainable Development. New York: Columbia University Press.
4 To those readers who would like to learn more about nature as a complex system of complex ecosystems I recommend the following books: Gordon Dickinson, Kevin Murphy (2007). Ecosystems. London and New York: Routledge. For an illustrated description see Rachel Ignotofsky (2018). The Wondrous Workings of Planet Earth: Understanding Our World and its Ecosystems. New York: Ten Speed Press.
5 A detailed account of the condition and prospects of marine ecosystems has been made within the United Nations Millennium Ecosystem Assessment. See: UNEP (2006). Marine and Costal Ecosystems and Human Well-Being: A Synthesis Report Based on the Findings of the Millennium Ecosystem Assessment. Nairobi: UNEP. See also: Tasman P. Crowe, Christopher L.J. Fried eds. (2015): Marine Ecosystems: Human Impact on Biodiversity, Functioning and Services. Cambridge: Cambridge University Press.
6 Cf. Donald G. Reid (2020). A New World System: From Chaos to Sustainability. London and New York: Routledge.
7 See Friedrich Schmidt-Bleek (1998). Das MIPS-Konzept. Weniger Naturverbrauch – mehr Lebensqualität durch Faktor 10. Munich: Droemer. For a description of the MIPS-concept in English language see Christa Liedtke et al. (2014). Resource Use in the Production and Consumption System: The MIPS-Approach. Resources, 3, 544–574.

8 For a stimulating analysis of the role of material and its flows in the history of mankind see Vaclav Smil (2013). Making the Modern World: Materials and Dematerialization. Chichester: Wiley.

9 See https://libquotes.com/karl-deutsch/quote/lbw7m8b

10 See https://www.futurepolicy.org/climate-stability/japans-top-runner-programme/

11 Readers that are particularly interested in the migration to cities and the problems associated with it could read Shlomo Angel (2012). Planet of Cities. New York: Columbia University Press.

12 For a broad discussion of the role of cities in sustainable development see Steven Cohen, Guo Dong (2021). The Sustainable City. New York: Columbia University Press. Alan R. Shark, Sylviane Toporkoff, Sébastian Lévy (2014). Smarter Cities for a Bright Sustainable Future: A Global Perspective. Washington, D.C.: Public Technology Institute. Marco Bontje (2016). Inventive City-Regions: Path Dependence and Creative Knowledg Strategies. London and New York: Routledge. David Miller (2020). Solved: How the World's Great Cities Are Fixing the Climate Crisis. Toronto: University of Toronto Press. Peter Nijkamp, Julia Siedschlag eds. (2013). Innovation Growth and Competitiveness: Dynamic Regions in the Knowledge-based World Economy. Berlin-Heidelberg: Springer.

13 See Dickson Despommier (2010). The Vertical Farm: Feeding the World in the 21st Century. New York: Picador. Quotation from page 135.

14 A detailed description of the lifestyles, ideas and desires of the "creative class" is offered by Richard Florida (2002). The Rise of the Creative Class: And How it's Transforming Work, Leisure, Community and Everyday Life. New York: Basic Books.

15 An encouraging view on a bottom-up approach is offered by Matt Ridley (2016). The Evolution of Everything: How New Ideas Emerge. New York: Harper Collins.

4 From the Wealth of Nations to the Wealth of People

A stimulating look at what economic sustainability might mean is offered by examining the foundations of Western societies in the history of ideas, more precisely in utilitarianism and the Greatest Happiness Principle. Utilitarianism is an important philosophical pillar of Western societies and classical economics. The Greatest Happiness Principle was one of the two basic principles of utilitarianism. This principle demands that social action must always be aimed at creating the greatest possible happiness for the greatest possible number of people. The purpose of economics in this sense is not only to promote the wealth of nations, but the wealth of people. As the development of inequality in Western societies after the Second World War shows, the Greatest Happiness Principle has not survived well in modern Western societies.

This is reflected in the logic of governments' distributional activities. Apart from among market-radical economists and politicians, the need for some equalization of inequality by government and its income policy is widely accepted. But in practice equalization works poorly. The state has been very active in distributing wealth in Western societies and has long since become a distributive state, but this promotes inequality rather than reducing it.

In the view of contemporary neoliberalism, the distributive state is the product of the proliferation of the welfare state. This is not even half the truth. The distributive state encompasses all areas of state action. This is especially true of the activity that even market-radical economists and politicians regard as one of the core functions of the state, namely the definition and protection of property rights. On the other hand, the distributive state fails in many countries in the very area in which it is widely recognized to have a distributive function, namely in income policy and social policy.

While government in Western societies can neither realize the Greatest Happiness Principle nor reduce inequality to an economically and socially reasonable level, this is done in a rather perverse way by the "nickel-and-dime economy". We have discussed this already in the first chapter and established that the "nickel-and-dime economy" leads to an environmental, economic and social dead end. The abolition of the nickel-and-dime economy must therefore be an urgent goal of any sustainability strategy of Western societies. To gain a

DOI: 10.4324/9781003261421-4

viable idea of how this could be done, we need to look more closely at the logic of the "nickel-and-dime economy" and its alternatives. That is one of the two central themes of this chapter. The other one is the future of work.

From what we discussed in this book so far, we can gain a clear idea of what we are aiming for: We are aiming at building a new economy geared to high value instead of high volume. The new economy must move from mass production to customer-oriented production and from short-life cheap products to long-life, high-quality products. This requires replacement of the structures of the industrial age which are strongly dominated by large enterprises by more medium-sized structures which are based on collaborative networks and on work systems that promote creativity and personal responsibility. Realization of this model could solve one of the central problems of the coming years, to wit work.

We can hardly forecast the development of work in the coming years and decades, but one thing seems to be clear: Digitization, microsystems technology and biotechnology are likely to destroy a large proportion of jobs in industrial production in the next few years. In contrast to what has often been the case in the past, these job losses will not be offset by new jobs in the technologies that trigger the losses. This does not have to mean that Western societies are inevitably running out of gainful employment. It just means that Western societies need to create new economic structures that offer new sustainable employment opportunities. In such structures, digitization, microsystems technology and biotechnology may turn into powerful drivers of new, sustainable employment.

Like all changes in social systems, development of a new economy must take place from within existing structures. These changes can be driven by innovative companies through competition, but government must do its part too. Government support is particularly necessary to help many SMEs make necessary organizational and technical changes and increase their innovation capacity strongly and sustainably. But this is not primarily a matter of financial support, but rather one of organizational and legal support of implementation of collaborative structures.

The Neglect of the Greatest Happiness Principle

The Greatest Happiness Principle comes in its traditional form from Jeremy Bentham, the actual founder of classical utilitarianism, who published it in 1789 in his work "Introduction to the Principles of Morals and Legislation". Utilitarianism laid major philosophical foundations for liberal social theory, which is the philosophical basis of Western societies and their democratic constitutions. The Greatest Happiness Principle, in turn, was the basic principle of utilitarianism. According to this principle, the goal is not only to make the nation's prosperity as great as possible, but rather to allow as many members of society as possible to share in this prosperity. This principle is crucially important even today because it teaches that growth is not the goal, but a fair distribution of fruits of growth. The goal is not primarily to raise the wealth of nations but the wealth of people.[1]

The second basic principle Utilitarianism, the principle of individual freedom, was established about 100 years before utilitarianism by John Locke, who is considered the founder of liberalism. The principle of individual liberty is incorporated in the constitutions of the United States and of revolutionary France and has found its way into most constitutions of Western societies. According to Locke's principle of liberty the state may restrict individual freedom only to prevent harm to others, but is otherwise obligated to protect individual liberties. This principle was firmly connected with utilitarianism, especially by David Hume. However, he represented a radical view of the principle, which corresponds to today's American libertarianism and to neoliberalism. Another great proponent of utilitarianism and one of the most influential thinkers of liberalism, John Stuart Mill, saw things quite differently. He set clear limits to individual freedom where people's actions cause harm to other people. In economics, such harm is called a negative externality if it is caused by economic activity. Externalities are considered as market failures which must be prevented or compensated by government regulation. A major negative externality is damage to environment. We will come back to this point below.

I mention only in passing that there are also positive externalities, that is, benefits to an actor from a transaction in which it is not involved. While this is important from a market perspective, it is hardly important from a sustainability perspective.

The two basic principles of utilitarianism have entered liberal social theory to varying degrees. The principle of liberty has become the core tenet of the theory and has been adopted in all liberal constitutions. The Greatest Happiness Principle, on the other hand, no longer plays a central role in the liberal social theory that emerged from utilitarianism. However, as an idea, not as a concrete statement, it does play a role in the liberal social theory that emerged from the philosophical thought of the French Revolution. The idea manifests itself in the motto of the French Republic "liberté, égalité et fraternité" (liberty, equality and fraternity) and in the European concept of the welfare state.

The principle of liberty has also become the philosophical basis of classical economics, which emerged from utilitarianism, while the Greater Happiness Principle plays only a partial role. A certain exception is ordoliberalism, a German school of economics which emerged in the middle of the last century. Ordoliberalism declared competition, social security and social justice to be major issues which governments' regulatory framework of the market must solve. It developed the concept of a social market economy. Similar, but more limited ideas and concepts are also represented by other schools of economics that have been grouped under the term neoliberal. While they mostly rejected the idea of a welfare state many accepted a limited role of government in fighting poverty. But in the 1980s and 1980s neoliberalism increasingly focused on market liberalization and rejected all government interventions in the market following the philosophy that the distribution of income and wealth must be left to the market.

However, current neoliberalism is highly controversial in economics. Prominent economists, such as Anthony Atkinson, Heather Boushey, Marcel Fratzscher, Thomas Piketty, Jeffrey D. Sachs, Joseph Stiglitz and Jean Tirole, argue that inequality beyond a certain level is economically and socially harmful. It hurts growth and employment because more inequality is associated with higher savings rates and lower consumer spending because people with higher incomes save a bigger share of their income than people with lower incomes. High inequality also affects investment and innovation although high incomes and their accumulation of wealth make more capital available to finance investment and innovation. However, the overall low level of consumer spending and the price-oriented purchasing behavior of many low-income people also leads in many sectors of the economy to what Karl Marx called the tendency of the rate of profit to fall. The returns on capital that can be generated by using capital for investment and innovation are declining. High inequality also inhibits educational opportunities and human capital development because many people cannot invest enough in their children's education. This is true not only in the US, with its expensive elite universities and private schools and kindergartens, but also in Western European countries with extensive public education systems. Even in Belgium, Germany, France, Hungary and other countries, children from wealthy families are favored in education. This is partly due to the family environment, but also because families with lower incomes have fewer opportunities to compensate for their children's educational weaknesses or deficits in their children's kindergartens and schools through tutoring, private childcare and private tuition, private schools and other measures. These options have gained prominence in the wake of the Covid-19 pandemic. In the long run, inequality in real educational opportunity can lead to declining levels of educational attainment in society and declining productivity and creativity in the economy. Growing inequality also inhibits sustainable consumption and promotes distributional conflict.[2]

These situations are also found in a problem that Tyler Cowen, an influential American economist, calls the great stagnation. His main point is that weak innovation dynamics in many areas also lead to weak growth. The talk of the great stagnation is pointed, but not exaggerated. For a long time, weak innovation and low growth rates have been associated with stagnating incomes, a growing low-wage sector and growing wage inequality.[3]

Social inequality is by no means merely a matter of the market but is also promoted by government action. An example: as Thomas Piketty reports, growing income inequality is primarily the result of the decoupling of the salaries of top managers from general income trends. This, in turn, is the result of little restriction of the power of top managers by US corporate law, which has led to a rapid increase in managerial salaries, first in the US and then in many other countries. According to Joseph Stiglitz, American law allows managers not only to determine their own salaries to a large extent, but also to help determine their supervisory boards. Stiglitz calls this a clear case of regulatory capture. Regulatory capture means that powerful interest groups gain strong influence and even control over regulation and regulatory agencies.

Another case of regulatory capture is the privileging of derivatives in the case of bank insolvency or the deregulation of financial markets in American law. Another example is the final withholding tax in Germany. This is a flat tax on capital gains of 25%. With this tax, the state refrains from subjecting capital gains to the much higher income tax in order to counteract capital flight abroad. The German state is thus depriving itself of substantial tax revenues in order to prevent rich people from cheating it out of taxes.

A glaring example of regulatory capture and state promotion of inequality is the so-called Riester pension in Germany. This pension was introduced in 2002 to compensate for a reduction in the pension from the state's compulsory pension scheme through private pension provision. The pension was offered in various forms, e.g. classic private pension insurance, savings programs of banks or funds. The state paid subsidies to this pension to an eligible group of people which essentially comprised persons who were members of the compulsory state insurance scheme. Other persons, such as many self-employed people, cannot profit from the Riester pension. The concept of the pension has been under massive criticism for years. The particularly interesting point of criticism in our context, which is repeatedly raised by academics and other experts as well as trade unions and other organizations, is that the Riester pension brings little added value, often even losses, for many people who take it out. At the same time, however, it offers the financial industry good profit opportunities through high fees. Some economists go so far as to describe the Riester pension as a subsidy for the banks and insurers offering it and a waste of taxpayers' money. It is often argued that it is not so much the insured who earn money from the Riester pension as the financial sector, the state pension scheme and, indirectly, employers. In this respect, we are dealing with a clear case of redistribution from the bottom to the top.

As this example also shows, Joseph Stiglitz is right in his thesis that inequality does not arise only from the operation of market forces, nor merely from the fact that the state regulates the market badly or does too little to reduce high inequality. It also provides opportunities of rent seeking for people with high incomes and wealth and the organizations associated with these people. Rent seeking is the attempt to obtain income and other benefits without delivering anything in return. The term is most often used in connection with the state. This does not apply to the many people who receive pensions from state social security systems, because they first have to pay many years of contributions to the system. Rather, this relates to the many that use their power to attain tax privileges, subsidies and protection. Rent seeking and regulatory capture have aggravated inequality considerably.[4]

The counterpart to the successful rent-seeking of actors is the fact that the state in Western societies has long since developed into a distributive state, distributing a variety of goods and services as well as other useful benefits. This is demonstrated, among other things, by the fact that government spending as a percentage of gross domestic product in the member countries of the European Union ranges from 40% to 65%. Only Ireland is significantly lower. It is also above 40% in the USA and slightly below that in Switzerland. The United States and Switzerland are countries that are not known for having a political culture that encourages a great deal of government activity.

The distributive state is the product of threefold inequality. This is first the large inequality of income and wealth. This translates into concentrated economic and political power. The political power of social interests is measured, as the German sociologist Claus Offe noted many years ago, by the services that interest groups can offer or deny to politicians and public administrators. These benefits include donations to political parties and individual politicians as well as to public institutions, the provision of specialized knowledge and information to politicians and public administrators, participation in government projects and measures, the mobilization of economic support or opposition for major political or administrative projects and policies, decisions about investments and the siting of facilities and projects, and personal benefits for politicians and administrators and their families and friends.[5]

Economic and social inequality is linked to a second form of inequality that we have already discussed in detail in the first chapter, namely the unequal ability to organize social interests. We noted in the first chapter that the special interests of small privileged groups are much easier to organize and thus to intermediate politically than the general interests of broad sections of the population. The small and privileged groups at the upper end of the income and wealth scale not only have more power, but they are also better able to apply it politically and make it work. This provides these groups with even higher chances of rent-seeking and regulatory capture. But not only that, there is third kind of inequality which enhances the possibilities for rent-seeking of these groups. These are systematic inequalities of the institutional context of interest intermediation. In the first chapter, I have argued that interest groups operate, for the most part, without competition. I will differentiate and qualify that a bit now.

Many social interests compete in that they are mutually contradictory and they cannot be satisfied simultaneously. But this fact does not become noticeable, because special interest groups each represent their interests in exclusive interactions with special politicians and small special parts of the bureaucracy. This allows them to pursue their interests in a covert and hidden manner. Their exclusive interactions with politicians and bureaucracy are hardly visible in public. Moreover, regulations favoring these groups are placed in laws or regulations where the "ordinary citizen" does not expect them. The lowering of the "guaranteed interest rate" for the Riester pension, for example, took place in a law on insurance supervision.

In contrast to that, groups representing the general interests of larger parts of the population cannot represent their interests in exclusive interaction and in a covert and hidden manner. The reason is simple: General interests affect many special interests and concern responsibilities of larger parts of public administration. Regulations that accommodate their interests can hardly be hidden in any special laws. These interests have to assert themselves in competition with a larger or smaller number of special interests or even with other general interests. As a rule, this succeeds only in part or in a weakened form.

Regulative capture and rent-seeking is, as Joseph Stiglitz argues, much more widespread in the USA than in other countries and in Sweden probably much less than in other countries. In the USA, the Greatest Happiness Principle seems to be politically much less effective and the principle of individual liberty much more effective than in other countries. In Sweden it is the other way around. But the distributive state is vibrant in all Western countries.

The Logic of the Distributive State

Paradoxically enough, the distributive state is the child of that state which in the view of libertarians and modern neoliberals is its alternative, namely the minimal state. The minimal state is a state which at the first glance has nothing in common with the distributive state. It is a state which is reduced to the necessary functions of government in a free society. In the view of radical liberals like the American libertarians or the modern neoliberals, the only indispensable functions of government in a free society are the definition and guarantee of property rights, and the safeguarding of internal and external security. If governments serve these "core functions" adequately, economic and social affairs can be regulated by the market or other voluntary social interactions.[6]

Property rights define the ownership and use of a defined resource or good. They determine on one side what good is owned and how the owner may dispose of the good. On the other side, they determine what a buyer of a good may expect to buy. This seems to be rather simple but it is not at all. Ownership and use of resources or goods is restricted by economic regulation which sets safety standards, quality standards, environmental standards as well as social standards and other properties which restrict the ownership and use of property. The reason for the restrictions is the protection of the rights of buyers and other people. In order to protect buyers, cars to be sold for example must ensure a certain condition, otherwise the owner may not buy them or only under certain conditions. To protect the general public, cars must meet certain emission standards, otherwise the owner is not allowed to use them on public roads. In effect, all these kind of regulations are an implicit part of the definition of property rights because they restrict trade and use of goods.

Over the period in which the political institutions of Western democracies have developed, the main focus has been on regulating the ownership of physical resources and goods. This alone has become more complicated because many physical goods have become more complex. For example, food today often contains a higher or lower number of chemical additives or a genetically modified basic product. In order to protect buyers and at least inform them on what they buy, it is necessary to regulate for each foodstuff what additives or genetically modified substances it may contain and how it must be labelled. This is difficult from a purely factual point of view. Recipes of foodstuffs are often complex. Moreover, nowadays new recipes and substances as well as genetic modifications are constantly developing. Therefore the regulation of foodstuff has to be continually adapted to change. The definition of food constituents is, hence, often not a one-time affair but an ongoing and substantially difficult process.

In this process, many actors with different, sometimes conflicting interests are directly or indirectly involved. These include the manufacturers of food and additives and their interest organizations. This is not a uniform group: organic and conventional farmers, for example, have completely different interests. Such differences also exist in food trade. The interests of food trade often collide with those of producers. Large trading companies, for example, put farmers under such massive cost pressure that they cannot survive economically without factory farming or the heavy use of fertilizers and pesticides. This puts them in opposition to many consumers and animal welfare groups. There are also significant differences between consumers and their interest associations. Some consumer groups consider animal welfare whilst others are primarily interested in low prices and good bargains. In addition to interest groups, there are also different bureaucracies involved, like the ministries of agriculture, environment and economics and their subordinate authorities. These bureaucracies each pursue their own, sometimes conflicting interests. Finally, the courts also frequently have a say.

In this situation almost any decision over property rights made according to political majority rule or by public bureaucracy benefits certain interest groups and impairs others. The definition of property rights, thus, usually involves minor or major conflicts of interest. In effect, this makes the definition of property rights as much a distributive activity as any other government activity, including subsidies and welfare benefits in particular.

Almost any relevant decision will face dissatisfaction from a smaller or larger number of interest groups. Dissatisfaction leads to various attempts to challenge laws, decrees and other regulations by means of initiatives to change those regulations, and attempts to influence administrative interpretations and implementation of regulations, often with resort to legal action and public campaigns. Such activity is often quite effective and results in minor or major modifications to regulations and their execution. However, modifications often create further dissatisfaction which again stimulates counter actions. This induces considerable instability and insecurity in regulation.

Since the second half of the last century, the problems addressed here have become much more acute because intellectual property and data have gained enormously in importance. Intellectual property includes literary and artistic copyrights, patents and trademark rights and property rights for plant varieties. Data is concrete information about almost everything that exists in the world: people, animals, things, relationships, natural and social developments, knowledge and institutions.

Intellectual property and data are intangible goods which are difficult to grasp and often complex. They are, therefore, difficult to define. Moreover, they are frequently subject to rapid innovation and novel usage. This adds significantly to the substantial complexity of intellectual property and data. Substantial complexity comes in tandem with political complexity. Knowledge and data have become the most important resources in the knowledge society and in the process of digitalization. These resources are used for an almost infinite number of activities, processes and products in many areas. The regulation of intellectual property and data has a far-reaching impact on the economy and society. It is, therefore, associated with an even larger variety of different and often diverging economic and social interests and a higher potential for distributive conflict than physical goods.[7]

Since the definition of property rights is as much a distributive activity as any other government activity, the concept of a "minimal state" is a dangerous illusion. Under the conditions of modern industrial society, the minimal state is doomed to rapidly grow far beyond its "core functions". This has long since led to the opposite of a minimal state. Government has developed into a big and complex machinery which distributes the gains and losses of the definition of property rights as well as of any other governmental activities, even including defense. This is what I refer to above as the distributive state.

Economists and politicians often associate big government with the welfare state but the modern distributive state has little or nothing to do with a welfare state. On the contrary, it is counterproductive for the functions of the welfare state. What drives big government and the distributive state is the production of public goods and the fact that public goods are not as public as the term suggests.

Although public goods are, in principle, accessible for all citizens of the state, they are by no means equally beneficial to all. Rather, they yield large benefits for some people and organizations but also significant disadvantages, costs and risks for others. This is the same kind of problem which we discussed earlier in relation to environment as a common good. A good example is the case of subsidies for renewable energy, including photovoltaic systems on private homes in Germany. Until 2022, these subsidies have not been financed through taxes but by a levy on energy price. This has benefited the somewhat wealthier households that own private homes and can afford the investment in a photovoltaic system. For all other households, these subsidies have created additional energy costs and probably impaired their living standard. Soaring energy costs in the wake of the Ukraine war have forced government to eliminate the eliminate the levy.

Above I have explained the problems that lead to big distributive machinery as a result of substantial complexity on the one hand and complex social interest structures on the other. But this is only half the story. The other half is the institutional mastery of social complexity, or, more prosaic, the openness and social diversity of Western societies. As we discussed at some length in the first chapter, mastering social complexity means on one side to reach decisions on the solution of social problems and to maintain social conditions which are widely accepted in spite of the high potential for social and political conflict of pluralistic societies. On the other one it means to be able to exploit these societies' high potential for creativity and social learning to find solutions of social problems which are adequate to the substantial complexity of the problems and suitable to solve the problems effectively and sustainably. This is, as we have already noted in the first chapter, what the political institutions of Western societies are failing to do.

In past years and decades, there has been a fashionable response to insights on government failure – leave it to the market. In theory, this is a sensible response in our specific case. Theoretically, the market can easily cope with complexity because it regulates production and distribution of goods and services, and thus indirectly also of income and property, in a society without requiring a collective decision to do so and without prior consensus. In principle the market may also create a pattern of production and consumption which is sustainable in environmental as well as in economic and social terms. However, this only works under two preconditions, namely an adequate regulatory framework and reasonable chances for people to participate in markets.

The regulatory framework must assure that there is effective competition in all markets. There should be no oligopolistic or even monopolistic condition both in relations between producers and their suppliers and between producers and consumers. Moreover, there should be no significant externalities and the regulatory framework must define clear standards of information. Standards give buyers security that they are reasonably informed about the product they want to buy and to enable them to make reasonable decisions on what they buy at which price. In economic textbooks, this is called consumer sovereignty and is considered an important precondition of effective competition. Last not least, the regulatory framework must gear the market to the common good, to sustainable development in particular. In the view of this book, the regulatory framework should gear the market at sustainable development by a resource tax which adds a valid environmental price tag on all products and services. In this way, market prices would reflect the non-renewable natural resources used for the production of goods (including rucksacks). Goods with low resource consumption would gain a significant competitive advantage on the market.

Reasonable chances for people to participate in markets means that they receive an income, above all an employment income, which enables them to acquire the goods and services which they need for a reasonably decent life in the market. The principle should be that income from a full-time job must meet this criteria without supplementary welfare payments. Supplementary welfare payments in effect are a subsidy to employers. This provides a positive externality to these employers which leads to market failure. The regulatory framework should prevent this by defining minimal wages rather than encourage it by supplementary welfare payments.

Unfortunately, the market is not the elegant solution to our problem which it could be theoretically. The cause is that governments in Western societies fail to establish a reasonable regulatory framework for the same reasons they fail otherwise. The ability of government to design an adequate regulatory framework is massively impaired by regulatory capture and the largely disproportionate influence and power of well-organized special interests. This I have known for many years. In 1982 Mancur Olson published a book entitled "The Rise and Decline of Nations" in which he argued that the strong influence of well-organized specialized interest groups leads to inefficient government regulation of the market. This in turn hinders growth and enhances stagnation, unemployment and inflation. This argument has not lost topicality since.[8]

This throws us back to government failure. In modern Western societies government failure is not an occasional event, but a systemic feature. The basic principles underlying the political institutions of Western societies emerged in a time when both the social complexity and the substantive complexity of politics were much lower than nowadays. Since that time the political institutions of Western democracies have become geared towards formal legitimacy. The general principle is that decisions are legitimate not because of their substance but because they are decided by majority voting based on formally free and equal participation of all citizens and on political competition. This concept assumes that formally legitimate decisions are binding for the entire society and widely accepted. In the times in which the basic principles of modern democracy were created, majority rule was a great and often hard-won achievement.

Today, the institution of majority rule is coming under increasing pressure because Western societies have become more open and diverse and their political culture has changed significantly. The individualization and rationalization of Western societies is also manifested in the fact that formal legitimation by majority rule does no longer mean that the respective decisions are also materially accepted or even represent a common understanding. Also, it does no longer mean that conflicts are really solved by majority decisions. Although many conflicts disappear from the political agenda after political decisions have been made, they remain in the background. Different understandings of ends, ways and means in the population at large and between organized interest groups do not simply disappear after majority decisions. It is certainly possible that outnumbered groups will adopt the majority decision, but this is by no means guaranteed. Often outnumbered groups (especially if they are well organized) do not just accept majority decisions to which they are opposed, but will try to reverse, modify, amend or evade them. In most cases, they do not need to reach a new majority decision. Well organized interest groups may simply use their capability of regulative capture to change a decision in its implementation in their sense.

This points to another fundamental change in Western societies since the times in which their basic institutional principles emerged. The possibilities and abilities of social groups, especially small, privileged groups, to get well organized have increased dramatically, as have their possibilities to acquire and exercise power.[9]

There are policy areas in which organized interest intermediation is more directly competitive. These are areas with high economic and social relevance, such as labor law, social security or environmental protection. In these areas, usually several well-organized interests clash. So there is definitely a strong competition of interests. But this does not have the beneficial balancing effect that the pluralist model ascribes to it. Rather, it leads to mutual blockades or weak compromises. Mutual blockades often hinder that regulation and other activities are only slowly adapted to scientific, technical, economic and social change. This creates new problems and conflict. Weak compromises have similar consequences. In the end, this again leads to an unsteady and short-term pattern of policymaking.

As we discussed in the first chapter, the strong influence of well-organized special interest groups and the related patterns of lobbying are likely to lead policymakers into a complexity trap. To remind: As a complexity trap I describe a situation in which political institutions increase the substantial and social complexity of problems rather than reducing them to a manageable level. This stimulates a permanent process of institutional change which often deprives institutions of their acceptance, reliability and efficacy. The more this is the case, the more contingent becomes social development and the more it evades direction. The complexity trap makes up for a fundamental challenge to the efficiency, legitimacy and acceptance of government in Western societies. Moreover, it is the driver of a big distributive state and leaves little or no room for consistent and effective strategies of threefold sustainability. This danger also manifests itself in the "nickel-and-dime economy."

The "Nickel-and-Dime Economy" Revisited

In the first chapter, I defined the "nickel-and-dime-economy" as a developed economy that has adapted to a prolonged period of stagnating or even falling incomes of a significant part of the population through fierce price competition. This has long since ceased to be a market niche for people with a low income, but rather has become an economic form that in some Western countries makes up a considerable part of the economy and that reaches far into the middle- and upper-income groups. Neither the establishment of the "nickel-and-dime-economy" nor its increasing outreach are really a surprise.

It is the expected reaction of the market to the fact that there are a large number of low-income people whose needs and wants correspond to those of the great mass of the population, but whose income is insufficient to satisfy those wants and needs. These people represent a considerable market potential that can be tapped by lower prices and special deals. It would be astonishing if there had not been companies, especially retail companies, that had recognized this potential and developed a suitable business model for it. In some countries discounters in food retailing entered markets shortly before or after World War Two. Their business model was based in particular on mass purchasing and rapid turnover of a limited range of products, as well as simply designed and intensively used salesrooms. As the relative number of people with low or stagnating incomes increased, this business model became a great success, especially since more and more price-conscious shoppers with medium incomes were taking advantage of the discounters' low-price offers too. Discounters have responded to this trend with temporary bargains on high-quality products. This made them attractive to more people from middle- or even higher-income groups. Many supermarket chains too adjusted to the changing income structure by enlarging their low-priced segment or newly introducing such a segment. Suppliers of discounters and supermarkets adjusted their pricing policies or even introduced no name versions of their brand products.

Similar business models have also been developed in a growing number of other sectors of the economy, even for technologically high-value products that fit the nickel-and-dime economy. For many of these products, for example cell phones, the costs of materials and material processing are low while the costs for research and development as well as for software and design are high. Therefore, manufacture of these products involves high fixed costs and low variable costs. Once the fixed costs are paid, these products can be sold at relatively low prices in large quantities. They can therefore be sold relatively expensively when they are new and come onto the market with interesting novelties to customers who value the latest technical state of the art or the latest craze in fashion. Afterwards they can be sold at much lower prices. Moreover cheaper versions of the product may be sold under a different brand name. Indeed, reduced versions of the new technology may also be used to offer lower-priced models. This is the strategy that can be observed with many suppliers of electronic products. It once again strengthens the nickel-and-dime economy. Nowadays there is in most Western countries a large nickel-and-dime economy with sharp price competition.

Even in the case of technologically advanced products, and much more so in the case of simpler mass-produced products, fierce price competition has led to three conditions that are extremely undesirable from a sustainability point of view. The first condition is that the intense price competition gives companies that have gained strong market power a considerable advantage. Strong market power allows companies to push down the prices of their suppliers as well as wages and working conditions of many of their workers.

This creates strong incentives to achieve and maintain high power in markets. The effect of this may be observed in the form of oligopolistic structures in the IT-industry in Silicon Valley and elsewhere and in food trade in Germany and many other countries. A particularly illustrative case is Amazon. As Brad Stone describes in his book "Amazon Unbound: Jeff Bezos and the Invention of a Global Empire" Amazon has become in less than a decade the world's largest online retailer and a company with almost uncontrolled power over the retail sector and the supplying businesses.[10]

The power of its major actors perpetuates the nickel-and-dime economy because it keeps many wages low and working conditions poor and maintains precarious jobs even for skilled workers like software developers and programmers. Remarkably, in retail, logistics, agriculture and other sectors of the economy wages often remain low even though there is a significant shortage of relevant labor, but no shortage of profit. This suggests that economic power and cartelization have long since undermined labor markets. In Germany and other countries, this is further supported by the state in that people who fall below the poverty line despite full employment (working poor) receive social welfare – another illustrative example of regulatory capture. All this reinforces social inequality and keeps large parts of Western economies on a path of development which is neither economically nor socially sustainable.

The second condition is relocation of large parts of production to countries with wages that are much lower and with working conditions that are even worse than those in the low-wage sector of Western countries. International labour standards, including the ban on child labour, are systematically violated. This amounts for massive economic exploitation which strangles development of the countries concerned. The resulting miserable living conditions in many African, Latin American and Asian countries create massive incentives for migration, especially for younger and active people. This leads on one side to migration flows that the USA and Europe can no longer cope with socially and politically and, on the other side, to a loss of active and often skilled people in developing countries which they would need for their development. This is a state of affairs that is anything but sustainable and can hardly be considered sustainable. This is not a new insight, but obviously the interests of the nickel-and-dime economy carry much more weight politically.

The third condition relates to the really disastrous environmental consequences of the "nickel-and-dime economy" which we already discussed in chapter one, notably strong incentives to produce in an unsustainable way and the environmental division of society in bottom and top. The environmental division of society is also reflected in fundamental value orientations. In his 1977 book "The Silent Revolution," the American political scientist Ronald Inglehart diagnosed a shift in Western societies from "materialist" to "post-materialist" values. He found this shift confirmed in later research. Values are the principles by which people orient their actions.[11]

Materialist values are strongly oriented toward goals such as income, wealth, status, physical and social security, economic growth and economic stability. Post-materialist values are characterized by goals such as quality of life, attractive working conditions, more opportunities to have a say, freedom of expression, and self-actualization. Inglehart's empirical research showed that especially people with higher incomes and good education develop post-materialist values. Inglehart found the explanation for this in the hierarchy of needs identified by American psychologist Abraham Maslow. From this hierarchy, Inglehart drew the conclusion that post-materialistic values develop when people's material needs are largely satisfied. In a later book, Inglehart brought together his many empirical studies into a theory of cultural evolution. In this theory, he postulated a general connection between economic wellbeing and social and physical security on the one hand, and basic social and political attitudes on the other. If one follows this theory, which fits well with the evolutionary approach of this book, a continuing decline in prosperity and economic security, as well as growing economic and social inequality, produces a greater emphasis on materialistic values. The silent revolution, so to speak, is being reversed. This manifests itself, Inglehart argues, in authoritarian, anti-democratic, anti-women and xenophobic attitudes and populism.

This is not merely an abstract problem, but a very tangible one. In a society where a large part of the population does not develop post-materialist values, it is difficult to reach an understanding on effective measures and programs for environmental sustainability. There are no broad political majorities and no strong market signals for such activities.

Strictly speaking, the nickel-and-dime economy is not the cause of the environmental division into bottom and top, nor of the reversal of value change. The causes are economic inequality and the concrete material conditions of life in Western societies that gave rise to the nickel-and-dime economy in the first place. But the nickel-and-dime economy disguises inequality while exacerbating it. It disguises it by offering lower- and middle-income groups consumption options that are similar to those of higher income groups – albeit with massive cutbacks in quality and environmental standards. At the same time, it exacerbates it because it entails low wages and poor working conditions as well as low prices in the purchase of agricultural and other products. It thus stands in the way of sustainable development. Therefore, dissolution of the nickel-and-dime economy and its replacement by a high value economy is an urgent task of public policy for sustainable development.

This however is a difficult task because the nickel-and-dime-economy is deeply entrenched in industrial production structures, in procurement and distribution of the retail sector and in the consumption behaviour and budgets of many consumers. Its replacement by a high value economy requires a lot of change and this brings a high potential of conflict. In order to reduce this potential and keep conflicts rather small, it makes sense to apply a strategy that is incremental but nevertheless effective.

An incremental strategy is also recommended because the dismantling of the nickel-and-dime economy entails significant losses in living standards for lower- and middle-income groups if it is not accompanied by income policy measures. However, a massive redistribution in a short period of time is likely to lead to strong conflicts in most Western countries and to fail as a result. As we will further discuss in chapter 5, reducing inequality to an economically meaningful and socially acceptable level should be combined with fundamental tax reform leading to a tax system that systematically curbs inequality. This needs time.

Against this background, the best strategy to dissolve the nickel-and-dime economy in the short run is probably the continuous raising of quality standards and social standards, and of minimum wages. In combination with a dynamic resource tax, this will ensure that the opportunities for action for companies in the nickel-and-dime economy are increasingly dried up. The continuous raising of quality standards removes cheap products step-by-step from the market. The continuous increase of social standards and minimum wages eliminates gradually the possibility for companies to secure their competitiveness through bad working conditions and low wages. As both are done successively, companies and consumers have time to adapt. In the end, a new economy geared at high value rather than high volume may emerge.

A New Economy

We do not know what the economy of the future will look like. In chapter 3, we roughly sketched a possible spectrum of future developments. In this chapter, we discuss what the new economy should look like as the goal of a strategy of threefold sustainability, why it should be so, and what can be done to guide development towards this model. As we noted earlier, our goal is an economy focused on high value and high resource productivity across the value chain. High value means high technical quality, high design quality and high customer orientation. Both high value and high resource productivity require a high level of innovation.

This is what Friedrich Schmidt-Bleek and I call a tailored economy. We define this as an economy that, like a tailor-made suit, is precisely tailored to our needs and desires and whose consumption of natural resources is precisely tailored to nature's possibilities. A prime example of this is individualized medicines that precisely match the molecular biological constellation of the individual patient and can therefore deliver high efficacy with low side effects. Modern biotechnology will also allow them to be produced with a low consumption of natural resources. So they operate at a low MIPS.

The new economy cannot be an economy dominated by traditional large companies and corporations. Traditional large corporations follow the opposite principle of a tailored economy which is the principle of a throughput economy. This is an economy that pushes through in a given amount of time as much material as possible to produce as much goods as possible. This also applies for a more customer-oriented form of mass production called mass customization. Mass customization uses flexible computer-aided manufacturing techniques and combines them with mass production methods. This allows some companies to tailor their products to individual customers without greatly increasing their production costs. Tailor-made suits may be at least partly produced in this way. However, despite flexible techniques, these options are organizationally limited because mass customization is also associated with standardized work and production processes and with the procurement, distribution and logistics structures typical of mass production. As soon as these structures of work, production and logistics are abandoned, large companies may lose their advantage as manufacturing companies unless they fundamentally change their organizational structures.

The real problem for many large companies is their structures of management, organization and communication and the associated ability to learn and innovate. When I talk about large companies here, I am not primarily referring to size in the sense of the usual definition based on employee numbers and sales, but size in the sense of complexity. A company is large if it has many employees which work in a centralized organization with a multi-level hierarchy and which are attached to long lines of communication and management. Such a company is large because its activity and development are simultaneously influenced by a multitude of interactions at different levels that are only formally coordinated. It is large because it requires a multitude of rules and instructions to guide the behaviour of its employees and its organizational units toward specific organizational goals and to direct its operation. It is large not least because it requires a large apparatus to manage and control its employees and organizational units.

Such organizations can be managed and controlled only to a limited extent because the organization's management has only limited information. Information flows through the hierarchy only within a formally prescribed framework and in formally prescribed ways. Much information is not captured at all, and much more is captured only selectively. The individual hierarchy levels act as more or less selective filters, passing on only that information which they absolutely have to and which corresponds to their understanding and interests. In these structures, not only is a great deal of control lost, but also a great deal of commitment on the part of the employees.

In the view of Peter Wickens, these are the pillars of a successful corporate organization. In the 1980s, Peter Wickens, the head of human resources at Nissan Motors United Kingdom, was instrumental in building up what was then one of the most successful automotive plants. In his book "The Ascendant Organization" you find the sentence "There is no absolute 'right' size for an organization. There are only well and badly managed organizations, whether they may be large or small". What this means Peter Wickens demonstrated at Nissan Motors UK in Sunderland. The company has adapted and further developed the Japanese system of lean production to British and European conditions. The company has installed a decentralized organization with a flat hierarchy. At the core of this organization are manufacturing cells, each of which is responsible for the production of an entire component (e.g., an engine). Work is done in autonomous work groups, which have a relatively high degree of independence and personal responsibility. They can help shape work processes and workplaces, organize their work largely independently, but are also responsible for the quality of their products, the functioning of their equipment and their consumption of energy and materials. This is the commitment pillar. The control pillar was formed in particular by clear targets at all levels from management down to the work groups, regular reviews of target achievement, public display of the teams' performance values, the strong role of supervisors (the lowest level of management), and relatively close contact between management and the workforce.[12]

With such organizational forms, large companies can be made much smaller from a complexity standpoint. There will probably be many large companies that apply these forms to retain their traditional structures but modernize them technically and organizationally in the way that Nissan Motors UK and other companies have done. We should however be aware that Nissan is still a mass producer, also a customized mass producer to some extent. Accordingly, the Nissan way is a model to reorganize mass production, make it more flexible and more customized. But it is probably not a suitable model for companies moving from high volume to high value.

Large companies on the way from high volume to high value may be well advised to change their organization more radically. They should make it into a network of companies managed by a head company. The head company could concentrate largely on the strategic planning and management of the entire company, the specification and control of goals and framework conditions for the subsidiaries, and the performance and organization of a few higher-level activities. These could be fundamental innovation projects, the early assessment of technological, economic and social developments, or the planning and maintenance of common technical systems and infrastructures. Individual companies could be focused on specific products and customers. Digitization, 3-D printing, microsystems technology and biotechnology offer many opportunities for this, as we saw in chapter 3 with regard to biotechnology and chemistry. Consistent use of these opportunities can ensure lean but effective management and a high strategic capacity to act for the entire company on the one hand, and a high level of product, process and customer knowledge and expertise for the subsidiaries on the other. By focusing the individual subsidiaries on specific products and customers, a common understanding of tasks and problems can ensure good integration of the various functions, e.g. research and development, procurement, production or quality control.

The structures outlined here, in conjunction with digitization, 3-D printing, microsystems technology and biotechnology, offer large companies many opportunities to localize their global or national structures more strongly and to become much more customer-oriented. In some cases, it will make sense to set up joint local production centres for the entire company;

in other cases, it will be more reasonable to let subsidiaries to do this on their own or with other companies. In still other cases, it might be more advantageous not to create fixed local production centres, but to use mobile centres or to use external production service providers. This could go so far as to have companies focus entirely on research, development, design, marketing and customer services, and outsource production altogether. To the point: As far as large companies are concerned our new economy will be much more differentiated and diverse than the economy of the industrial age.[13]

The SME economy too will change fundamentally. Many SMEs will have to become embedded in network structures. In their conventional form, many SMEs are unable to cope with the problems of the knowledge society, especially with rapid development of knowledge and technology, and rapidly changing markets. They are poorly equipped for this in terms of finance, personnel and technology. They usually have only a few levels of hierarchy, but nevertheless their management and communication structures are often rigid and hierarchical. But even well-organized, well-equipped and well-managed SMEs often reach limits in terms of personnel and finances which are far too narrow to be able to survive in the knowledge society with its environmental, economic and social challenges.

Alone many SMEs also cannot take advantage of the opportunities which the key technologies of the early twenty-first century, particularly digitalization, 3-D printing, microsystems technology and biotechnology offer to realize new business ideas, eliminate weaknesses and further develop strengths. Such opportunities could provide many SMEs with new impetus for competitiveness and growth. Yet, to use these opportunities, they must engage in some form of networking which helps them to overcome their limitations.[14]

To overcome too narrow financial limits, for example, they may use crowd funding, forming attractive funds for institutional investors with the help of capital management companies, or seeking venture capitalists for ambitious innovation projects. With crowd funding, start-ups or companies look for private investors interested in a new product or the company in general. Capital management companies establish and manage investment funds for third parties. Venture capitalists are companies, funds or private investors who are willing to invest a lot of money for very demanding and therefore risky projects. SMEs often do not have such opportunities on their own, but can mobilize them for themselves in an attractive group of companies. If, for example, a larger number of plumbing and heating installers join forces to jointly develop a new plumbing and heating system with high resource productivity that can then be 3-D printed locally, they are likely to be of interest to many investors.

SMEs can connect in the form of a network of cooperating independent companies or of a network company. In the latter case, they form a joint head company, but retain a great deal of independence and individual responsibility. What makes SMEs collaborating in strong networks reasonable is not only that together they have a lot of technical knowledge and a lot of experience and can serve a large market, but also that in the network they can greatly increase their innovative capacity and tackle challenging forward-looking innovation projects.

A particularly interesting opportunity for many SMEs is to set up powerful open innovation systems and thus harness a great deal of external knowledge for themselves. Open innovation is the term used to describe corporate innovation processes in which external players can also participate. In many companies, openness is limited to customers and external experts. However, there are also open innovation networks that are open to all actors who can make a significant contribution to the project in question and accept the rules of the network. This kind of open innovation is particularly attractive for networks of SMEs.

All these possibilities can also be used by start-ups and by self-employed people. Start-ups or self-employed people with an innovative idea and some, but not all, of the knowledge needed to realize this idea can, for example, use an open innovation network to gain partners with additional knowledge and expertise and thus considerably increase the chances of financing and realizing their idea. In addition, 3-D printing and microsystems technology offer many new and attractive opportunities for self-employed work. For example, self-employed people can develop or design digital models for items, such as jewellery or tableware, and equipment, such as kitchen appliances or machines, for individual customers or companies, which the customers can then produce in a 3-D centre or on their own 3D printer. The amount of these opportunities is likely to be huge. Harnessing these opportunities will be a key driver of jobs and employment. I further discuss this in the next part of this chapter.[15]

If all the possibilities described in this part are used wisely, a diverse economy with a wide range of different forms of organization and cooperation could emerge. In such an economy, concentration of economic power could be contained and competition better reinforced and guided than in the economy of the industrial age. Paradoxical as it may sound at first, it is precisely the many cooperative elements of the new economy that make competition stronger, not weaker. These elements ensure that there are many strong but less dominant companies. Moreover, their diversity can durably improve the new economy's social learning and innovation capabilities.

Therefore government support for the networking of SMEs, start-ups and self-employed people is justified and reasonable both economically and in terms of sustainable development. Government support should involve financial as well as organizational and infrastructural measures. Financial resources are probably the least of the problems. Although significant investments are likely to be made for the realization of the cooperation, e.g. in 3-D printers or new software, these investments may be privately financed by crowd funding, an investment fund or venture capitalists if the network has a promising product or business model. Financial resources are then only needed for the costs of the formation of the network which still may be significant.

A significant problem for many SMEs, start-ups and self-employed people is that they lack human capacity or skills as well as the information and knowledge to form such networks. They also may lack knowledge on possible partners and on the legal and organizational possibilities and pit-falls of cooperation and cannot get this knowledge themselves due to a lack of personnel capacities and competencies. For the same reason, they cannot conduct the often complex negotiations on the cooperation without external advice. For large companies, these are all minor problems, but for many SMEs, start-ups and self-employed people they are large, hardly sol-vable problems because external advice is often costly. They therefore need organizational support by government.

To provide organizational support for the networking of SMEs, start-ups and self-employed people, government can set up information platforms and, together with business, science and other stakeholders and experts, create efficient consulting and support facilities. Models for this exist in some countries from government support for the formation of clusters or projects of smart specialization. Clusters are spatial concentrations of com-panies, research institutes and other actors from a particular sector of the economy that are linked to each other by business and other exchange rela-tionships. Smart specialization is an EU program to promote the focusing of economic development strategies of weak regions on relative strengths and the formation of corresponding networks.

Support for the networking of SMEs may also come from actors other than government. These may be financial investors looking for investment opportunities in companies and networks with a strong potential for growth, local associations for promotion of the local economy or even large, but also decentralized companies looking for creative milieus for some of their smal-ler subsidiary companies. But this can also be many cities, companies and other organizations that want to build strong innovative milieus in their realm. Last not least it may be a variety of actors who want to build up strong local or sectoral structures for sustainable development.

Whether the kind of new economy described above will emerge or the "nickel-and-dime economy" survives, or something else will happen does to a large degree depend on government activity. This refers not only to the provision of support described above, but also the government's ability to establish a better regulatory framework for sustainable development. As long as government tolerates or even supports cheap mass production and a "nickel-and-dime economy" it may well be that powerful economic and political profiteers of the old economy and its entrenched structures will capture large parts of the economy in strong path dependencies which in the end not only hinder or even prevent development of a new economy, but of sustainable development at all.

Development of a new economy described in this part will probably not avoid the loss of many jobs in industrial production, especially at larger companies. However, it may create new jobs in customer-related services at large companies. Most probably, it would also create many new jobs in SMEs and start-ups because these enterprises become more innovative and competitive and therefore may grow considerably both in established and new businesses. New jobs may also be created in organizational services for cooperation among companies and self-employed people. In addition, the environmental transformation of the economy is likely to create many new jobs in any case.

How the new economy copes with work and employment is a matter of how development of a new economy is shaped. Given the difficulties of shaping social developments, it is of crucial importance to develop a widely accepted understanding of the new economy as early as possible. Nothing would be worse for all the players involved and for society as a whole than flying blind into the new economy. But development of a widely accepted understanding will require much time and much public debate. A good measure to initiate this process and keep it in progress would be a series of citizens' assemblies, consensus conferences and consensus forums which could not only be organized by government, but also by NGOs, cities, institutional investors and other actors. As I will explain in the last chapter, this needs some regulatory framework which secures that all such activities must follow the basic principles of mini-publics and deliberation.

A Key Issue: The Future of Work

The future of work is key issue in sustainable development because work and employment are important aspects of the social dimension of threefold sustainability. Beyond that it is a key issue because massive problems of employment and work may well cause climate change and sustainability to quickly disappear from the political agenda in most Western societies, or at least to be pushed far back. Even if this is not the case, massive employment problems will create many economic and political conflicts that will greatly inhibit sustainability and climate neutrality activities.

With additive manufacturing (3-D printing), rise of robots, internet, internet of things and artificial intelligence, digitalization leads into a new machine age. The same is true for microsystems technology and biotechnology. There is no doubt that the new machine age will change work and employment significantly. In the previous chapter, I demonstrated this using the examples of biotechnical and chemical industries.

As social evolution in general, these changes can only be predicted to a limited extent. This is particularly true since digital technologies are highly flexible and may be used in a variety of different ways. For actors that want to apply these technologies, this is certainly a nice thing. But for people who want to predict how the new machine age will look, this is as bad as it can be. High flexibility of digital technologies means that a lot is possible and, hence, little is predictable. This is reflected in a variety of different predictions on the impact of digital digitalization on work and employment.[16]

Some of the predictions are rather optimistic with respect to work. They argue, for example, that intelligent machines will make life for most people much more easy and pleasant. People have to work less and working conditions may be much better. Moreover, they may enjoy much more freedom and opportunities for self-actualization. They may enjoy a much better work–life balance. A good example of this optimistic thinking on the digital economy is Don Tapscott who argues that "with ubiquitous broadband, society now has the most powerful platform ever for bringing together the people, skills, and knowledge needed to ensure growth, social development, and a just and sustainable world". But at the same time he warns that there are not only promises, but also perils, and that positive development needs positive leadership. Similar views are expressed by other thinkers.[17]

The opposite view is that intelligent machines will destroy a large, even overwhelming proportion of current jobs. Even highly skilled jobs, like chemists, tax consultants, bankers, architects and IT-workers may be replaced fully or partly by algorithms and robots. For many people, this could mean poverty and loss of meaning and self-esteem. This will raise fundamental issues of inequality, social security, purchasing power and the absorption capacity of economies, but also of social cohesion. Current inequality of income wealth which is already high compared with the middle of the last century and before will further increase. Mass purchasing power may decline or at least stagnate. Living standards between permanently employed and well paid people and people with occasional jobs or low wage jobs will heavily diverge. Many people may do reasonably well only if they exploit themselves. Working conditions may decline for many workers.[18]

There is also a middle-of-the road view, namely that there will be big problems during a transition period. But during this period, new economic structures shaped by innovative self-employed, small firms or cooperatives who collaborate in networks, common workspaces and other open forms of organization will emerge. They become the major drivers of innovation and the core of a highly customized economy. They will create new forms of work and employment, new economic structures and new understandings of the meaning of life. As a result, large parts of manufacturing may become decentralized. Small firms, often connected in collaborative networks, may replace big ones. Nimble factories may replace traditional factories. Many manufacturing companies particularly in the industrialized countries may focus on development and design of products and leave physical production to other, mostly small firms. This may enhance customization in many industries and suppress traditional mass production. Consumers may increasingly become prosumers. A new financial system with social capital, crowd funding and peer-to-peer credits may be rising. A sustainable post-scarcity economy will emerge. This is obviously the kind of new economy advocated in the previous section.[19]

But in the transition period the opposite is possible as well. In the early stage of industrialization at the beginning of the nineteenth century, mechanization provoked violent conflicts by the luddites. The luddites were the textile workers whose jobs and social status were threatened by mechanization. They lost in the end because they could destroy machines, but had no power. But the "losers" of tomorrow's machine age, Bankers, IT-workers, chemists and other skilled persons, may have much more in their toolbox. Instead of blind violence, their reaction could be smart striking back against former employers and established business. This may be creative forms of strike or sabotage (e.g. hacking of the programming of robots or the internet-based organization or many small attacks on energy supply or payment transactions). It may also be development of new, competing business models by displaced skilled workers – or many other possible responses. This opens up a large variety of possible future development. There may be years of heavy industrial and political conflict, anti-technological movements and building of massive innovation barriers, but also a long period of economic recession and a period of creative destruction and radical innovation.

A most horrible possibility would be a nightmare which Israeli historian Yuval Noah Harari describes in his book Homo Deus. It is a world in which mankind succeeded to eliminate famine, plague, and war mostly. But it is also a world in which bioengineers may produce changes in human DNA and intervene directly in human evolution. This may be used to create intellectually powerful "superhumans". Moreover, information technology may develop artificial intelligence to a level which is comparable to human intelligence. Above all, it could become a world in which a class of "superhumans" will govern over a large class of useless people. This class is formed by three types of people. These are, first, the people who drive and control knowledge production, that is, the top researchers and the top science managers. Second, they are the people who drive and control the use of knowledge, i.e., the top business managers. Third, it is finally the people who develop and control the highly intelligent machines that make most other people economically redundant. The redundant people belong to the genus Homo sapiens, the knowledgeable human being, which is still considered the most highly developed human genus today. As these people lose their economic importance and becomes "useless" they will, as Harari fears not without reason, lose their human rights and their freedom.[20]

Given that the "losers" of tomorrow's machine age have a much better toolbox at hand then the luddites, the rule of the "superhumans" may not last too long and end in a much better world than that which Harari fears. There may be years of severe industrial and political conflict and rebellion, but in the end a world may emerge in which people's livelihood and standard of living no longer depend on their work. Rather highly automated factories and service companies, robots and algorithms generate the money necessary to secure an unconditional basic income for all people in society with which they can finance a good standard of living. Then, people only have to work if they want more than an unconditional basic income or if they simply want to have fun and satisfaction from their work.

Although much of these and other visions sound like science fiction, they may become true within two or three decades or even less. The enormous speed of scientific and technological development may put into reality possibilities which are imagined today by a few avant-gardists only. This enormous speed is the core of the problem. Modern societies are not helplessly exposed to future developments. While social development can neither be fully predicted nor controlled, it may be shaped and directed by smart institutions. But the problem is that politics and large parts of business in the Western societies (and all the more in autocratic states) are far too entrenched in the present.

The present seems to offer a clear picture. There is in the United States and in much of Europe a significant labor shortage which inhibits economic growth. Especially in Europe, this may not only be a transient, but a structural problem. But even if we assume that it is a structural problem, we should not conclude that it is a lasting problem and none of the negative development of employment and labor will take place. Quite on the contrary, we should consider that this problem may produce in the medium and long term the kind of massive job losses which the above-mentioned pessimistic views predict. Why? Because many, particularly large companies which assume that there will be lasting labor shortages will invest more rapidly and more heavily in automation. This may turn the current situation on which these companies based their investment to its opposite.

Given all this insecurity on future developments, it is of crucial importance here too to get a clear, early picture of possible and even seemingly impossible developments of work and of the conditions which make one scenario likely to become reality and others not. The idea is not to predict development, but rather to prepare to cope with any scenario may it be "probable" or "unthinkable" and to develop for each of these an adequate strategic response. This would be great job for a citizens' assembly or even for a series of citizens' assemblies which could, for example, be jointly organized by unions and employers. The mini-publics would have, as usual, a randomly selected panel and audience. They could, however, differ insofar as the hearings should in addition to experts also include groups of randomly selected workers and employers as stakeholders.

Social models are rarely realized one-to-one. However, much would be gained for employment if a dynamic resource tax and dynamic technical, environmental and social standards were quickly introduced in Western societies. By this the transformation of Western economies from high volume to high value would be set in motion. At the same time, consideration should also be given to social security systems that could absorb high employment losses in a transitional period or even in the long term in an economically and socially acceptable way.

The Deliberative Way: Making Small Beautiful Again

The new economy I propose in this chapter is new because it is supposed to be different from the established economy. In terms of ideas, however, it is not new. In 1973 the German-British economist Ernst Friedrich Schumacher published a book with the title "Small Is Beautiful: A Study of Economics as if People Mattered". In this book, Schumacher argues for an economic system that handles natural capital and human resources with care. He criticizes industrial society for dealing with irreplaceable natural capital as if it were income that could be multiplied at will. He is particularly interested in human labor, which he sees as something much more than a means of earning a living. It conveys self-esteem, social recognition, solidarity and sociability. He therefore criticized technology that increasingly alienates people from their work and advocates work in smaller groups and intermediate technology. The fact that Schumacher's ideas are still pertinent to a new, sustainable economy illustrates how difficult social learning and the shaping of social development are.[21]

However, our model differs fundamentally from Schumacher's ideas in two respects. We no longer regard growth as a massive obstacle to sustainable development, but as a problem that can be solved in principle by decoupling growth and resource consumption – at least over a longer period of time. While Schumacher calls for a move away from "big" technology and toward intermediate technologies, we rely on the fact that today's key technologies, IT, biotechnology and microsystems technology, not only enable large-scale industrial applications but, on the contrary, promote a production system that is highly decentralized, relies on group work and has flat hierarchies.

This divergence does not mean that Schumacher's ideas have become obsolete, but merely that the technological progress of the past 50 years offers other and better ways to realize Schumacher's ideas. Schumacher's ideas have lost nothing of their topicality if only because these possibilities are used merely to a limited extent. Worse still, much of what was created in the 1980s and 1990s in the way of new flexible production systems with lean organization and a focus on high value has been rolled back in recent years in favor of global industrial structures, high volume and a nickel-and-dime economy. This too illustrates how difficult social learning and the shaping of social development are.

The realization of Schumacher's guiding principle "small is beautiful" is not easy. This can be seen in our model of a new economy. This model interlinks two principles namely competition and collaboration. This is not a new idea, but one which is already well established in business practice. In the retail sector, there have been purchasing associations for a long time. Some of these associations have now achieved a great deal of market power and are therefore not really the model for the cooperation which I am proposing. Much closer to my proposal is the cooperation between companies and their customers, including the cooperation between Airbus and Boeing and airlines in the development or improvement of aircraft, or the cooperation between medical technology companies and companies in the healthcare industry for the development of telemedicine. But what we really look for is cooperation between companies that are competitors in the marketplace.

Such cooperation is also nothing new. In the automotive industry, the German arch-rivals BMW and Daimler are cooperating on autonomous driving, where they want to achieve market leadership together; Ford and VW or Honda and General Motors are also cooperating on this topic; Daimler and Toyota are cooperating on drive technology, as are Toyota and Suzuki, to name just a few examples. In other industries, too, cooperation between competing companies is well established.

Interestingly however, cooperation between competitors is not yet common practice among the very companies that should benefit most from it, namely SMEs. This is particularly true for permanent cooperation in the development of specific technologies and products. While many SMEs cooperate with customers and suppliers in this regard, rather few do so with direct competitors on the market. If they do, cooperation is mostly confined to single projects of limited duration.

The great reluctance of many SMEs to engage in long-term cooperation probably has a lot to do with the fact that the owners and also many managers of these companies attach great importance to individual freedom, independence and personal responsibility. In the emerging economy of the knowledge society, however, these values can often be realized much more poorly through independence than through permanent cooperation with competitors and other companies. This may sound like a contradiction in terms, but there are three simple reasons. The first reason is the high speed and great breadth of the development of knowledge and technology, the second is the global networking of the large companies, manufacturing companies in particular, and the third is the financial restrictions of many SMEs.

The pace and breadth of knowledge and technology production overwhelms the ability of many SMEs (and also many large companies) to adapt and innovate in time. They are often unable to keep up with developments or are dependent on external help, which they often receive from customers or consulting institutions. Even if they are able to follow developments, they lack the human, organizational and financial resources to quickly implement new knowledge and technology in their products and processes, as we discussed above. Here, too, they are dependent on external help. In terms of technology and organization, they often receive this help from customers or consulting institutions. They receive financial help from government institutions, banks and investors, sometimes even from customers.

In a nutshell this means, that under conditions of the emerging knowledge society and its rapid knowledge production, SMEs are anyway tied into a network of multiple dependencies. In this situation, their individual freedom, independence and personal responsibility is merely a myth. The price for help by customers is often that SMEs are integrated in the customer's global innovation and production networks. In these networks, they are determined by others. In order to receive financial support from banks or government agencies they have to accept the conditions of these actors which are often rather restrictive and bureaucratic.

In a good network with competitors and other interested players, on the other hand, SMEs are equal and major partners. They can contribute their own ideas and interests and learn from their partners. Together with their partners, they are innovative and therefore attractive to customers and financiers. They are also major players for the state, because they in fact support government in its goal of promoting a strong and sustainable economy without making financial demands on it. Again to the point: In a good network with competitors and other partners, SMEs may remain "small" but become really "beautiful".

Notes

1 This is demonstrated well in David Pilling (2019). The Growth Delusion: The Wealth and Well-being of Nations. London and New York: Bloomsbury Publishing. See also Paul Allin, David J. Hand (2014).The Wellbeing of Nations: Meaning, Motive and Measurement. Mahbub ul Haq (1996) Reflections on Human Development: How the Focus of Development Economics Shifted from National Income Accounting to People-Centered Policies. New York: Oxford University Press.

2 See Joseph E. Stiglitz (2012). The Price of Inequality: How Today's Divided Society Endangers Our Future. New York and London: W.W. Norton. Anthony B. Atkinson (2018) Inequality: What Can Be Done? Cambridge, MA: Harvard University Press. Heather Boushey (2021). Unbound: How Inequality Constricts Our Economy and What We Can Do about It. Cambridge, MA: Harvard University Press. Marcel Fratzscher (2016) Verteilungskampf: Warum Deutschland immer ungleicher wird. München Carl Hanser. Jeffrey D. Sachs (2017). Building the New American Economy: Smart, Fair and Sustainable. New York: Columbia University Press.

3 Tyler Cowen (2011). The Great Stagnation. How America Ate All the Low-Hanging Fruit of Modern History, Got Sick, and Will (Eventually) Feel Better. New York: Dutton.

4 Cf. chapter 2 of Joseph E. Stiglitz (2012). The Price of Inequality: How Today's Divided Society Endangers Our Future. New York and London: W.W. Norton.

5 See Claus Offe, Politische Herrschaft und Klassenstrukturen: Zur Analyse Spätkapitalistischer Gesellschaftsstrukturen. In Gisela Kress, Dieter Senghaas eds. (1972). Politikwissenschaft: Eine Einführung in ihre Probleme. Frankfurt: Fischer.

6 The concept of the minimal state and the theoretical argument underlying it is explained in James Buchanan (1975). The Limits of Liberty: Between Anarchy and Leviathan. Chicago and London: University of Chicago Press.

7 An introduction to intellectual property, its definition, regulation and problems is provided in Aram Sinnreich (2019). The Essential Guide to Intellectual Property. New Haven and London: Yale University Press. Siva Vaidhyanathan (2017). Intellectual Property: A Very Short Introduction. Oxford and New York: Oxford University Press. For a concrete explanation of intellectual property and related problems see Claudy Op den Kamp, Dan Hunter eds. (2019). A History of Intellectual Property in 50 Objects. Cambridge UK: Cambridge University Press.

8 Mancur Olson (1982). The Rise and Decline of Nations: Economic Growth, Stagflation, and Social Rigidities. New Haven and London: Yale University Press.

9 This is demonstrated in a vast and diverse literature on the influence and power of organized interest groups in Western democracies. See for example Frank R. Baumgartner (1998). Basic Interest: The Importance of Groups in Politics and in

Political Science. Princeton, NY: Princeton University Press. Mark P. Petracca (1992). The Politics of Interests: Interest Groups Transformed. Abingdon and New York: Routledge. Paul S. Herrnson, Stacey L. Joyner, Clyde Wilcox eds. (2012). Interest Groups Unleashed. Los Angeles and London: CQ-Press. Rinus van Schendelen (2004). Macchiavell in Brussels: The Art of Lobbying the EU. Amsterdam: Amsterdam University Press. Irina Tanasescu (2010). The European Commission and Interest Groups: Towards a Deliberative Interpretation of Stakeholder Involvement in EU Policy-Making. Bruxelles: ASP Academic and Scientific Publisher.

10 See Brad Stone (2021). Amazon Unbound: Jeff Bezos and the Invention of a Global Empire. New York: Simon & Schuster.

11 Cf. Ronald Inglehart (1977). The Silent Revolution: Changing Values and Political Styles Among Western Publics. Princeton: Princeton University Press.

12 Cf. Peter D. Wickens (1995). The Ascendant Organization: Combining Commitment and Control for Long-term, Sustainable Business Success. Basingstoke and London: Macmillan Press. Quotation from page 63.

13 See Martina Fuchs (2016). Industrial Transition: New Global-local Patterns of Production, Work and Innovation. London and New York: Routledge.

14 On the importance of cooperation for innovation see Jason Potts (2019). Innovation Commons: The Origins of Economic Growth. Oxford and New York: Oxford University Press.

15 See Edmund S. Phelps (2015). Mass Flourishing: How Grassroots Innovation Created Jobs, Challenge and Change. Princeton: Princeton University Press.

16 The new machine age is described in Erik Brynjolfsson, Andrew McAfee (2016). The Second Machine Age: Work, Progress, and Prosperity in a Time of Brilliant Technologies. New York: Norton.

17 Don Tapscott (2015). The Digital Economy. Rethinking Promise and Peril in the Age of Networked Intelligence. New York: McGraw-Hill, p. 53. See also Robert D. Atkinson, Michael Mcternan, Alastair Reed eds. (2015). Sharing in the Success of the Digital Economy: A Progressive Approach to Radical Innovation. London: Rowman & Littlefield International. Max Neufeind, Jaqueline O'Reilly, Florian Ranf eds. (2018). Work in the Digital Age: Challenges of the Fourth Industrial Revolution. London: Rowman & Littlefield International.

18 See for example Richard Baldwin (2020). The Globtics Upheaval: Globalisation, Robotics and the Future of Work. New York: Oxford University Press. Judith Bessant, Rys Farthing, Rob Watts (2017). The Precarious Generation: A Political Economy of Young People. Abingdon and New York: Routledge. Kendra Briken, Shiona Chillas, Martin Krzywdzinski, Abigail Marks eds. (2017). The New Digital Workplace: How New Technologies Revolutionize Work. London: RedGlobe Press. Martin Ford (2015). The Rise of Robots: Technology and the Threat of Mass Unemployment. New York: Basic Books. Simon Head (2003). The New Ruthless Economy: Work and Power in the Digital Age. New York: Oxford University Press.

19 See Chris Anderson (2012). Makers: The New Industrial Revolution. London: Random House; Peter Marsh (2012). The New Industrial Revolution: Consumers, Globalization and the End of Mass Production. New Haven and London: Yale University Press; Jeremy Rifkin (2014). The Zero Marginal Cost Society: The Internet of Things, Collaborative Commons, and the Eclipse of Capitalism. New York: Palgrave MacMillan.

20 Yuval Noah Harari (2017). Homo Deus: A Brief History of Tomorrow. London: Vintage.

21 E.F. Schumacher (1993). Small Is Beautiful: A Study of Economics as if People Mattered. London: Vintage Books.

5 A Social Contract for a Sustainable Society

Some philosophers and economists apply the concept of a social contract to describe emergence of social order. The concept was introduced in the seventeenth century in the wake of the Enlightenment. In a nutshell, it postulates that a society of free people is based on a contract that regulates the rule of society. The social contract is a simple picture for a complicated case. The case is that societies need a set of widely accepted basic understandings and rules for people living together and for societies to make collective decisions. In modern democratic societies, most of these understandings and rules emerge spontaneously. They represent an implicit contract. The ability to create and maintain such an implicit contract is what social cohesion is all about. This fits well with the theory of social evolution which assumes that social order evolves to a large extent spontaneously and must be reinforced again and again by everyday actions in society.

One of the leading modern contract theorists is John Rawls, who is also one of the intellectual foster fathers of the concept of deliberative society. In his book "A Theory of Justice" which he published originally in 1971, Rawls argues that a social contract requires justice as its basic principle. Justice means that each member of society enjoys the same indefeasible set of basic liberties. Social and economic inequality is only permitted under restrictive conditions. I agree on this argument, but define justice somewhat more empirically as widely accepted basic social and economic conditions and as social institutions which are widely considered to safeguard reasonably fair representation of different interests in political decision-making and civil society.[1]

If these conditions are given, a social contract could provide a viable basis for social cohesion. It could do so not only by defining the rules of the game of society but even more by embedding them in a core model of society. This provides an effective frame for social actors. In the social sciences, framing is the embedding of the actions and situations in a context of meaning provided by shared understandings and voluntarily followed rules. Framing does not only mean restriction of possible action and, by this of possible development of society (or any other social systems to which the frame refers). Far beyond that, frames help social actors to understand society and to appropriate it to some extent.

DOI: 10.4324/9781003261421-5

Many Western societies seem to have been losing their ability to create effective frames for their members and especially for their elites for many years. Lack of framing leads to a loss of representativeness of democratic institutions. The democratic institutions of almost all Western democracies are based on the principle of representation. According to this principle, the political institutions of Western democracies are supposed to function in such a way that political decisions and government action reflect the will of the people, or at least the majority of the people. This is, as we discussed in the previous chapter, difficult in a pluralistic society. The established institutions of most Western democracies fall short of this.

A prime case is the inability of Western democracies to keep social inequality within a framework that makes economic sense and is socially acceptable. In his book "Capitalism and Freedom" Milton Friedman proposed to avoid poverty through a negative income tax and to offer all members of society the possibility to satisfy their needs largely through the market. This is actually a sine qua non for leaving social distribution largely to a well-regulated market economy. If this prerequisite is not met, there will always be more or less strong efforts to solve distribution problems politically.[2]

As serious as these material problems may be, culture may become an even greater problem. For some years now, we are observing that in many Western societies, fundamental understandings and rules of society and its political system are being called into question. Sometimes it is "merely" populist currents and smaller parties that do this, but sometimes it is governing parties and governments. The latter often generate massive polarization, which weakens the respective countries to the point of incapacity to act. This cannot be blamed solely on the populist currents and parties, but must be understood as a problem of society as a whole in dealing with other interests and ideas. The more general problem is that politics in almost all societies leaves far too many citizens materially or culturally behind.

The Underpinning of Cohesion

Contract theorists assume that all people have the natural right to pursue their individual happiness and to protect themselves and their loved ones. In the view of Thomas Hobbes this would lead to a war of all against all, which is why, for their own protection, people enter into a social contract that gives absolute power to a ruler. The duty of the ruler is to ensure peaceful coexistence in society and to protect individual rights. In contrast to Hobbes, John Locke, and after him the utilitarians, rejected the idea that in the state of nature there would be a war of all against all, but argued that the social contract would arise spontaneously and would be observed voluntarily. Therefore, he calls for rule which is limited and dependent on the consent of the ruled. Liberal economists, such as Friedrich August von Hayek and James Buchanan, argued even more radically that the state should be limited to a minimum of functions and that society could spontaneously order itself on the basis of clearly defined property rights. As we discussed in the previous chapter this is an illusion.

At the core of this illusion is the assumption that all people in a society have a genuine interest in peaceful order. While this is certainly true, it does not imply that societies are capable of agreeing spontaneously on social order. Human history is full of examples of social order being challenged and rejected. Recently, we can observe this in some Western societies, in particular in the USA which seem to be deeply divided over fundamental principles of democracy and open society. In Poland and Hungary autocratic governments are about to eliminate important principles and institutions of democracy and rule of law. In other Western countries right wing and populist parties work to the same end.

This is far from surprising. The social contract defines the rules of the game in society, and these rules determine the chances of social groups to assert their interests. In a pluralistic society, it is therefore quite unlikely that a widely accepted agreement on the rules of the game of society will easily emerge spontaneously. We are dealing here with the same common good problem that we discussed in the first and second chapters with regard to nature and sustainable development. Social order is abstractly speaking in the interest of all members of society, but in concrete terms, it brings great advantages to some social groups, while others are permanently on the losing side.

This is the expression of the fact that political and social power is unequally distributed in all societies, not least in capitalist societies. In most Western societies, this has become worse and worse since the 1970s due to the enormous concentration of wealth. Accordingly, the consensus on the basic principles and rules of the game in Western societies seems to erode more and more. We will come back to this further down in this chapter.

This situation underlines the principal validity of Rawls argument: A viable social contract requires some minimal level of justice. In an evolutionary view this means that basic social conditions must be widely perceived as fair and social institutions considered to safeguard reasonably fair representation of different interests in political decision-making and civil society. These conditions must be reinforced in day-to-day experience and communication of citizens. This is where the problems of Western societies lie.[3]

The Western society represents a unique model of society. It is profoundly liberal, but with a secularized Christian legacy and a social component which intellectually may be traced back to both Christianity and the roots of liberalism. It is based on a specific set of understandings and rules which describe Western society as a society based on individual freedom and equality, limited government, democracy, and openness and tolerance. For some time now, due to high inequality, the social deprivation of the middle classes and other factors, trust in basic understandings and rules has been suffering more or less severe damage in most Western societies. This is aggravating the structural problems of cohesion which Western societies have due to their social and cultural diversity.

As we already discussed in relation to the definition of property rights, these problems have a substantial and a social side. With respect to the basic understandings and rules of Western societies, the substantial side is that the principles of individual freedom and equality, limited government, democracy, and openness and tolerance do not fully match, but are partly conflicting. The principle of individual freedom, for example, limits government's right to restrict individual property, but keeping inequality in socially accepted scope often requires significant redistribution. Individual freedom, to take another example, includes freedom of speech, but this freedom is also often used to bully or discriminate against other people, which violates their freedom rights and against which the state should intervene. To do this, however, it must restrict freedom of expression. The social side is the social and cultural diversity of Western societies which we have discussed in detail in the previous chapter.

In these conditions, spontaneous emergence and reinforcement of a social contract cannot be taken for granted. Rather, we must assume that the everyday interactions of members of society involve considerable variation with respect to the basic understandings and rules of society. Members of society will, for example, interpret and weight understandings and rules differently. Some will give greater weight to freedom than to equality, others will do the opposite, and still others will give priority to equality only when inequality has exceeded a certain level. Society members will also spontaneously react differently to these variations, so that even more variation will occur. There is no reason to assume a priori that the different understandings will always be brought together in the process. On the contrary, it is more likely that the understandings will differentiate. Differences may remain in rather narrow limits or aggravate over time. They may build up to the point where a social contract can no longer be maintained. This seems to be the situation the USA is currently facing.

In terms of sustainable development, this is much more dramatic than it might seem at first glance. It means nothing less than that societies lose the ability to make widely accepted decisions. Rather, they get caught up in a maelstrom of conflicts, which need not even be serious in individual cases, but which, taken together, massively impair the ability of society and its political system to act effectively and consistently.

What really happens depends largely on how strong the framing is in society. Framing does not only mean restriction of possible action and, by this of possible development of society. Far beyond that, frames help social actors to understand society and to appropriate it to some extent. It's like a picture frame. The picture frame does not simply mark the border of the picture, but encloses the picture and emphasizes its context. A social frame also encloses a picture, in our case a picture of a society. The picture describes the essential principles and structures of that society and explains their meaning. It conveys, in other words, a concrete idea of what constitutes society. This idea is partly transmitted only orally, partly it exists in written form, for example, in the form of a constitutional document. The fact that a frame is created only or mostly through oral transmission does not mean that it is less effective. The United Kingdom, as is well known, does not have a codified constitution; in the USA, a large part of the law consists of common law codified only in the form of judicial decisions.

Since good frames make society understandable and its logic comprehensible, they contribute to the prevention of alienation of society members from society. In his book "Homo Sociologicus", the German sociologist Ralf Dahrendorf described society as an annoying fact. It is an annoying fact because it restricts the freedom and self-realization of the members of society and is associated with many constraints. In this respect, there is always a greater or lesser degree of alienation between the members of society and society. However, alienation is much less when members of society understand and accept the meaning of the restrictions and constraints. This also helps social actors to act in society and to realize their own interests within the given social constraints.[4]

Frames also have another important function. They are intended to direct the actions of elites toward their task and duties as well as toward the public interest. The elites' actions are difficult to control if only because they have power and exclusive knowledge. This offers them many opportunities to place their own interests, especially their power interests, at the center of their actions. The CEO of a large company, for example, can tailor the entire organization of the company to secure her or his power. This repeatedly leads to subordinates selectively informing their boss and not reporting problems or only partially to her or him. The VW diesel scandal, and the role of CEO Martin Winterkorn in this scandal, are an illustrative example of this. This scandal has done a lot of damage to the company, the environment and, above all, to trust in the elites. Similar cases, for example cases of political corruption and fraud or insider trading, can be found quite often. Effective framing of elites is, thus, an important prerequisite for the acceptance of the social order.[5]

Many Western societies seem to have been losing their ability to create effective frames for their members and especially for their elites for many years. The social contract of these societies is questioned. In the US this is evident, among other things, in the frequent inability of the two major parties to reach workable agreements, not even on major national issues. In the EU this is manifested, among other things, by the fact that permanent breaches of EU law by Poland, Hungary and other member states remain largely without consequences. This situation is leading Western societies into decline.[6]

Since the rules of the game are no longer accepted and framing is weak, it is almost impossible to make political decisions that are widely accepted. Political decisions therefore often have a very short expiry time. We have been able to observe this in the USA for quite some time. Newly elected presidents spend their first days and weeks revising decisions made by their predecessors. New parliamentary majorities are first busy repealing laws passed by the old majority and pushing through their own laws, which significantly violate the interests and rights of a considerable part of the population. In order to spare the new majority this fate after the next election, they often also change the allocation of constituencies in such a way that their own majority is preserved. In the European Union, Poland and Hungary have been doing the same thing for years. In Poland, not only are laws changed, but the judiciary is also changed, and in Hungary the media are brought under the control of the government. Thus, both countries violate the EU Treaty, i.e. the constitution of the EU. However, this has not generated any strong reactions from the EU so far. In most other Western societies, the problems manifest themselves less dramatically in the fact that political decisions are repeatedly questioned and revised.

Effective framing of elites and other actors may facilitate shaping of social development strongly. Much can be left to spontaneous coordination by the market and social self-organization. Hierarchical coordination by the government also becomes easier. Political actors have more common understandings and thus greater common ground. The wishes and demands of their constituents and other clients move within a narrower framework. The social complexity of politics is thus reduced. In order to explain this in more detail, I will first make a digression into institutional theory.

The Shaping of Social Development

In social science two basic forms of social coordination are distinguished, namely hierarchical and spontaneous coordination. Hierarchy is the typical form of coordination in government, companies and other organizations. Spontaneous coordination may take two different forms, namely markets and culture. Somewhere in between are social self-organizations and networks. Both rely mostly on voluntary participation but usually have some element of hierarchical decision-making. With respect to the whole society, these forms are in principle spontaneously coordinated unless, although some regulatory framework may gear them to a defined common good.[7]

Hierarchical coordination is purposeful. It seeks to coordinate social interactions to achieve specific goals of the company, the state, a government or another organization. Goals are determined and controlled by an authorized actor, maybe a person or a body of persons. In a company, it may be the board or an executive officer, in government and public administration goals may be defined by legislative action or an executive actor. In order to be effective, hierarchy requires clearly and operationally defined goals and an organization which implements goals and controls achievement of goals. This in turn needs much and reliable information about the interactions that are to be coordinated, available opportunities and instruments of coordination and their mode of action, possible problems of coordination and other situations, as well as regular feedback on the effects actually achieved. The great need for information is the sticking point of hierarchical coordination.

Formally, this is not a big problem in most organizations. Most organizations have clear rules about the content, forms, paths and timing of information and communication. However, all organizations have an informal side in addition to the formal side. The informal side consists of many personal relationships, interests, understandings, experiences, external contacts and dependencies, and similar factors. For example, the engineers in the development department of a company see many things differently than the business people in the accounting department and therefore evaluate information differently. Officials in the Ministry of Economics may have different goals than those in the Ministry of Environment which inform them accordingly. Perhaps the engineers in the development department or the civil servants in the Ministry of Economics also have negative experiences in dealing with higher levels and superiors and therefore inform them very cautiously. Last but not least, most actors and organizational units in companies or public administration also have an interest in not fully sharing their knowledge but in maintaining a knowledge edge. This illustrates that the informal side of an organization acts like a large filter system for information and communication.

How and how strongly this filter system works depends on the framing of the respective organization. A strong framing in the form of a shared understanding of the organization's mission and a shared open organizational culture ensures communication that is focused on fulfilling the mission. Even today, this is probably found in relatively few well managed companies. It is probably found particularly in those innovative SMEs that Hermann Simon so well describes as hidden champions.[8]

The opposite, a lack of framing by shared understandings and a rigid organizational culture is mainly found in large companies and in public administration. In both types of organizations, one often finds highly formalized structures. Moreover, public administration is often still managed in a rule-oriented manner and not in a goal- or performance-oriented manner. This favors communication that is formal and aligned with individual interests of the respective actors and their organizational unit. Again, this is particularly common in public administration because each agency has a specific "clientele" on whose support they depend. Before discussing what this means in our context, let's first consider spontaneous coordination.

Spontaneous coordination differs in three respects from hierarchical coordination. It is not purposeful, it is not based on explicit collective decisions and it does not require defined goals and much information. Spontaneous coordination produces implicit social decisions for example in the form of certain resource allocation on markets or certain informal rules. The decisions emerge retrospectively from social interactions and are not based on defined goals. All involved actors act on the basis of their own goals and their own knowledge.

A simple example for the difference between hierarchical and spontaneous coordination is food trading. In supermarket chains, the price of a certain product, let us say white asparagus, is determined by the sales management of the chain and the individual stores have little or no ability to adjust the price of asparagus to daily demand. The amount of asparagus sold, and the profit made with it depends among other things on whether the sales management has estimated supply and demand well. At a local weekly market, each trader has his own price that she or he can adjust throughout the day to match supply and demand at the market. In textbooks at least, at the end each trader may sell all the asparagus she or he wants and get a reasonable income, and all buyers get the amount of asparagus they want at a reasonable price. But this is a very idealistic view with low correspondence to reality.

In an evolutionary view, spontaneous coordination is a process of social evolution that continuously generates and changes social structures. Social structures are social understandings, rules and resource allocations that guide the behavior of a more or less large part of the population. Spontaneous coordination does not mean that the social decisions resulting from the spontaneous coordination of a society are respected by the whole society. The opposite can arise just as well: Spontaneous coordination may also lead to a structural diversification or even division of society. The development of prices on the housing market, for example, is currently leading to strong segmentation in many cities, which is reflected, among other things, in the fact that in some neighborhoods the established population is being driven out by gentrification, while other neighborhoods are experiencing massive social decline.

However, spontaneous coordination by markets can be influenced in the sense of achieving desired states and avoiding undesired states. The vehicle for this is the fact that markets only function if there are clear and binding rules for them. These include property rights and competition rules. In the modern world, these rules are determined by a regulatory framework set by the state. This framework can be used to direct the coordination through markets to certain generally formulated goals, e.g. resource productivity. As we discussed in chapter 3, this could be done for example through a dynamic resource tax.

For the second form of spontaneous coordination, culture, this possibility does not exist. Culture here refers to the many shared understandings and informal rules (values, norms) that no society can do without. Many of these understandings and rules are followed as a matter of course by most members of society. Most members of society also expect others to follow the rules and to have similar understandings. An example of cultural coordination which is particularly interesting with respect to social cohesion is the social understanding of social justice. These understandings determine, among other things, the acceptance of social inequality in societies and vary considerably across Western societies. In the US, the understanding of social justice has long been shaped by the American Dream, the notion that every American has the chance for a career from rags to riches. This idea corresponds to a widespread understanding in the US of far-reaching individual freedom and a limited state, which is deeply rooted in the history of the US and in many stories of its inhabitants. This understanding results in a great tolerance for social inequality and a widespread rejection of state social policy. A stark contrast to the USA is Sweden. The Swedish understanding of social justice is based on the principle that all people have the same right to a decent life and that the state is therefore obligated to provide its citizens with equal living conditions and an adequate minimum income. This is associated with relatively low tolerance of social inequality and the widespread advocacy of a strong welfare state.

Such understandings emerge totally spontaneously. Culture does not require a regulatory framework set by the state; rather the rules of the game of culture emerge spontaneously as a broad consensus, and they are reinforced on a day-to-day basis by the fact that they are observed by almost all people belonging to this culture. If this affirmation no longer takes place, cultural divisions arise. In modern Western societies, this often happens without any significant problems arising from it. Society simply continues to differentiate itself culturally. A good example is the approach to understandings and rules concerning sustainable development in the sense of threefold sustainability.

As Ronald Inglehart argues in his book "Cultural Evolution: People's Motivations are Changing and Reshaping the World", these understandings and rules on one side reflect people's current and past living conditions, social security in particular, and related cultural divisions, but on the other one changes of these understandings and rules may induce far reaching cultural, social and political changes. The high prosperity and social security of the post-war period has advanced positive orientations towards environment and diminished misogyny, homophobia, xenophobia and racism. Now the latter are on the rise again and practical support for environmental change weakens again because job insecurity and inequality which threaten people's living standards and social security have been increasing for many years.[9]

This development should not be underestimated. While cultural differentiation can be quite conducive to social development because it can promote creativity and the ability to learn, it becomes problematic when it comes to a few basic understandings and rules. Probably the most important basic rule of Western societies is tolerance. Tolerance is the indispensable prerequisite for the openness and pluralism of Western societies. If this rule no longer applies, Western societies sink into a maelstrom of conflict. This endangers or even destroys their cohesion and with that their ability to successfully cope with the challenges of sustainable development and the knowledge society. The current developments in the USA. and in Europe are warning examples of this.[10]

Particularly in modern Western societies with their openness and diversity, culture must provide a large part of the social coordination that is necessary for sustainable development. Societies and the problems of sustainable development are simply too complex to be controlled hierarchically. Markets, too, quickly reach their limits when they have to be aligned with sustainability solely through the regulatory framework. Culture can extend these limits by influencing demand through a strong social awareness of sustainability. By this, it can thereby create a strong framing for the market and for government. In order to create this strong framing, however, it must also create a strong piece of framing for itself. It must reconstitute its basics.

This brings us back to Rawls and the preconditions for a social contract, namely widely accepted basic economic and social conditions and institutions which are widely accepted as reasonably fair. In recent years and decades, most Western societies have failed to maintain these conditions. This is evidenced by the great inequality and the growing dissatisfaction with institutions and elites. But much more has happened: In most Western societies, the social and political climate has tilted.

Western Societies in the Face of Decline

In the 1960s and 1970s, in a number of countries predominantly young people rebelled against culture and structures of that time. This development was not uniform, but rather varied considerably across countries. The common ground was some vision of a more open, egalitarian, livable and sustainable society with high quality of life, social and cultural diversity, good working conditions, more political participation, better education and more self-fulfillment.[11]

Development started in the United States back in the 1950s with the civil rights movement. By civil disobedience, black Americans tried to end racial segregation and to win recognition of their constitutional rights. In the second half of the 1960s, escalation of the Vietnam War induced a rising anti-war movement which was supported primarily by students. This movement in turn gave birth to the hippie movement. The hippie movement was directed much more broadly against existing social settings and their associated ways of life. Its aim was explicitly an open and livable society. In the aftermath of these developments, a variety of new social movements emerged.

The strong individualistic culture in the United States provided a favorable milieu for many ideas and activities of the hippies and of the students' movement. There are, in particular, remarkable substantial links between these movements and the libertarians. For example, many of these people shared the idea of a minimal state. The minimal state, to remind readers, is one which is confined to protect peoples' security and rights. The state does not otherwise intervene in the economy and society, and in peoples' lives. Yet, the different individualistic, anarchistic and libertarian currents in American society could not prevent the American state from departing far from the minimal state. But they produced a lot of creative and innovative milieus in science, technology and economy as well as in the arts.

In Germany, a strong student movement emerged in the 1960s. It was a predominantly left-wing movement rebelling against the rule of conservative and even fascist "bourgeois" forces in universities, politics, business and the media. Right from its beginnings the students movement understood itself as a broader "extra-parliamentary" opposition disputing dominant political, social and cultural conditions in the Federal Republic. The movement reached its peak in 1968. About a year later, it begun to dissolve into different ideological and political camps. But at the same time, it also gave birth to variety of new social movements which developed in the 1970s, growing environmentalist movements in particular.

In France, 1968 was a year of even more and broader social unrest than in Germany and other European countries. Unrest started in fall 1967 at the University of Nanterre, a poor suburb of Paris, with student protests against bad working conditions, and alleged restrictions to the right of free speech. The university reacted by closing of the faculty of arts. In response to that, students at the Sorbonne, the famous university of Paris, joined the protest. They occupied the Sorbonne which then was cleared by police with brute force. This provoked widely shared indignation and motivated the unions to call for a general strike. This was, however, not an act of solidarity with the students' protest. Rather, it was the expression of a general social dissatisfaction. Various protests and actions of civil disobedience across the whole of France followed. Finally government and employers reacted constructively and signed the agreement of Grenelles to end the general strike. The agreement left the students alone and their protest gradually came to an end.

There are differences between developments in Germany and France which are important in our context. In France, student protests led quickly to a much broader protest. This forced government, business and the unions to come to an agreement. The immediate result was that the protest ended as quickly as it begun. But this also reinforced existing social structures and hindered more fundamental reforms until today. In Germany, the government responded to student movements with police force. Subsequently, a part of the students radicalized and become violent while the much larger part dissolved into a variety of different groups and movements. Some became actively involved in the building of a new party, the "Greens". In the 1970s, from all these developments a broad, multifaceted reform movement accrued. This movement led to a significant cultural change, but also to many institutional changes. Even today, Germany profits economically and socially from this.

Similar developments to those in Germany and France took place in several European and other countries. Developments varied considerably with respect to causes, participation, goals, means and impact. But they often brought about considerable cultural and structural changes. An example is the change of values from "materialist" to "post-materialist" values which Ronald Inglehart (1977) described in his book "The Silent Revolution". We discussed this in the fourth chapter. Although in empirical terms value change was not as dramatic as the title of Inglehart's book suggests, it showed that departure to a new society become culturally increasingly corroborated. A growing number of people in the Western countries adopted cultural principles (values and norms) which were conducive to sustainable development.[12]

As Inglehart's data show, post-materialism is primarily a matter of younger and educated middle-class people. These people also dominated most of the movements of the 1960s and 1970s. As a result, values, the aspirations and interests of the middle class spread in public debates and public policy. A more equal distribution of income, opening of education, increase of skilled labor and social mobility were crucial aspects of this.

These changes certainly did not create a beautiful, ideal world. But they justified hopes that the world, at any rate the Western world, was on the way to achieving livable and sustainable societies. This opened up new opportunities for environmentally more sustainable development of economy and society. Western societies became more open and tolerant. This long period of prosperity has shaped expectations and attitudes of most members of society.

Much has been accomplished in these years, but half a century later, the good departure came at least for the time being to a bad end. This is not to say that today everything is worse than 50 years ago or that liberal societies are already in an existential crisis. But the liberal societies have erased a large part of their population from the aim of a livable and sustainable society. Developments in the second half of the twentieth century in North America as well as in Western Europe contained strong promises of living standards, quality of life and social chances, but these promises have not been kept. This is, as Robert Reich argues, a systematic problem.[13]

In most Western societies, many people suffer from stagnating or even declining real income and declining living standards. For many, particularly young and often well-educated people, jobs are becoming more insecure or even precarious. Many others work in a growing low-wage sector and even poverty even though they work full time. There are also many people realizing that the educational opportunities and social chances of their kids are dwindling. An increasing number of people fall ill more frequently as a result of work because psychical or material working conditions have declined. A considerable part of the middle class experiences social deprivation or fears social deprivation for themselves or their kids. Social deprivation means that people or social groups perceive that their income, wealth, living standard or social chances is in decline in relation to that of other people or groups. For those affected, relative deprivation means that their acquired standard of living and the associated social status are lost or endangered, whereas many people in their social environment do not have to go through such experiences. In most of the Western societies, social relegation or social deprivation is a particularly serious problem because middle class is a culture-forming and stabilizing factor. As a result of this development, in many countries there is a growing sense of injustice and dissatisfaction with political and economic conditions particularly among the middle class. All this is true to varying degrees in different countries, but it seems that not one of the Western countries really can provide the living standard, quality of life and social chances which was almost taken for granted in the past years and decades.[14]

In Western democracies, an unfavorable personal or general economic situation is blamed not only on the economy but also on the government or, more generally, on the "system". The term "system" usually refers to the entire social order which includes the political and economic conditions in a non-specific way. This blaming often remains diffuse and unreflected. However, this does not make the whole thing better, but worse. The diffuse feeling can then be adopted by various political and social forces, provided with an "explanation" and instrumentalized. This scenario is playing out in the USA and in Europe, currently exploited by populist forces.[15]

I do not want to dramatize the current situation of Western societies, although the United States seems to quickly approach a condition of ungovernability because of sharp polarization and the unwillingness or incapability of the two parties to bridge and contain it. A number of countries, Italy as the permanent example, face severe problems of political stability and consistent policy-making. In other countries, Poland and Hungary as prime examples, democracy is in distress. But for almost all Western societies what I just sketched out should be understood as warning signals that their foundations are threatened by erosion.

There are more warning signs in this regard. These include the many news stories about minor and major breaches of market rules and laws by reputable companies, which have been almost commonplace for years now. In no market economy in the world are its rules respected by all actors. Breaking the rules is always part of the game. As long as this is kept within limits, it is not only unproblematic, but even quite useful. Sanctioning rule-breaking reinforces the rules. What we have observed in recent years, however, is much more than the usual rule-breaking by a few black sheep in business and politics. It is the widespread breaking of rules by bellwethers in business and politics. These include renowned automobile companies that cheat on exhaust gas measurements, no less renowned banks that sell their customers non-transparent and risky products or help them with tax evasion through cum-ex and cum-cum transactions or even with money laundering, companies from various industries that do not look very closely at the working conditions of their suppliers or subcontractors, and also many companies that do not take the sustainability of their supplier products very seriously.

These may not all be dramatic events individually, but the continuous news of such events can lead to dramatic changes in fundamental understandings and rules in the long run. We have already talked several times about the fact that such understandings and rules can only endure if they are confirmed again and again in everyday social life. If, on the other hand, they are regularly violated, their validity gradually erodes. This danger is naturally especially great with the many understandings and rules of culture. Here, as we will discuss in detail later in this chapter, a silent drama is emerging in both the US and Europe.

To a larger or lesser degree, this has led in Western societies to a growing disenchantment with politics and a loss of confidence in the state among a considerable part of the population. This is accompanied by a massive loss of credibility and prestige of the political elites and administrative management. The political system and the parties are losing social support. Acceptance of political and administrative decisions is declining. Even more problematic, however, could prove to be the anti-secular and anti-liberal character associated with the growing right-wing populism. As Peter Berger argues, such normative conflict constitutes a fundamental challenge to pluralist societies, which can be mediated by some societies but on which many others fail.[16]

New Topicality for Milton Friedman

At the beginning of this chapter we identified two conditions for the emergence of a social contract, or more prosaically a broad consensus on basic understandings and rules of social order, in democratic society. The conditions are, first, widely accepted basic social and economic conditions and, second, social institutions which are widely considered to safeguard reasonably fair representation of different interests in political decision-making and civil society. We further explore the first condition in more depth in this section, the second one, in the following section.

The first condition relates to a problem that we have already discussed in detail in previous chapters, namely inequality. In this chapter, we sharpen this discussion to the question of how to reduce inequality to a level that is widely accepted and to do so in a way that is also widely accepted. The real goal is to reduce both the potential for conflict and the harmful consequences for consumption and growth with which inequality is associated. Both, to reiterate, are essential for sustainable development. But it makes no sense to try to achieve this important goal in a way that first creates strong conflicts because this will most likely lead to the failure of these efforts.[17]

However, reducing inequality always involves distributional conflicts because it always requires redistribution. This is not only about income and wealth, but also about status and power. In the current culture of Western societies, a high income and great wealth also ensure a high social status and the means to materially demonstrate singularity. This is often more important than the monetary value of income and wealth. For many wealthy people, it is less about how much they earn and how much wealth they have than about how much more than others they earn or have and how much more this helps them to manifest their singularity.

A high income and, above all, a large fortune also confer a lot of economic and political power and a lot of power in civil society. Only a few people and organizations hold power sufficient to influence or even determine the actions of governments, large corporations and other organizations, many companies as well as media. Many more people and organizations have enough power to exert a lot of influence on parties and politicians, on government agencies and

bureaucrats as well as on many smaller and larger companies and other organizations. However, the power and influence of most wealthy or even rich
people is limited to a rather narrow social environment, to individual politicians, local party organizations, to local or regional governments and other
local organizations.

The latter, the small fish among the rich, are often a bigger problem than
the big ones. Many of the individuals and organizations with large assets are
broadly integrated into the economy and widely affected by general economic and social developments. Their actions are therefore often also
aligned with these developments. This may well mean that, within certain
limits, they support political measures to reduce inequality if this seems
economically and socially appropriate. The interest of many small ones, on
the other hand, is quite naturally often more limited and focused on securing and increasing their relatively small fortune and the status and the little
bit of power associated with it. They will therefore often use their limited
influence to locally initiate resistance to political attempts for redistribution.

The implication of this situation is that political measures to significantly
reduce inequality usually face rather broad resistance from a variety of different people, groups and organizations with a variety of interests. This
includes, on the one hand, wealthy retirees, heirs of smaller and larger
estates and ordinary people who have saved up a small or larger fortune, and
on the other, the owners of many SMEs and many self-employed people
who have their fortune invested in their company. In addition, there are
financial advisors, banks, funds, tax consultants and other players involved
in the management of these assets. Together, they form an informal alliance
that is heterogeneous and, for that very reason, politically difficult to overcome. With its various actors, it is widely represented in different parties
and interest groups.

There are two ways to overcome this alliance, which are not mutually
exclusive. One is to divide the different interests by designing activities to
reduce inequality accordingly. The second is the opposite, namely to link the
activities to a larger project in which most of the members of the alliance are
interested.

The first way is not a perfidious manipulation but economically and socially
sensible. The various stakeholder groups involved have very different economic
and social relevance. SMEs and the self-employed are a particularly important
group of actors in the economic outlook represented in this book. It therefore
makes sense to design activities to reduce inequality in such a way that the
entrepreneurially invested wealth of this group is not diminished. For other
groups, such as heirs or others who simply invest their money as safely and
profitably as possible, there is no economic or social reason for an exception.

The second way is the strategy proposed in chapter 3, namely to install a
dynamic resource tax which strongly drives resource productivity and compensates negative effects on the purchasing power and the living standard by
a corresponding cut of income tax for lower- and middle-income groups,

and only for these groups. In most Western countries, there will be a more or less large group of taxpayers whose tax liability is less than the income loss from the resource tax. The number of people in this group will grow as the resource tax increases. In order to nevertheless reimburse these people for the loss of income due to the resource tax, the negative income tax proposed by Milton Friedman, which we briefly discussed in the third chapter, comes into play.

The intention of Milton Friedman's proposal is somewhat different from mine. He suggests a negative income tax to lift peoples' income to a level which on side secures a minimal standard of living and their ability to satisfy the corresponding needs by market transactions. But on the other side the income reached with the negative income tax should still entail incentives to find a better job and earn more income. I find this proposal very thought-provoking because a negative income is an effective and easily to administer means to secure a certain minimal standard of living. It requires no complicated application procedure and no large administration.

My intention is to compensate people with a tax liability which is lower than the income loss by the resource tax. This makes administration of the negative income tax somewhat more difficult. The reason is that the amount of the negative tax is not so easy to determine as the difference between one's own income and a defined threshold. Rather, the income losses resulting from the resource tax must be calculated. But this problem can be easily solved by using statistical averages for income groups. This also has a desirable side effect. It creates an incentive for resource conservation, because actors with below-average resource consumption are credited more in taxes than they actually loose, and vice versa. The mere knowledge of this situation will probably give many actors an additional incentive. With the resource tax, Friedman's original intention by no means loses its meaning. It must still be used to raise low incomes to a level that ensures a minimum standard of living. This simply means that for people with a low income, not the concrete income but the threshold is taken as the basis for income. The threshold should be above the official poverty line.

The negative income tax in the sense of Friedman, however, has an important weakness. It provides incentives for employers to rent-seek by paying unskilled workers wages that are below the threshold of the negative income tax. This is by no means a far-fetched fear. In Germany, for example, fully employed workers receive government subsidies for their living costs if their income is too low to provide a defined minimal standard of living for themselves and their families. Government thus offers them a subsidy that they do not even have to apply for. For many entrepreneurs, this is a temptation to rent-seek they cannot resist. This problem may be solved by defining a general minimum wage that is above the threshold for the negative income tax.

Such an approach offers a good entry point into a policy to reduce excessive income inequality. This entry point is likely to generate little conflict in most Western societies because it builds on established socio-political principles of those societies. It also makes a significant contribution to reducing bureaucracy. This is an aspect of Milton Friedman's proposal that is thought-provoking beyond the concrete problem. It suggests thinking about whether the many government benefits and subsidies could be replaced with income policies with more effectiveness and less bureaucracy. Instead of unemployment insurance, the income losses caused by unemployment could be replaced by a negative income tax.

The first step in reducing income equality through the negative income tax can and should be rapidly complemented by abolishing the subsidies and tax privileges for people with higher incomes for which there is no important social or economic rationale. There are many more of these in most Western countries than one might think. In many countries, for example, capital gains and the private use of company cars are tax privileged. Also, people with higher incomes often benefit more from tax breaks on international flights and aviation fuel than those with lower incomes. Abolishment of all these subsidies and privileges saves a lot of money which can be used to finance the negative income tax.

Friedman's rationale for the negative income tax is to provide all people with an income which allows them to settle their needs through the market. Behind this is a clever insight that many a neoliberal and libertarian should open up to: Those who want the market to play the dominant role in the allocation of resources must ensure that this role is also recognized by (almost) all members of society. But this will only be the case if (almost) all members of society can also satisfy their relevant needs through the market. If this is not the case, there will be pressure on the state to provide for the satisfaction of these needs.

This is not only true for democratic societies. However, democratic societies provide a platform on which this pressure can be manifested. Especially in multiparty systems, this pressure is often quickly adopted. This should be a self-evident insight. However, this is, as the ideas and understandings of many neoliberals and libertarians demonstrate, not the case. These demands and ideas are caught up in textbook models which reflect a neat bourgeois world and hide the real living conditions of the poorer part of society.

The same insight also says that whoever wants sustainable development must also ensure that all members of society can afford it. Otherwise, resistance to a policy of sustainability will quickly form and be exploited by some political forces. This, too, should be a self-evident insight. However, if you look at the demands and ideas of many environmentalist and green politicians, you will see that this is not the case either. These demands and ideas are also caught up in a neat bourgeois world.

If the real living conditions of the poorer part of society are not ignored, the first step towards reducing income inequality described above is an essential part of a sustainability strategy and thus a major and important step. Tax experts will certainly point out further possibilities to reduce income inequality to an economically reasonable and socially acceptable level. The use of each of these options can bring Western societies closer to the goal of sustainable development by further reducing the environmental division of society into top and bottom discussed briefly in the first chapter. We should, however, be aware that even the first step will overstrain the political decision-making capacity in some Western democracies. A fortiori, more far-reaching measures will do this. We will return to this in the following section of this chapter.

A different case exists with respect to inequality of wealth. Wealth is much more concentrated than income and big fortunes provide much more economic and political power than high income. This implies that strategies to reduce inequality of wealth to an economically reasonable and socially accepted level have only to target the very top. In order to reduce inequality of wealth in the long term, the inheritance tax is a particularly effective tool. This does not apply to those who have acquired their wealth through their own efforts, but to future generations. If these generations have to pay tax on inheritances as income, the large fortunes will be lost within a few generations. In this context, the commitment of parents to their children can be honored by generous allowances. It is important, however, that assets that remain invested in companies are exempt from tax and only are taxed when they are withdrawn from the company and consumed. This is particularly important in order to secure the capital base of SMEs in the medium and long term.

This approach tackles the politically most powerful part of the wealthy. However, since only a small part of the rich and an even much smaller part of the broader population are concerned and since only the heirs of the rich and not the rich themselves are concerned, this should be feasible. However, tax experts will have to find solutions to prevent the outsourcing of assets to tax havens and the exploitation of other tax avoidance schemes.

The proposals made in this section are obviously based on the assumption that almost all people that want to work can find reasonable employment and pay taxes. However, if the gloomy forecasts about the future of employment come true, these considerations would be in vain. In that case, a different solution will have to be applied. This could be an unconditional basic income for all citizens.

Philosophically, the unconditional basic income could be considered as society's dividend for the many services that civil society, not the state, provides to the economy. These include the education of children, the maintenance of a culture conducive to economic performance, and the production of a vast store of experience and social knowledge that is indispensable for the economic application of knowledge. Accordingly the unconditional basic income could be financed by a reasonable share of dividends and profit withdrawals in privately owned enterprises. To clearly separate taxes from the social dividend, funds for the unconditional basic income should be administered by an independent agency similar to the central banks. Government's role should be that of custodian and warrantor of the agency. The unconditional basic income could replace most of social security and other welfare payments. The money which government saves by this should also be used to finance the unconditional basic income.[18]

Representing Pluralist Societies

The second condition for the emergence of a social contract, namely social institutions which are widely considered to safeguard reasonably fair representation of different interests in political decision-making and civil society is difficult to realize in modern Western societies and their pluralistic structures. After all we have said in the previous chapters about these structures and their evolution, this is not a surprising insight.

As we discussed in the first chapter, we are not talking about formal legitimacy, but about material acceptance of institutions. Institutions no longer secure their acceptance by bringing about formally legitimate decisions, but by ensuring that the decisions made on their basis adequately reflect the interests of the vast majority of the population. This need not apply to every single decision, but it must be true on the whole. If this is not the case on a regular basis, there is a great risk that low acceptance of political decisions will lead to a deterioration of attitudes toward the political elites or even "the system" and that trust in both will be lost. As can be readily observed in some Western societies today, confidence in the rationality of politics and its ability to solve societal problems in a timely and effective manner is dwindling in broad sections of the population, especially among younger educated people. This manifests itself in right-wing populism and market radicalism as well as in growing disenchantment with politics and declining political commitment.

This brings us back to one of the core arguments of this book namely that the established democratic institutions of Western societies are not up to the social and cultural diversity of modern Western society, nor to its knowledge and development dynamics. They can neither cope with the many associated conflicts nor exploit the great social learning and innovation potentials that are also linked to them. They can therefore no longer adequately cope with the factual and social complexity of these developments. They are also no longer able to meet the demands of many well-educated and committed citizens with regard to the rationality of politics and the opportunities for political participation.

The institutional cornerstones of legitimacy in Western democracies are equal suffrage, party competition and elections, as well as majority voting and parliamentary control of state activity. The institutional structures determined by these cornerstones are designed neither for material legitimacy nor for the generation of materially widely accepted decisions and actions. This can be properly understood by contrasting party competition and competition in markets.[19]

In principle, competition on markets ensures that every market participant can get the good she or he wants. However, they do not necessarily get it at the price they want, but at the price that is formed from supply and demand. Elections and party competition have nothing in common with a market except that there are competing "offers". However, they function according to the winner-takes-all principle. Only those who have voted for the winners can expect their wishes for politics to be fulfilled to some extent. But even that is not assured. The market is about concrete goods and their quality. If the market were to function like party competition, consumers would not have a choice between goods, but between shopping centers where they would have to buy all the goods they need and with which they would also have to sign an exclusive supply contract lasting four years and more. If this exclusive supplier does not deliver what consumers want, they can voice their displeasure and perhaps even go to court, but they have no possibility of choosing another supplier until the next elections.

The comparison is even worse when you consider that the shopping centers cannot really guarantee their offer and its quality. It is not clear and well-defined in the first place, because the owners of the shopping centers fall into factions with different ideas about the type, scope and quality and can only agree on a fairly general sales program. In most parties there are several different factions and in countries with proportional representation there are coalition governments with several parties that have several factions. The individual parties and also coalition governments therefore operate on the basis of wordy but ultimately rather general and vague programs. To make matters worse, the realization of the programs can only be controlled to a limited extent by the owners of the malls (the parties), because it is carried out by many shops (bureaucracies) that pursue their own interests and have their own networks and affiliations.

There is another important difference: shopping centers that compete with each other in the market would probably offer broad and similar assortments. Maybe they would offer some special deals that make them particularly attractive to certain groups of shoppers, but the competition would largely be on price. In party competition, there is no price and no price competition, only products. The parties have to compete on their products and product quality, clearly differentiating themselves from each other. Product quality means above all issue competence. This is the ability to solve problems on a given issue. Issue competence cannot be separated from the ideological or substantial approach of a party.

The parties must ultimately make it clear that they have a higher issue competence precisely because of their fundamental orientation, which distinguishes them from the other parties. Parties have to do this because many of their potential voters are more or less strongly ideologically and programmatically bound to a party or at least vote for it regularly. They have to reinforce this again and again during the legislative period by marking opposites in concrete decisions. In most democracies, this is done within the framework of common basic understandings and rules.

For some years now, we have been able to observe more frequently that democratic parties and democratically elected governments deliberately violate hitherto widely accepted basic understandings and rules as well as the interests of broad sections of the population in order to increase their election chances or to secure their power. In Europe, the post-communist countries Poland and Hungary are particularly glaring examples, which I have already mentioned here repeatedly. Another drastic example is the USA, the oldest democracy in the world in terms of modern democracy, and for a long time a model of democracy with its system of checks and balances and party consensus on important national issues. In Donald Trump's presidency, violating or questioning basic understandings and rules as well as the rights of broad sections of the population became an integral part of the toolbox. This seems to be finding more and more imitators in the states. In the UK, the Johnson government is developing significant authoritarian tendencies in the form of attacks on freedom of expression and assembly. A new Police Act, for example, gives the police considerable powers to restrict peaceful demonstrations; schools were asked to avoid anti-capitalist material as it was anti-democratic. One example that makes me particularly sad is my home country, Switzerland, which is considered the second oldest democracy in the world. Switzerland has generated a lot of interest through its deliberative elements in politics. These elements include direct democracy as well as the non-competitive election of governments at the federal level and in the cantons (states). The latter is a core element of consociational democracy. All major parties in parliament participate in the government. The government makes decisions as a collective body and the decisions are generally supported by the parties involved. For years, however, the Swiss People's Party has been deviating from this rule, thereby also calling concordance democracy into question. This has not harmed but benefited the party in federal elections – since 1999 it has been, with some 20% of the votes, the largest party in the Swiss National Council.[20]

Developments in the USA, Hungary and Poland, as well as in Switzerland, and the strength of right-wing populist parties in most European countries illustrate that acceptance of established political institutions is crumbling in Western democracies. For the most part, this is not yet dramatic, but it is a problem that must be taken seriously. It is a serious problem above all because Western societies can only meet the challenges of sustainable development and the knowledge society with a policy that is able to bundle social forces and to resolve the many social conflicts associated with these developments without restricting pluralism. This is where the silent drama that I mentioned briefly above evolves: Western societies seem to be losing the social cohesion they need to achieve sustainable development and a knowledge society that is as efficient as it is livable.

A Key Issue: Culture

In an evolutionary view, culture can be understood as a system of informal understandings and rules that are reflected, among other things, in ways of life, language, literature, art, architecture and technology. But culture is more than a system of understandings and rules. It is the framework for the social construction of reality. It shapes human thinking and makes it not only an individual, but a social phenomenon. It aligns individual thinking to common understandings, but far beyond that to common principles of the construction of reality. The culture of Western societies assigns, for example, high value to the principle of rationality that is the principle of reasonable, purposeful action which is an important element of Western culture since the enlightenment. This is the more general form of the economic principle of rational action and of the principles of science and the scientification of society.[21]

In a different perspective culture is, as the American sociologist Ann Swidler argues, a toolbox which provides people with symbols, rituals, forms of communication, knowledge, stories, and understandings with which to construct their patterns of action. What this means can be illustrated by the example of the connection between social origin and educational success. In the conventional understanding of culture, which is oriented toward values, children from lower social classes lack the achievement- and education-oriented values that characterize the education-oriented middle class. If, on the other hand, Swidler's understanding is taken as a starting point, children from the lower class have fewer opportunities even if they have high achievement and educational motivation because they lack cultural tools, such as certain behaviors toward teachers, communicative skills, an individualistic social understanding, or self-confidence.[22]

The culture of every society, but also that of every company and other social system, has a specific identity. As the German sociologist Niklas Luhmann argues, social systems, including culture, gain their identity through their distinction from their environment. This is not something that is ontologically defined, for example by certain basic values. Of course, one can identify specific values for each culture at any point in time that distinguish it from other cultures. But no society loses its identity because these values change. It only loses its identity if these changes are rejected by large parts of society and therefore lead to divisions.[23]

In every culture, thus, there are boundaries of change, the transgression of which leads to conflicts and divisions, and identity. These boundaries are not fixed, but can change greatly over time. At any given moment, however, they are first given and cannot be crossed without the threat of massive conflict. This is an important insight that actors who want to achieve social change should not ignore. This insight does not mean that society can only be changed within these limits, but only that the avant-gardists of change must take the large part of society with them on the path across the borders. However, this brings the avant-gardists themselves to their cultural limits.

Actors who want to achieve fundamental social change form a subculture in their society that differs from their social environment in that they reject important understandings and rules of society and want to change them. This gives them a special identity from which they gain the strength to oppose society. Standing against society is not easy socially and psychologically. It is often associated with a lot of rejection and social exclusion. Being part of one's own subculture can compensate for this. If the avant-gardists want to take a large part of society with them on the path of change, they must first accept understandings and rules that they actually reject. That is a great balancing act which is difficult to accomplish once conflicts have erupted. It is more feasible at an early stage of the aspired change process than in a later stage. In an early stage, however, conflicts often are not visible.

In a diversified society, actions that do not conform to established understandings and rules are something commonplace. It is equally commonplace that such actions meet with acceptance from some actors and rejection from others. This is unproblematic as long as it does not lead to the formation of antagonistic subcultures. That is the rule in open societies. Deviant behavior is also tolerated by many of the actors who in principle reject it. This can lead to this behavior spreading and gradually becoming an accepted and common form.

When I was a child, I lived for a few years with my grandparents, who lived in a small town in the Swiss canton of Bern. My grandmother was a teacher, which was just starting to become common in most parts of Switzerland at the time. She was a truly respected person in the town. Nevertheless, she was not legally independent. Every Friday, my grandfather had to collect her wage from the town hall. My grandfather owned a small stationery shop and ran the family household "on the side". So he was the househusband. He also enjoyed great respect in the town and the way in which my grandparents lived was accepted, even though it was very unusual in those days. Today it is quite common.

However, all this can also go quite differently. Acceptance and rejection of actions that contradict established ideas and rules can lead to the formation of antagonistic subcultures. This is most likely the case if understandings and rules are concerned which are highly important for larger parts of society or defined social groups. In this case, people that rejected relevant actions are likely to communicate the reasons of their rejection. By this, people will mutually reinforce their rejection and the underlying understandings and rules. In this way, they delimit themselves more and more from the people who have accepted the relevant action. This in turn can create social divisions that massively impair social cohesion that is the ability of societies to make widely accepted collective decision-making and their ability to act. Subcultures may also develop if people who are in a closer or looser social context are repeatedly confronted with actions which they reject. Such contexts are nowadays easily established through communication in the social media. I will explain both cases in more detail below with concrete examples.

As long as the formation of subcultures remains limited to the cultural level, i.e. to informal understandings and rules, this need not affect social cohesion in pluralistic societies. In these societies, the coexistence of subcultures is a matter of course. However, things become dangerous for cohesion when rejected changes are brought about or secured by political decisions. As a rule, these are decisions taken by political majority which in the concrete case may or may not represent a majority of society. In any case, it naturally violates the interests or concerns of a smaller or large part of society.

In contrast to cultural decisions, political decisions are also binding for those actors who reject them. They cannot simply withdraw into their sub-culture and live there according to their own understandings and rules. The majority decision is also binding for them. They must therefore not merely tolerate the changes they reject, but must also act accordingly if necessary. This can lead to a permanent cleavage that is manifested in a permanent opposition of the concerned subculture to the policy of the party or parties responsible for this decision. In some cases, it may even be opposition to the ruling elite and, in extreme cases, to the "system" as a whole. This can be an interesting mobilization potential for parties, especially populist parties and radical social movements. We are witnessing at present such kinds of developments in several Western democracies in relation to achievements of the social movements of the 1960s and 1970s, namely gender equality, the dismantling of sexual discrimination and multiculturalism. Misogyny, homophobia, xenophobia and racism are on the rise again, or at least more openly shown. In effect, they have never disappeared from the cultural underpinnings of Western societies.

In the first chapter I explained this setback by saying that the movements of the 1960s and 1970s forced many changes with narrow majorities and failed to carry many people along. In retrospect, this is a good explanation that also offers an important insight for present and future action. If you want to change society permanently, you have to take as many people with you as possible. But for the actors of the time, this insight would not have had much practical use. For them, the option of taking as many people with them as possible did not really exist. There were three main reasons for this. The first reason was that the social structures of the time in many Western societies were encrusted and therefore offered little opportunity for mean-ingful and purposeful dialogue with a large part of the population. In addi-tion, the thinking and actions of most actors on both sides were strongly biased towards the competitive concept of conflict resolution. The second reason: Discrimination against women, and even more so sexual and racial discrimination, was enshrined in law, which greatly impaired the social agency of those affected. Homosexuality was a criminal offence in most countries until the 1970s. In Poland, Latvia and other countries, state perse-cution of homosexuals continues to this day. Homosexuals who went public sometimes risked and still do risk punishment and professional dis-advantages. The elimination of these legal bases of discrimination was therefore urgent. The third reason is that the struggle for equal rights for women and against sexual discrimination and racism had a long and grueling history. Understandably, this left little room for patience. The relevant actors wanted to achieve success even if this was only possible against a large part of the population.

Two lessons should be learned from these observations. The first is that fundamental social changes are always associated with the danger of oppositional subcultures forming if significant parts of the population are not taken along. In these subcultures, the old understandings and rules are preserved, as it were. This can lead to bitter setbacks years later. Therefore, it is advisable to involve as much of the population as possible in such changes, even if it takes a lot of time. In the end, the desired changes are often achieved faster and more securely. The second lesson, however, is that this is not always possible. The possibility of being able to openly discuss the state of society and desirable fundamental changes is itself an important cultural achievement that has to be reproduced again and again in everyday social action. This achievement is an important foundation of the cohesion of pluralistic societies. In some Western societies, however, this foundation has never been fully established, in others it has been crumbling for years. This is manifested in the rise of right-wing populism in the USA and in Europe.[24]

A good example of this is racism in the USA. The fight against racism has been largely political and legal, but hardly about broader social debates. On the legal level, equality for black Americans has progressed, but culturally it has largely remained stuck. This is currently manifesting itself in a fierce cultural battle over the teaching of history in schools. On the one hand, there is a movement of educators and other actors who want to overcome racism through education in history classes. On the other side is an equally broad movement of conservative and patriotic citizens who see this as a threat to the country's reputation and identity, but also openly racist groups such as evangelicals and white supremacists. Republican states, like Texas, Oklahoma, Florida and Idaho, intervene in this debate by bills or other rules which restrict teaching of sexism and racism. There is an ideological underpinning for both sides. For the anti-racists this is, among other things, critical race theory, for the racists social Darwinism, which has nothing to do with Darwin and the modern theory of evolution in the social sciences, but understands evolution as linear progress whose most developed result is the white race.

In Europe, too, debates on misogyny, homophobia, xenophobia and racism seem to have become increasingly hostile, especially in the social media. This is not only the case for right-wing populists, but also for those who fight against misogyny, homophobia, xenophobia and racism. People who express deviating opinions or differentiated viewpoints get hit with a shitstorm and other verbal attacks even if they reject misogyny, homophobia, xenophobia and racism. This does little to help the cause, but rather promotes further division and polarization. Even worse, it contributes to an erosion of the foundations of pluralistic society.

A particularly difficult problem for Western societies is immigration and multiculturalism, i.e. the coexistence of clearly demarcated cultures in the same space. Cultures are clearly demarcated when they differ from each other in important and easily perceivable understandings and rules and by language. The coexistence of such cultures is a major problem above all because the advocates of multiculturalism and politics often fail to recognize it as an integration problem, or recognize it too late. A good coexistence of these cultures only develops spontaneously to a limited extent. Instead of multicultural coexistence, parallel societies often develop. This is not at all surprising when one considers that social coexistence is only possible through some common understandings and rules as well as through communication. Multiculturalism therefore needs integration, not assimilation, in the form of common understandings and rules and language skills to develop these together. It is a task for politics and the state's educational mandate to provide necessary infrastructures, programs and rules.

In most of Europe the problems of multiculturalism are often neglected or even sugarcoated. This largely gives free rein to the cultural tensions and divisions that have been developing for years between migrants from different European countries or former European colonies, and even more so between people with a Muslim migrant background and locals. Tensions and divisions manifest themselves in development of parallel societies, political cleavages and right-wing populism as well as with spreading xenophobia and aggressions among both people with a Muslim migrant background and the native population. This is no wonder since Islam includes values and understanding which are in opposition to important values of Western societies. I am not talking of the opposition between Islamic and Christian values and understandings, but of the opposition between Islamic values and values of Western civil societies, such as secularization, gender mainstreaming, freedom of sexual orientation and individual liberty, and of views of the world.

Migrants and locals alike suffer from these problems, not least the many people with Muslim migrant backgrounds who have now integrated well in their European countries. These problems have become a growing threat to the culture and social cohesion of many European countries and the European Union because they stimulate xenophobia and racism, but also increasing intolerance of those that fight xenophobia and racism and engage in political correctness. This problem is also a major threat to sustainable development in Europe.

The cohesion problems described in this part and in this chapter as a whole make one thing very clear: From the point of view of cohesion and governance, the prospects of Western societies for sustainable development seem to be not particularly favorable and those of the USA seem to be even poorer. Western societies urgently need reframing in order to meet the challenges of sustainable development and the knowledge society.

The Deliberative Way: An Alliance for Reframing

At the UN Climate Change Conference 2021 in Glasgow, many thousands of young people protested against the slow progress in the fight against climate change. The figurehead of the young activists, Greta Thunberg, called the conference a greenwashing festival. German journalist Petra Pinzler said in a column in the German weekly "Die Zeit" that she was wavering between growing despair and desperate hope. What makes her despair are the leaders of the Western countries, China and Russia, who know well the dangers and prospects of climate change and give great speeches on it, yet do so little about it. Her desperate hope is based on the many companies, organizations, initiatives, networks, individuals and other actors who are working hard against climate change and for sustainable development. This is a concise description of the current situation, which I can only agree with on the basis of my scientific work on the subject, except for one point. The only point I do not agree with: My hope is not desperate, but cautiously optimistic. If things go well, we can see in the next few years that a well-educated and emancipated civil society, markets driven by innovative companies, creative scientists, engineers, designers and other people and, last but not least, many cities with many large and small inventions, activities and projects will nevertheless achieve sustainable development, including climate neutrality, by the middle of this century. In doing so, they will drive politics before them rather than be led by it.

The great opportunity of all these actors lies not only in what they do concretely, but in what they achieve with it. With their many activities they will reframe society in one way or another. It can lead to a situation where, precisely because of many well-meaning activities for sustainability, society remains divided or becomes even more divided. But it can also lead to the emergence of a social contract for sustainable development. The first case is likely to emerge if the different actors convey divergent, controversial, and mutually detrimental messages to society. This would impair or even destroy the credibility of the common cause, play into the hands of actors who want to prevent a consistent sustainability and climate protection policy for economic or political interests, convey a lack of orientation instead of framing, and exacerbate societal divisions and conflicts or even create new tensions and conflicts. In short, it would do lasting damage to sustainable development. The second case, on the other hand, is likely to occur if the actors convey appropriate messages and thus a coherent picture of sustainable developments. This picture may well show that there are still open questions and individual controversies, as long as it makes clear that there is a clear common basic understanding and an agreement to resolve the questions and controversies amicably and reasonably.

For the second case to be the likely one, the relevant actors should form alliances that are as broad and comprehensive as possible. These alliances would have to include as many actors as possible from different areas and with different interests. For example, they would have to bring together environmental organizations and activists with industrial companies, energy suppliers and institutional investors pursuing convincing sustainability strategies. Scientists from biotechnology, genetic engineering and nuclear technology who are working on new technologies that are or could be important for sustainable development should also be involved.

This is much easier said than done. Many of the relevant actors have years and even decades of disputes and sometimes fierce conflicts and hostility behind them. This is true even for the relationship between environmental organizations and activists, and much more so between these actors and actors from business and academia. For many environmental activists, for example, institutional investors are the embodiment of capitalism, whose greed for profit has been a major cause of environmental destruction. That institutional investors, of all people, should be the spearhead of an environmentally oriented financial capitalism in pursuit of their economic interests will be difficult for many environmental activists to accept at first. Conversely, for companies from the biotechnology or financial sectors that pursue convincing sustainability strategies, environmental organizations such as Greenpeace, Conservation International, The Nature Conservancy, World Wildlife Fund or even Extinction Rebellion are often not exactly obvious discussion partners or even partners for an alliance that also serves their own business goals.

To build alliances, preferably even a single comprehensive alliance, to bring about a social contract for sustainable development and thus drive sustainable development across the board, the diverse actors involved in sustainability must switch from conflict mode to deliberative mode. That certainly won't happen overnight. But even if it takes a few years, it's worth the effort. That would be the most promising way to achieve sustainable development by the middle of this century. It would also create a deliberative model for society as a whole. Apart from that, the way to build such alliances would also be part of the goal, because that already conveys messages of deliberative practice and of a new spirit into society.

Even the formation of viable alliances is a difficult task, but no less difficult a task awaits these alliances. They must involve in their concrete activities and projects for sustainable development as many of the people affected and other stakeholders. In order to achieve this, they must deal with the interests and arguments of their opponents in a constructive and solution-oriented way. This is essential because the social contract, as we discussed at the beginning of this chapter, must be confirmed again and again in everyday actions. This too requires a deliberative switch. In the first chapter I briefly described a number of deliberative methods and practices such as mini-publics and online deliberation that could be applied for that purpose.

An essential element of this approach is the establishment of a permanent dialogue on new technology, gene technology and atomic energy in particular. As we discussed in previous chapters, new technology plays a key role in sustainable development. This includes bio- and gene technology and probably even atomic energy. These are technologies that many environmentalists, as well as many other people in Western societies, are critical of or even dismissive of. They are also technologies that, in addition to great opportunities for sustainable development, also entail great technical, economic and social risks. A comprehensive technology assessment is needed so that these opportunities can be used sensibly and the risks minimized. This must not be a matter for expert commissions and similar bodies alone, but must be organized as a broad social process. There are deliberative solutions for this, too, as the use of mini-publics in Denmark shows.

Notes

1 Cf. John Rawls (1999). A Theory of Justice: Revised Edition. Cambridge, MA: Harvard University Press. See also John Rawls (2001). Justice as Fairness: A Restatement. Cambridge, MA: Harvard University Press.

2 Cf. Milton Friedman (1962). Capitalism and Freedom. Chicago: University of Chicago Press.

3 Perception of justice and fairness is a rather complex social psychological process which I do not discuss here. Readers who would like to learn more about that could for example read E. Allen Lind (2019). Social Psychology and Justice. London and New York: Routledge.

4 Ralf Dahrendorf's book was first published in 1974. To my knowledge, there exists no English translation. For a recent German version see Ralf Dahrendorf (2006). Homo Sociologicus: Ein Versuch zur Geschichte, Bedeutung und Kritik der Kategorie der sozialen Rolle. Wiesbaden: VS Verlag für Sozialwissenschaften.

5 An impressive story of the Volkswagen scandal and the role of Winterkorn is offered by Jack Ewing (2017). Faster, Higher, Farther. The Inside Story of the Volkswagen Scandal. London: Penguin Random House.

6 For a broad discussion of the decline of Western democracy see Peter Mair (2013). Ruling the Void: The Hollowing of Western Democracy. London and New York: Verso.

7 Major concepts of governance, including those addressed in this book are defined in Mark Bevir (2008). Key Concepts in Governance. London and Thousand Oaks: Sage. Readers who would like to know more about modern institutional theory in social science which is applied in this book could read John Groenewegen, Antoon Spithoven, Annette van den Berg (2010). Institutional Economics: An Introduction. London: Red Globe Press. Ronald L. Jepperson, John W. Meyer (2021). Institutional Theory: The Cultural Construction of Organizations, States, and Identities. Cambridge UK and New York: Cambridge University Press. Patricia H. Thornton, William Ocasio, Michael Lounsbury (2012). The Institutional Logic Perspective: A New Approach to Culture, Structure and Process. Oxford and New York: Oxford University Press.

8 Cf. Hermann Simon (2009). Hidden Champions of the Twenty-first Century: The Success Strategies of Unknown World Market Leaders. Dordrecht and Heidelberg: Springer.

9 Ronald F. Inglehart (2018). Cultural Evolution: People's Motivations are Changing and Reshaping the World. Cambridge and New York: Cambridge University Press.

10 For the United States, this is analyzed by Robert B. Reich (2019). The Common Good. New York: Vintage Books.

11 There is a vast literature on social movements which we cannot discuss here. See for example Stefan Berger, Holger Nehring eds. (2017). The History of Social Movements in Global Perspective: A Survey. London: Palgrave Macmillan. Donatella Della Porta, Mario Diani (2010). Social Movements: An Introduction. Malden: Blackwell. Jeff Goodwin, James M. Jasper eds. (2014). The Social Movements Reader: Cases and Concepts. Malden: Blackwell.

12 Cf. Ronald Inglehart (1977). The Silent Revolution: Changing Values and Political Styles Among Western Publics. Princeton: Princeton University Press.

13 Cf. Robert B. Reich (2020). The System: Who Rigged it, How We Fix it. New York: Alfred A. Knopf.

14 An analysis of this development with a special focus on the middle class is provided by Joshua Kurlantzick (2014). Democracy in Retreat: The Revolt of the Middle Class and the Worldwide Decline of Representative Government. New Haven and London: Yale University Press. Wallace C. Peterson (1995). Silent Depression: Twenty-five Years of Wage Squeeze and Middle Class Decline. New York and London: W.W. Norton. Robert D. Putnam (2016). Our Kids: The American Dream in Crisis. New York: Simon & Schuster.

15 This is described in Anne Applebaum (2021): Twillight of Democracy: The Seductive Lure of Authoritarianism. New York: Anchor Books. David Renton (2019). The New Authoritatians: Convergence on the Right. London: Pluto Press. Marco Revelli (2019). The New Populism: Democracy Stares into the Abyss. London and New York: Verso.

16 Peter L. Berger (1998). Conclusion: General Observations on Normative Conflicts and Mediation. In Peter L. Berger ed. The Limits to Social Cohesion. Boulder, CO and Oxford: Westview Press.

17 There is much literature on the role of inequality and the welfare state for political legitimacy and social cohesion. See for example Anthony B. Atkinson (2018). Inequality: What Can Be Done? Cambridge, MA and London: Harvard University Press. Bent Greve (2019). Welfare and the Welfare State: Central Issues Now and in the Future. London and New York: Routledge. Steffen Mau, Benjamin Veghte eds. (2016). Social, Justice, Legitimacy and the Welfare State. London and New York: Routledge. Mike Savage (2021). The Return of Inequality: Social Chance and the Weight of the Past. Cambridge, MA and London: Harvard University Press.

18 There is a lot of literature on the basic income. See for example Brian McDonough, Jessie Bustillos Morals (2019). Universal Basic Income. London and New York: Routledge. Philippe van Parijs, Yannick Vanderborght (2017). Basic Income: A Radical Proposal for a Free Society and a Sane Economy. Cambridge, MA: Harvard University Press. Malcolm Torry (2018). Why We Need a Citizen's Basic Income: The Desirability, Feasibility and Implementation of an Unconditional Income. Bristol: Polity Press.

19 I do not discuss the established structures and principles of representative democracy and the theories of these systems here in detail. Readers who are interested in that could read for example Robert A. Dahl (2020). On Democracy. New Haven and London: Yale University Press. Arend Lijphart (2012). Patterns of Democracy: Government Forms and Performance in Thirty-six Countries. New Haven and London: Yale University Press. For a more critical assessment see Christopher H. Achen, Larry M. Bartels (2017). Democracy for Realists: Why Elections Do Not Produce Responsive Government. Princeton and Oxford: Princeton University Press. Adam Przeworski (2011). Democracy and the Limits of Self Government. Cambridge UK and New York: Cambridge University Press.

20 See for example Daniele Albertazzi, Davide Vampa eds. (2021). Populism and New Patterns of Political Competition in Western Europe. London and New York: Routledge. James M. Curry, Frances E. Lee (2020). The Limits of Party: Congress and Lawmaking in a Polarized Era. Chicago: University of Chicago

Press. Catherine E. de Vries, Sara B. Hobolt (2020). Political Entrepreneurs: The Rise of Challenger Parties in Europe. Princeton and Oxford: Princeton University Press. Swen Hutter, Hanspeter Kriesi eds. (2019). European Party Politics in Times of Crisis. Cambridge UK and New York: Cambridge University Press. Yuval Levin (2017). The Fractured Republic: Renewing America's Social Contract in the Age of Individualism. New York: Basic Books.

21 Cf. Ronald L. Jepperson, John W. Meyer (2021). Institutional Theory: The Cultural Construction of Organizations, States and Identities. Cambrige UK and New York: Stanford University Press. John W. Meyer, Ronald L. Jepperson (2000). The "Actors" of Modern Society: The Cultural Construction of Social Agency. *Sociological Theory*, 18: 100–120. Gill S. Drori, John W. Meyer, Francisco O. Ramirez, Evan Schofer (2002). Science in the Modern World Polity: Institutionalization and Globalization. Stanford: Stanford University Press.

22 Ann Swidler (1986). Culture in Action: Symbols and Strategies. American Sociological Review, 51, 273–286.

23 See chapter 5 of Niklas Luhmann (1996). Social Systems. Stanford: Stanford University Press.

24 The study of right-wing populism reveals how great the problems of cohesion in Western democracies have become. See for example Chip Berlet, Matthew N. Lyons (2000). Right-wing Populism in America: Too Close for Comfort. New York and London: Guilford Press. Allan Laine Kagedan (2021). The Politics of Othering in the United States and Canada. London: Palgrave Macmillan. Michael Malice (2019). The New Right: A Journey to the Fringe of American Politics. New York: Saint Martin's Press. David Renton (2019). The New Authoritarianism: Convergence on the Right. London: Pluto Press. Marco Revelli (2019). The New Populism: Democracy Stares into the Abyss. London and New York: Verso.

6 Mastering the Knowledge Society

We have already discussed the knowledge society and the opportunities and problems associated with it in the first chapter. We established that the transformation of the industrial society to a knowledge society, as well as development of a sustainable society and social change in general, can only be predicted and controlled to a limited extent. In this chapter we will explore what possibilities there are to steer further development of the knowledge society in such a way that corresponds to our ideas of sustainable development. We will also discuss how these possibilities can be used sensibly.

In the view of Lester Frank Ward, one of the two founders of American sociology, social evolution becomes increasingly predictable and controllable through knowledge. It is shifting from genesis, the spontaneous evolution, to telesis, the purposefully controlled evolution. Although this is too techno-cratic, it is an interesting concept supposing that telesis is not understood as a deterministic development, but as a possibility. Ward's basic assumption that knowledge opens up more possibilities for shaping and controlling is correct, but overlooks two facts. First, scientific knowledge, new knowledge in particular, does by its very nature not provide the certainty which telesis in the sense of Ward would require. Second, it is above all the use of knowledge that makes social evolution unpredictable and only controllable to a limited extent.

Science is a social system whose evolution corresponds in an almost ideal way to our theory of knowledge-driven evolution which we discussed in the first chapter. It represents a complex learning process which is driven by a tough competition of ideas. In this process, new knowledge is often subject to multi-layered debate and controversy. New knowledge is, therefore, often associated with considerable uncertainty on the science side. Uncertainty is magnified by the fact that new knowledge usually can be applied in different, even contradictory ways. Telesis becomes, therefore, a question of the social handling of knowledge. The central problem is how to deal with uncertainty. Uncertainty must be systematically included in the shaping of social devel-opment. This requires thinking in alternatives and the ability to consider the unthinkable as a possibility.

DOI: 10.4324/9781003261421-6

Transformation of industrial to knowledge society is a complex process that eludes Ward's model. In order to intervene into this process, we need to identify feasible gateways. Gateways are areas that play an important role in this transformation and can themselves be shaped. Given the importance of knowledge and its application, an obvious gateway is human capital and education. We first look at this gateway from the demand side and discuss the likely or desirable composition of human capital. The likely patterns of rationalization in the digital economy as well as the development of a new economy as outlined in chapter 4 requires significant restructuring of human capital over the next years. Basic general knowledge, a basic understanding of the world and the mastery of basic cultural techniques will continue to play an important role but creativity, learning capacity and the ability to cope with uncertainty, dispositional ability and social competence will become equally important.

Significant changes on the demand side will require at least as significant changes on the supply side. A quite obvious change is to increase educational attainment significantly. But it is not enough that many young people achieve a high level of education, but students from different social classes and ethnic backgrounds should acquire this level together, i.e. in the same schools and in the same learning groups and classrooms. Common learning may make schools to a microcosm of pluralist society. This is likely to first create social conflict in schools and learning groups, but if students learn to resolve these conflicts by deliberative methods they gain much in social competence and experience superior learning opportunities.

The transformation of industrial to knowledge societies is associated with a far-reaching change of the form and dynamics of innovation. In the traditional form of innovation which is called linear innovation, basic research at universities and other academic institutions and down-stream industrial research and development are clearly separated stages. This has long complemented or even been replaced by a non-linear form of innovation in which basic academic research and applied industrial research and development run interactively. This form is associated with the parallel development of technology and markets. Economic development becomes simultaneously pushed by technology and pulled by markets. Like many developments this one too not only has a positive, but also a negative side. The negative is that a considerable and important part of findings and experience of basic research is privatized and removed from public basic research for a shorter or longer period of time. This may inhibit basic research and knowledge production quite heavily. It also may endanger acceptance and use of technology. This may be detrimental to threefold sustainability.

In the emerging knowledge society education becomes more important than ever both for economic and social development, and for individual social chances. But in the knowledge society education no longer just means kindergartens, schools and universities although these continue to be of crucial importance. Rather, education must include learning which is institutionally anchored in everyday life. This is not a matter of individual learning alone, but one of organizational learning. The inevitable turbulence of the knowledge society forces organizations of all kinds to acquire a high capacity of adaptation and innovation and, thus, a high capacity of organizational learning. However, today many organizations in business, politics and civil society fall far short of being learning organizations. There is a large literature on learning organizations which offers a lot of practical advice to transform organizations to learning organizations. In addition to these possibilities and going far beyond them, deliberative procedures open up great new ways to develop and advance learning organizations and a learning society.

Development of modern industrial society and modern Western democracy would hardly have been possible without the Enlightenment in the eighteenth century. The central theme of enlightenment was reason as the universal authority of judgement. Its guiding principle was that people who use their reason can develop into mature personalities and attain freedom of action. This was associated with the idea that a society of reasonable citizens could gradually solve the important problems of society. The Enlightenment has triggered great changes in Europe and America. But today the ideas of Enlightenment experience severe setbacks in some Western societies. Regrettably this is also true for the United States, the country which based its constitution and its political system on the principles of enlightenment. But currently, this country experiences social and political polarization which leaves little room for reasonable argument and sensible solutions to problems. The UK seems to approach a similar condition. Other Western societies have similar, albeit not so heavy problems. The spirit of enlightenment calls for getting to the bottom of the causes of polarization and to eliminate them as far as possible. This is a core problem of Western societies that can probably only be solved through a new enlightenment. A core element of this new enlightenment is deliberative practices, mini-publics in particular.

From Genesis to Telesis

In evolutionary theory and in modern systems theory, the control problem of social evolution has a name, to wit contingency. Contingency means that the consequences of a certain action or a certain event are in principle open. Simply speaking, contingency means that in a given situation a certain event may happen, but the opposite is also probable. We discussed a nice example of contingency in the first chapter using Schumpeter's process of creative destruction. We argued there that the introduction of a significantly improved product on the market can lead to established products being pushed out of the market, as Schumpeter assumes. But the opposite is also possible: The new product cannot prevail because competitors sharply lower the prices of their less good products. We saw something similar over and over again in the Covid-19 pandemic. Well-intentioned measures came to nothing because too many people did not see the point or did not want to see the point and therefore circumvented them. As these examples under-line, an important cause of the contingency of developments is what Herbert Spencer described as the major quality of social evolution, namely the ability of social actors to anticipate variations and evolutionary developments, to react to them in a purposeful way, to learn from them and act strategically.[1]

Interestingly, Lester Frank Ward, drew the opposite conclusion from Spen-cer's insights. In his two-volume work "Dynamic Sociology" and other books, he argues that social developments can take two forms, namely genesis and telesis. In the course of social development, telesis gains in importance over genesis because social actors have more and more theoretical knowledge about society and its laws. This increases their opportunities to plan and shape social development. On this theoretical basis, Ward developed the concept of a the-oretically based applied sociology which develops intervention instruments for the control of social evolution. His theory, however, has found little resonance in sociology, which has long been European in character.

If one accepts that knowledge opens up possibilities for action, Ward's concept of a theoretically grounded applied social science makes sense in principle. It reflects, however, the technocratic thinking of the early industrial age which is long outdated by the modern theory of evolution, especially by our theory of knowledge driven evolution. This thinking far overestimates the predictability of social development. Yet this is no reason to completely throw out Ward's concept. Rather we could understand it as an invitation to what the American futurist Barbara Marx Hubbard calls a conscious evolution. In her visionary view we have a huge social potential to shape the world in positive way. This may be over optimistic but a lot of optimism is what is needed to positively shape the knowledge society and to reach sustainable development – and optimism is, in our context, not unfounded.[2]

Since the invention of Ward's concept, more than a hundred years have passed and social science and related fields, such as interdisciplinary complexity theory, have made great progress. Even with all this knowledge, social devel-opments still cannot really be planned. They are still contingent and will remain so in principle – precisely because new knowledge always creates new possibi-lities for action. But currently available theories, methods and data help to better understand and assess these developments. Modern theory of evolution and of complex adaptive systems provide a reasonable understanding of the development of social systems and of the opportunities to shape them. They can systematically cope with contingency and the "chaotic" element which this brings into social development. Advanced techniques make it possible to simulate complex social developments or the effect of certain measures and instruments to steer developments. Such models can also take into account that social developments are contingent. Last but not least, deliberative processes offer good opportunities to use the diversity of Western societies productively to achieve widely accepted solutions for social developments. Widely accepted solutions reduce contingency because they align people's behavior to this solu-tion and its underlying understandings. We will come back this further down.[3]

As we have already noted in previous chapters, the prime problem of shaping societal development, especially sustainable development, is not knowledge, but the use of knowledge and societal capabilities to do so. Two capabilities are particularly important: the constructive handling of the contingency of social developments and the productive use of social diversity to achieve widely accepted solutions. These capabilities are closely interrelated. The contingency of social development cannot be dealt with by technocratic planning, but by integrating it and its sources into decision-making processes.

Contingency essentially arises from the fact that social actors perceive and evaluate things differently and that social subsystems are subject to different logics of action and decision-making. This can only be limited by bridging different perspectives and interests and bringing them together in common solutions. If this is not done or not possible, any social decision will provoke a number of different responses including opposition and resistance to the decision. In the longer run, this may make the decision obsolete.

An example which we discussed already in the first chapter: If the German government passes a law to subsidize the construction of photovoltaic panels on the roofs of private houses and finances this through a levy on electricity prices, this increases the electricity costs of many households that do not benefit from the subsidies because they do not own their own houses. In the end, this may lead to the government having to cancel the levy and finance the cost of the subsidies from tax revenues. This is a development that could have been foreseen if the government had considered how the law would affect different groups. But majority rule makes it too easy for governments to neglect such effects.

A society does not become a knowledge society because its knowledge production is enormous and because knowledge has become the central factor of production. A society only becomes a knowledge society when it has consistently geared its institutional structures to the production and reasonable use of knowledge. Western societies are still far from achieving this. In terms of their institutions, industrial societies are still industrial societies and still have a long way to go to become real knowledge societies. This is unintentionally expressed in a symbolic way when scientists, management gurus, politicians and other people talk about the second, third or even fourth industrial revolution in connection with information technology and digitalization. This illustrates that the use of knowledge is still firmly anchored in the thought and action structures of industrial society.[4]

A prime example of the institutional change required for the transition from industrial society to knowledge society is public bureaucracy. For Max Weber, one of the founding fathers of sociology, bureaucracy is the ideal type of rational and legal rule. It is characterized by the fact that its actions are clearly regulated by law and are exclusively geared towards implementing the law. Bureaucracies act according to general, reliable rules without arbitrariness. The rules are executed by civil servants who are integrated into a hierarchy with a clear division of labor and clear assignment of responsibilities and powers to each part of the organization. Bureaucrats act independently of personal interests and relationships. This is a similar concept of rational work organization as is behind Fordism in industry. Fordism denotes a work organization which is based on highly standardized work and highly standardized products as it was introduced by the legendary automobile producer Henry Ford after World War I. However, Fordism has largely become obsolete with the end of standardized mass production and modern flexible production systems.[5]

The classical model of bureaucracy which Max Weber describes has so far defied attempts for fundamental reform in most Western countries although it repeatedly fails at the complexity of problems and at the knowledge required to solve these problems. This does not mean that the model as a whole has become obsolete, but merely that its applicability in today's world is limited. It is the model that protects citizens from arbitrariness where the use of state coercive power is concerned, i.e. in the judiciary and the police – if its principles are consistently implemented and the responsible officials have the necessary professional competences. It is also works well where routine administrative tasks are concerned, for example in the tax offices, the social security authorities or the administration of public parks.

There are, however, a number of policy areas in which the classical bureaucratic model performs badly or is even doomed to failure. These are areas with one or more of the following characteristics: a high degree of factual and social complexity, a strong knowledge-sensitivity or high dependence on the cooperation of major actors in the area. Knowledge-sensitive areas are those in which the problems and conditions for action are significantly changed by new knowledge often and at relatively short intervals. In order for the classic bureaucracy model to function in these areas, the legal foundations of the relevant authorities would have to be adapted to change again and again. Otherwise they will quickly become obsolete. But this likely would overtax governments' capacities to act and often would simply result in increasing complexity of rules. Strong dependence on major actors in the field exists if either politicians or bureaucrats lack knowledge and are dependent on knowledge which the actors provide, or if implementation of the bureaucracies' activities require cooperation of major actors. In both cases, rapid and frequent adaptations of the relevant law can hardly be achieved through the usual legislative and regulatory channels. The definition of property rights discussed in chapter 4, especially intellectual property rights and data rights, is a good example of this problem. It is the problem which most regulatory authorities, such as the licensing authorities for new medicines, patent offices, banking supervision or cartel authorities regularly face.

The problem is even more pronounced for administrations entrusted with the execution of policies to shape social development, such as projects and programs for sustainable development, regional economic development or research and technology policy. The concrete activities of these projects and programs can usually only be determined in very general terms from the outset. This is particularly true for programs and activities that extend far into the future, such as programs for sustainable development. The activities of these projects and programs must be determined in concrete terms during implementation. This requires a great deal of specialized knowledge and also a great deal of social knowledge which often has to be provided by the relevant actors in the field. Often, these actors are also needed as active partners of the relevant programs. Programs for smart specialization of regions or programs for greening chemical industry, for example, are in vain, if major companies in the field are not partnering.

In several Western countries, in such cases independent agencies are set up which often perform not only executive but also limited legislative functions. An interesting example is the involvement of independent agencies in the American system of government. These agencies are located outside the executive branch and operate independently of it. They are not subject to presidential or departmental control. They are established by a statute passed by Congress that defines the agency's mission and goals. The executive staff of these agencies is appointed by the President with the approval of the Senate, but unlike the executive staff of departments and other executive agencies, they cannot be dismissed by the President. Examples include the Environmental Protection Agency, the Federal Communications Commission, the National Science Foundation, the CIA, the Federal Deposit Insurance Corporation and the Federal Reserve System, the US central bank. Similar institutions exist in other Western countries, notably the United Kingdom and France, as well as in the EU. Most central banks also have a similar status.

Such agencies usually have three important advantages over conventional bureaucracies, namely a high level of expertise, a high degree of political independence and good networking in their field. These are three characteristics that are extremely important in the developed industrial society and the developing knowledge society. They enable agencies to considerably reduce the substantial and, above all, the social complexity, and thus the contingency of government activity. This is increasingly becoming the decisive prerequisite for the ability of politics and political administration to shape social developments in the sense of telesis. Through their professional competence and their networking with relevant research and important actors in their field independent agencies can bring together a lot of theoretical, practical and social knowledge and develop relatively simple solutions to problems. Moreover, through their networking, they can bring about a broad reconciliation of interests in their decisions and thus significantly reduce the social complexity of the problems to be solved.

The case of bureaucracy, and of independent agencies in particular, suggests that it may be reasonable to introduce in government and the public sector similar forms of organization as we discussed in chapter 4 for a new economy. This is an organization characterized by flat hierarchies, flexible work organization and teamwork, strong delegation of authority and power to work units and groups with a high autonomy, but also with a high degree of personal responsibility, and last not least leadership through clear, operationally defined targets and consistent controlling of the attainment of targets. No less important is inclusion of all relevant stakeholders. Stakeholders here means all social actors whose activity is significantly affected by the activity of the concerned governmental agency. This can be done through representation of these stakeholders on agency boards, but also through the deliberative processes we will discuss later in this chapter, or a combination of both.

Coping with the Janus Face

Janus was the Roman god of the beginning and the end. His head is always depicted with a double face. This Janus Face is considered a symbol of dichotomy, of something that has two opposite sides. I use this symbol for the contingency of science. Science is contingent in a double sense. First, although science is a reasonably organized and planned process, its outcome is still open. As Austrian sociologist Helga Nowotny, an internationally recognized science researcher, puts it, research thrives at the cusp of uncertainty. Second, it regularly leads to findings that can be interpreted and used in different or even opposite ways at the same time. Science is not only open in terms of its production, but even more in terms of the application of its findings. Science, the key resource of the knowledge society, is regularly associated with much uncertainty. Accordingly, the knowledge society is a society in which contingency is commonplace.[6]

By its very nature, science always deals with the unknown, with what we do not know or know only insufficiently, do not understand or understand too little, and cannot explain or can explain only partially. Scientific research therefore always contains a more or less strong element of informed speculation about what might be, why it might be so, and how it might be captured by scientific methods and data. This speculation is called hypotheses. If these hypotheses are not trivial, which should not be the case in good research, hypotheses can be empirically tested in the particular research process. But a positive test means no more than that hypothesis is valid at the current state of knowledge. New knowledge time and again refutes knowledge that hitherto was widely accepted in the concerned discipline or even in the society.

Science as a social system is organizationally and culturally oriented towards the generation of novelties. On the one hand, it is characterized by a high degree of professionalism, often combined with pronounced idealism and even egocentrism, by strong competition for ideas and tough selection mechanisms, but on the other hand it is also characterized by a great deal of cooperation and a bundling of forces in projects, research groups and international networks. Unlike competition in economic markets, competition for ideas in science is not governed by a formal regulatory framework, but is inherent in a culture that arises, as it were, from the nature of the thing.

Knowledge is only special if it stands out from general knowledge, is new, and conveys new understandings and opens up new possibilities for action. Science constitutes itself as a social subsystem by continuously providing this new knowledge and thus contributing to the orientation and solution of social problems.[7]

The competition of ideas is the motor of the evolution of science. New theories, methods and knowledge, when received by the science system, represent variations, accepted or rejected. In effect, we are not talking here about the science system as a whole, but about disciplines, sub-disciplines, and even individual schools of thought. Already in antiquity and in the middle ages there were different fields of work in the science still called philosophy as a whole. In modern times these fields of work developed more and more into independent scientific disciplines and sub-disciplines. Moreover, different schools of thought developed within disciplines and sub-disciplines. Different schools are the result of the fact that new theories, methods or findings often were accepted in parts of the discipline or sub-discipline, while they were rejected in others.

Most evolutionary explanations of science are based on a Darwinian model. I however hold that especially in the scientific system, Witt's argument that selections are mostly not final, but trigger learning processes, is true. Only in the ideal world of some philosophers of science are there clear criteria and methods for evaluating and refuting new theories, methods and findings (in short novelties). The real world is much more complicated. On the one hand, different schools of thought in a discipline use different criteria and methods and therefore come to different evaluations of novelties, on the other hand, many scientists use objections of colleagues against their theories, methods and findings as suggestions for improvement. Furthermore, theories that are no longer generally valid according to the latest state of the art can still be useful in certain areas. A famous example are Newton's laws, which the physicist Isaac Newton published in the seventeenth century, and which are still applicable in classical mechanics today. Ironically speaking, the theory is at odds with new approved findings of physics, but it can still be used to build bridges or houses.

Since scientific reality is not as nice and simple as some philosophers of science would like it to be, science usually is associated with disputes and controversies on the meaning and relevance of its findings. Some of these controversies remain in place longer because they involve different schools of thought with lack of common criteria and methods, and accepted data. Controversies usually remain within the respective discipline or sub-discipline and are not communicated publicly – and if they do reach the public, they are often not understood. But when it comes to important practical problems and questions, the situation is different. Then a more or less large part of the public does perceive that there is disagreement in science. Since the background of the controversy is usually not comprehensible, only the impression of disagreement remains. This disagreement can be used in political debates and conflicts to give equal scientific legitimacy to opposing positions. The Covid-19 pandemic has provided some illustration of this.[8]

Although science is a prime example of social evolution as a complex learning process, it is reasonably predictable in broad terms. This is due to the fact that science is highly organized and quite transparent. Much research is conducted through projects, research groups, specialized institutes, and international networks. If these actors apply for grants to finance their activities, their major ideas and approaches become known to colleagues that act as reviewers or members of the decision-making body. The results of the research are discussed in refereed journals or at conferences and other events. The individual disciplines and sub-disciplines are organized in national and international professional associations, which create their own discussion contexts and also do some agenda setting for their fields. As a result, there are in many disciplines and sub-disciplines, especially in the natural sciences and technology, widely shared understandings of the most important problems and ways to solve these problems. Moreover, in most sciences, the natural sciences in particular, controversies are as a rule confined to research at the forefront. This does not exclude many unexpected results, but it does narrow contingency insofar as science, even cutting-edge research, largely proceeds along manageable trajectories. This is manifested, for example, in the fact that mRNA vaccinates are parallel developed and brought to market by several independent firms. What reduces predictability and may create uncertainty even in well-organized scientific disciplines is the speed with which knowledge production proceeds and cross-disciplinary effects of research. The high speed of knowledge production is based on high specialization which implies that many researchers know well what happens in their field of specialization, but may have little knowledge on what happens in other fields.

For society at large, contingency of science results mostly from the fact that many findings can be interpreted, evaluated and used in different or even opposite ways at the same time. This also and especially applies to the results of basic academic research, which are freely accessible, at least in Western societies. This means that in principle every social actor worldwide can use these results for applied research and development. Applied research and development is only public to a small extent. This is often even true for research and development that is financed or at least supported by public funds. The application of basic research results is therefore for many stakeholders and society at large not really transparent. This is also why their practical effects, and in particular their impact on economic and social development, are only recognizable outside expert circles once they have been manifested in concrete innovations. This is all the more problematic because the application of the results of basic research is strongly determined by values, interests, financial strength and power. This always carries the risk of applications that collide with public interests.

The state can and does influence this through regulation and public funding, but this involves two problems. The first is that guidance of research exceeds the knowledge and competence of the responsible agencies by far. In effect, this often means that relevant policies are determined by organized interest groups and uncontrolled expert committees. But this is only the minor problem. The major one is that guidance of research may limit contingency and this deprives science from one of its most important drivers: variations as stimuli for learning.

In social science, contingency is usually seen as a problem of social systems. It impairs social systems' capacity to provide the orientation which social action requires. The rules and understandings of social systems provide social actors with an enormous amount of knowledge on how to behave in everyday life and of what behavior they may reasonably expect from other actors. This contains everyday life mostly to an easy routine. Contingency disrupts and even destroys this easy routine. Social actors cannot be sure what they reasonably can expect in social situations involving significant contingency and how they should behave in such situations.

Traffic rules, to take a simple example, serve to ensure that every road user knows how to behave and how other road users will behave. If this is not the case, participating in traffic becomes much more difficult. You notice this when you are a car driver, cyclist or pedestrian in a foreign country with different traffic rules and signs. Since you don't know the traffic rules, everything you do in traffic becomes much more difficult. In many situations, you don't know how other road users behave and you have to learn by observation or by tentative attempts. What is easy at home can become a difficult thing in a foreign country. Even at home, contingency can make traffic a difficult matter. Contingency in traffic arises when traffic rules are obeyed in some situations and not in others, or when in a specific situation the rules are obeyed by some road users and not by others. If this happens often or even regularly, rules lose their reliability and ultimately their validity.

Against this background, it makes sense to consider contingency as a problem and to try to eliminate it. However, this is often done by adding to and differentiating the rules. This often makes the rules more complex, which allows more room for interpretation and increases contingency. In fact, this is often the problem: rules are too complicated and therefore unclear. A good example of an unclear situation in traffic is 4-way crossings or, in the USA and Canada, 4-way stops. There are clear rules for this, but they are not very simple. They specify that the first to arrive at the intersection is the first to proceed. But this of no help if four cars or motorcycles arrive at the intersection from all four sides at about the same time or if they do not really know who first arrived at the crossing. Reasonable road users will resolve the problem in the concrete case by communicating with each other by hand signals or other means. But the basic problem remains that the rules are regularly involving contingency. The basic problem, thus, is the weakness of the actual rules. Contingency is, in other words, also an indicator of badly designed rules.

From this simple case, we may draw an important lesson: While it is important to limit contingency in order to ensure reliability and validity of rules and thus their functioning, it is no less important to deal with contingency constructively. Dealing constructively with contingency means to first accept that contingency may point at weaknesses of rules. The complex regulatory structures of modern societies are prone to weaknesses. Their complexity often leads to inconsistency and contradictions. This opens up great scope for interpretation, which is naturally associated with contingency. This is how inconsistencies and contradictions are often first detected. In Western societies regulatory structures are often poorly adapted to the diversity of social interests and therefore prone to conflict. Conflicts are often manifested in disobedience to rules and resulting contingency. Contingency may serve as an early warning here. It may also serve the same function when rules are becoming obsolete. When we discussed Max Weber's model of bureaucracy earlier this chapter, we noted rapid changes in knowledge and action may make rules quickly obsolete which increases contingency. In this case contingency points early to the need for institutional reform.

Dealing constructively with contingency also means the deliberate use of contingency to signal social problems and to initiate social change. Many social changes have only come about, and continue to come about today, because individuals and other actors openly disregard rules. This is true for the civil rights movement in the US as well as for the student movements in European countries, for homosexuals and their supporters as well as for the environmental movement. The Friday for Future movement, to cite a recent example, also attracted attention and interest because students "skipped" school – and some principals, school authorities and politicians threatened them with punishment for doing so. For many social groups, even large groups, with moderate organizational and conflict skills, rule-breaking is a good tool to convey their interests.

In today's world, dealing constructively with contingency is an important prerequisite for successful telesis. This will not be telesis in the sense of Ward, i.e. telesis as a planned social development. However, today's knowledge about society and the methods that the social sciences have at their disposal help to estimate what could happen. With these theories and methods, we cannot predict developments in the long term, but we can nevertheless estimate different possibilities, their conditions of occurrence and the associated problems, and prospectively work out ways of solving these problems. We can develop scenarios for different conceivable developments. This requires another form of coping constructively with contingency, namely thinking in alternatives including the seemingly impossible or the unthinkable. This can reveal unexpected dangers and undesirable developments at an early stage, but also unexpected opportunities.[9]

For many people (including many politicians and managers), regularly considering the seemingly impossible or the unthinkable seems to be difficult. They rather look for certainties including "sound" predictions. Some turn to science, many turn to management consultants and other management gurus, as well as to religious leaders or charismatic politicians, and sometimes to "false prophets". This endangers the development of the knowledge society and sustainable development. Even more: As we have experienced again and again in recent times, it also endangers social cohesion.

Therefore, it is necessary to change institutional structures of societies, especially of Western societies, in such a way that they help as many members of society as possible to deal more constructively with con-tingency and uncertainty. This concerns education and science on the one hand, and participation structures in politics, business and civil society on the other. In effect, what is needed are learning processes that are anchored not only in educational systems, but also in the world of life and work, and in innovation systems.

A New Innovation Dynamism

With the high pace and broad scope of knowledge production, the form and dynamics of innovation are changing. The traditional form of linear innova-tion has long been replaced in many cases by a non-linear form. This is described in detail in two books of Michael Gibbons, Helga Nowotny, Peter Scott and others, which call the traditional form mode 1 and the non-linear form mode 2.[10]

Mode 1 is characterized by a clear separation of basic university research and downstream industrial application research. Somewhat ironically, the scientists sit in their ivory towers and do research for the sake of scientific knowledge. However, they are mostly integrated into international scientific networks and discourses. Their driving force is curiosity and the desire to understand some aspects of the world. The problems they deal with are academic problems. Nowadays, these are usually problems that arise from new questions resulting from actual results of basic research, in exceptional cases also problems that arise from a completely new question. For example, a researcher working on the development of social systems might have the problem that, although she or he shares the evolutionary approach in prin-ciple, analysis of the state of the art has led him or her to the conclusion that the theories, which are strongly oriented at the Darwinian model, fall short because they do not take into account the ability of social actors to learn and adapt. Perhaps she or he was inspired by Herbert Spencer's approach. Yet in his or her view Spencer's theory does not systematically take this ability into account because it is based on the theory of Jean-Baptiste de la Lamarck, the founder of the biological theory of evolution. This theory is based on the principle that species develop progressively through variation and selection which is also contained in Spencer's theory. This principle does not really fit the assumption that humans may anticipate developments, learn from selec-tion and act strategically on evolution. Against this background, the goal of the researcher in our example is to develop a theory of social evolution that systematically takes knowledge, human learning and creativity into account. The result of his research could be a theory of knowledge–driven innovation as described in chapter 1.

In mode 2, basic university research and applied research and development are interlinked. Basic research and industrial R&D run interactively. The scientists from the universities leave their ivory towers permanently or only temporarily and do research to solve important practical problems. The problems they deal with are very concrete real problems. They are driven by the desire to develop new, truly innovative products or to find new ways to solve important societal problems. Scientists from universities working in this mode also draw on scientific knowledge and theories, but at the same time also use practical experience. They are often closely networked with researchers and developers and other actors from the field. They often work together with researchers and developers from industry and other fields in projects or institutes. A mode 2 scientist working on the development of social systems, for example, would not deal with this development in an abstract way, but find a feasible way to broaden and accelerate the modernization process in an old industrial region. To this end, she would perhaps also rely on evolutionist approaches, but also on a lot of her own empirical and practical knowledge and on the knowledge and experience of partners from the field. In addition, she receives a lot of impetus from the fact that new scientific solutions are at the same time innovative products or are quickly converted into such products. This means that a lot of market knowledge flows into research.

At some universities and higher education institutions, basic research is already geared towards specific application contexts. For this purpose, research groups or institutes are often set up that work closely with industrial research and development. In some areas, especially in biotechnology and genetic engineering, but also in information technology, this is an almost inevitable development. In these areas, knowledge is often no longer just the basis of a product, but the actual product itself. If you know how microorganisms can produce a desired substance, then in principle you have that substance. In other areas, such as health technology or mechanical engineering, the dovetailing of basic research and applied research promotes the rapid development of new solutions to problems.

In the first chapter we briefly discussed that in the knowledge society successful innovations mostly depend on the parallel development of technology and markets. An important reason for this is that research-intensive companies can only recoup their high costs if they develop their markets in parallel with their technology and are thus on the market much faster than their competitors. From this we have drawn the conclusion that in the knowledge society economic development is not driven by technology alone, but also by markets. In this respect, mode 2 can be seen as an obvious and sensible reaction of science and business to the rapid and broad knowledge production of the knowledge society and the volatile dynamics of many markets. This makes mode 2 a positive development factor of the knowledge society.

Like so many things, it also has a less positive, not to say dangerous, downside. In mode 2, the findings and results of basic research are "privatized", at least temporarily, and thus withdrawn from basic research for the time being. As an extreme case of privatization, biopatents, i.e. patents on gene sequences and other biological material, are often named. But this not what really concerns me. In most Western countries, such patents are subject to restrictive conditions. Often there are rules that prevent patented material from being taken away from basic research. I cannot and will not judge how effective these rules are. The problem that concerns me here may seem much less dramatic.

Scientific knowledge consists only to a small extent of results in the sense of solutions to problems. To a large extent, it consists of the many insights gained on the way between the scientific perception of a problem and its solution. These are theoretical considerations, data, methodological insights, intermediate results that have changed the path, critical objections and debates and, last but not least, findings about failures and inconclusive controversies. All this flows continuously into the research process at different levels and in different ways and in different contexts. Since science has long been a global process, different cultural and social contexts also flow into it and provide additional discussion. All this makes up the evolutionary dynamics of basic research.

Even in mode 1, scientific research is not a completely open and transparent process. No scientist or research group discloses all their lukewarm deliberations, let alone their failures, on an ongoing basis. However, since mode 1 research is much more integrated into the open interaction contexts of the respective discipline and its many informal discussion contexts, a great deal of knowledge flows continuously into the discussion of the respective discipline.

In mode 2 research, on the other hand, this must systematically be prevented and the discussion must be restricted to a narrowly defined and controlled group of participants, while a large part of the relevant researchers must be excluded. In terms of evolutionary theory, this means that the scientific system is deprived of a more or less large part of the variations that continuously drive its learning processes. The worst thing about this is that it is not at all foreseeable how many and which variations are withdrawn. Mode 2 research thus intervenes in the evolution of science in a way that is hardly manageable and certainly not controllable. This may or may not result in a considerable slow down in progress of knowledge in the disciplines concerned. Anyway, this is not a problem that can be regulated by patent law or other law. Rather it is one of the many problems that cannot be formally regulated, but must be left to culture.

There is a second problem with mode 2, namely the negative impact of the spread of this mode on the social acceptance of new technology. New technology, especially biotechnology, genetic engineering and nuclear fusion, often encounters more or less massive acceptance problems in Western societies. This became apparent in the Covid-19 pandemic in the form of a considerable rejection of vaccination and many rumors about the danger of mRNA vaccines. In Germany, this also manifested in a massive rejection of nuclear energy including nuclear fusion as a serious contender of established technology. Other industries, such as the chemical industry, also repeatedly encounter acceptance problems. Although this usually only affects more or less large minorities, it creates a considerable potential for conflict that repeatedly impedes or prevents the introduction of new technologies.

An important reason why the problem is mostly confined to smaller minorities is that science enjoys a lot of prestige and trust in most Western countries. However, this trust could suffer if an increasingly large part of basic research takes place in mode 2 and thus in close connection with companies and economic interests. In order to counteract this, it would make sense to establish participation and communication structures that are suitable for creating public trust, especially for mode 2 research. The deliberative processes discussed in the penultimate part could be instruments for this.

A Key Issue: Restructuring Human Capital

We have already discussed in the first chapter that the transformation of the industrial society to a knowledge society creates many opportunities, but also many risks for sustainable development. We have established that how opportunities and risks materialize depends crucially on how this transformation is shaped, that is from successful telesis. However, the transformation is a very complex process which can hardly be shaped in a comprehensive manner. The question that arises from this insight is about possible gateways into this complex process. Gateways are areas that, on the one hand, play an important role in this transformation, and on the other hand can be relatively well shaped. Because of the central importance of knowledge and the use of knowledge, education and skills are two of the most important gateways into the transformation of industrial society. In this part of the chapter, we will first look at these gateways from the demand side, more precisely from the human capital requirements of the knowledge society. In the following part we will look at the supply side and the design of education and qualifications.

I define human capital here very broadly as what people bring to society in terms of knowledge, cognitive skills, cultural techniques and competences for their economic activity and their social and political participation. My analysis of human capital requirements draws on what we learned so far in this book about labor and skills, about civil society involvement and deliberative processes.

In the first chapter, we found that the technologies from which the necessary radical innovations for sustainable development are to come, in particular digitalization, biotechnology and microsystems technology, are causing massive and permanent job losses. At the same time they also may create new economic structures and new forms of employment and work. We also learned that job losses will not only affect unskilled labor but skilled labor as well. In the extreme, this could lead to a society in which gainful employment will lose its hitherto great social significance. We also talked about the key role of knowledge work and that knowledge work is not only work in production, but also work in the application of knowledge. In the first chapter, we also discussed the Western societies' problems of governing sustainable development and the need for greater involvement of civil society and a deliberative switch. In several chapters we have talked about the problems of uncertainty associated with the knowledge society and its enormous knowledge production. We have underlined that a constructive approach to uncertainty by society and its members is essential for the development of a knowledge society worth living in and for sustainable development. All this requires a far-reaching restructuring of human capital in the coming years and decades.

Based on this knowledge, we outlined in the fourth chapter a model of a new economy. The basic idea is to replace the "nickel-and-dime economy" with a tailored economy with a focus on high value and high resource productivity across the value chain. This model describes an economy which is shaped by innovative SMEs and their organizational principles, collaborative networks and work systems that promote creativity and personal responsibility. This not only involves a stronger role for SMEs, cooperatives and freelancers, but also new decentralized structures in large companies. Realization of this model may save jobs or create new jobs and new opportunities for self-employment. In every case it requires a far-reaching restructuring of human capital.

Many academics and other experts assume that in the course of digitalization not only low-skilled but also highly skilled workers will be affected by job losses. The decisive criteria is whether a job can be automated at reasonable cost or not. In the third chapter, we showed that the interaction of biotechnology, information technology and microsystems technology enables the automation of many activities in research and development and in production. This suggests that in the knowledge society other qualifications are required than in the industrial society. Jobs that require a high level of creativity, disposition skills or social competence and activities that can not be automated at a reasonable cost are pretty secure. We know the same from other sectors. An example: many activities of doctors, for example the evaluation of laboratory reports, can be easily automated, which by no means makes doctors superfluous, but rather a considerable part of their previous activities. On the other hand, it is hardly possible to automate the work of an electrician or IT-technician who installs, maintains and repairs electrical devices or installations or computer systems in small businesses and private homes. It may be even more difficult to automatize a formally less qualified cleaner who has to clean an operating theatre or a clean room in a laboratory. The installation of such rooms is complex and delicate while relevant wage costs are moderate. This is a bad case for automation.

If the experts' assumptions come true, human capital will develop differently than it currently does. In recent years, there has been a strong trend towards "academization" in most Western countries. For many jobs, higher educational qualifications are required. This is especially true in Germany, Switzerland and Austria. In addition their system of dual vocational training has gained high international recognition. This leads people who are formally qualified for college to no longer opting for vocational training but for university studies. With the increased focus on higher educational attainment, the business community has, to a certain extent, devalued its own internationally recognized training system. This is likely to prove to be a big mistake in the coming years, when the expected trend towards automation of many jobs, even highly qualified ones, gains momentum and the above discussed assumptions become true.

Given the situation which we just discussed, educational attainment will no longer be the sole decisive or most important criterion of demand for labor and people's job opportunities. At least as important will be creativity, disposition skills, social competence and non-routine as well as the relationship between wage costs and automation costs. These criteria apply equally to high and low-skilled jobs. Creativity is a multi-layered concept and includes finding new solutions, creating new, original, special or unique things, generating new knowledge and insights, breaking new ground and being able to react constructively to the unexpected and new. Dispositional competence is the ability to use the resources of a company or other organization effectively and efficiently and includes management, planning, organization and control. Social competence is again a multi-layered concept that refers to all skills that are necessary and useful in dealing with other people and that can be used to positively influence the behavior and attitudes of other people. These include teamwork and communication skills, empathy, the ability to compromise, and the ability to understand others and their emotions and behave appropriately towards them. Non-routine is simply the opposite of routine. Routine can be defined as actions that always follow the same pattern and are habitually performed by the actors.

Creativity, dispositional ability, social competence and routine exist to a greater or lesser extent in both high-skilled and low-skilled activities. Creativity is required in many activities in art, literature and science, in research and development, in design, in architecture, in branding, in game development and in arts and crafts. It is also required in many customer-related activities and services, e.g. in systems management, interior design, in the construction of individual furniture and other furnishings for homes and buildings, in maintenance and repair, for hairdressers and, last but not least, in the catering industry. Moreover, creativity is also required by many people who are constantly confronted with new problems in the most diverse areas. Lastly, a lot of creativity is demanded from many start-ups and self-employed people.

Dispositional skills are important for managers and some employees in the above-mentioned areas of companies and other organizations. But it is also important for many workers at different levels who work largely independently and hold responsibility in the flexible company structures and networks described in chapter 4. These workers are also required to be creative in solving problems. Finally, disposition skills are required of many workers who also operate largely independently and hold their own responsibility. Last not least, self-employed people need dispositional skills.

A certain degree of social competence is desired or required in almost every job. That is not what we are talking about here. Rather, we are talking about jobs for which a particularly high degree of social competence is required and is an important hiring criterion. These are social professions, teaching professions, customer-oriented activities and jobs that require a lot of communication. A high degree of social competence is also required for work in the structures and networks of a new economy mentioned above and other jobs that require a lot of cooperation.

A particularly high level of social competence is required in the developing knowledge society of managers who are supposed to lead "knowledge workers" and other creative people. Actually, high social competence should be expected of all people who are supposed to lead other people. In fact, however, one finds in companies and other organizations a considerable number of CEOs and other senior managers whose striving for power and egocentrism clearly exceeds their social competence. This has done the companies concerned and their environment no good in the past. In the future, it could cause a lot of damage in companies where knowledge work and other creative activities play an important or even decisive role. As we briefly described in the first chapter, knowledge workers and other creative people have a lot of power because they can withdraw their knowledge and creativity from the company at any time. Moreover, they are not available at will, but often in short supply. Managers who work in the decentralized organizational structures described in chapter 4 or in flat hierarchies in general also need special social competence. They must compensate for the loss of control through flat hierarchies and decentralized structures with socially competent leadership, an open corporate culture and charisma.

The skills discussed here are particularly important in the worst case, that many people will lose their employment in established businesses permanently. In this case, many people have to become self-employed or must start up a new business. This maybe particularly successful in fields which are not well served by established business, such as environmental protection, or in which established business does not provide high customization, for example in fashion. As we discussed before, modern technology, like miniaturization or 3-D printing may offer a wealth of such opportunities. But people need creativity, disposition skills and social competence to exploit these opportunities.

Whatever scenario on the future of employment and work we consider, one point seems to be clear: The demand on human capital in the knowledge society will change considerably. Basic general knowledge and a basic understanding of the world as well as mastery of cultural techniques will

remain important, but the acquisition of the competences we have just discussed will become equally important. Beyond that, in view of the dynamics of
knowledge and development and the associated uncertainty, the individual and
societal ability to learn and adapt will become much more important.[11]

With the implementation of these requirements, human capital adapts to
the presumed effects of automation in many sectors of the economy. It
increases the resilience of the labor market and society to far-reaching changes in employment and work, up to and including the case of massive and
permanent jobs losses as a result of digitalization. In this case, new economic
fields of activity and employment opportunities that escape automation must
be developed as quickly as possible. The emphasis is on the word economic.
In contrast to Jeremy Rifkin and other authors, I do not assume that we are
in a historical epoch in which more and more jobs will be permanently lost
and gainful employment will lose its previous central importance. But I do
not rule out this possibility either. Both are possible, to repeat my "mantra"
of the limited predictability and formability of social evolution.

Whether it is a question of creating new economic fields of activity (markets)
and employment opportunities or shaping a society in which gainful employment loses its central role, a great deal of creativity, learning ability and social
competence is required. This is all the more true as we currently live in a world
where these skills seem to be quite scarce in economic and political leadership
and therefore important problems such as climate and environment, growing
migration and its causes, poverty and underdevelopment, the future of work,
education and participation in education are tackled far too hesitantly and too
weakly. Therefore, these problems will come to a head in the coming years.
Solving them will involve even more uncertainty and risk, even more institutional change and social self-organization, and even more creativity, learning
and social competence.

Winning the Race

In their book "The Race between Education and Technology", Claudia
Goldin and Lawrence F. Katz describe the economic and social development
of the USA in the past century as a process driven by the relationship
between education and technology. They argue that during the first half of
the twentieth century, income inequality between skilled and less-skilled
workers declined while productivity and growth increased. Most people in
society benefited from this growth. In the second half, however, income
inequality has increased while productivity and growth rates have decreased.
The share of the population that benefited from growth declined.[12]

This development is often explained in the relevant literature by a skill-biased
technological change. According to this hypothesis, growing technology-related
skill requirements have increased demand for skilled labor and wages of
skilled workers. Goldin and Katz also refer to this hypothesis, but only
follow it in part. In their view, the problem is not on the demand side but on

the supply side. The supply problem is caused in particular by the lower educational participation of the native population. This is also due to the growing importance of social background for educational attainment, which has long been much lower in the USA than in most European countries. Accordingly, the educational participation of Americans, especially native-born Americans, must therefore be significantly increased in order to provide human capital that is commensurate to technological development and to counteract the growing income inequality.

I share this view insofar as broad participation in education is a must for the development of the knowledge society. But Goldin and Katz's argument falls short because it focuses exclusively on the supply of skilled workers for the economy and neglects the long-discussed problems of changes in employment and work in the course of digitalization, and the social conditions of the emerging knowledge society.

In a discussion about this issue, Hans-Günter Rolff, an educationalist, drew my attention to a point that I had not considered before, but which immediately struck me. He argued that it is not only important that as many young people as possible achieve high educational skills, but that people from different social classes and ethnic backgrounds acquire these qualifications together, i.e. in the same schools and universities. This has the potential to promote common understandings that transcend different social classes and groups and their interests. This in turn serves the common good, social cohesion and coping with the challenges of the evolving knowledge society described above. It also serves the acquisition of social competence.

Rolff's argument is a thought-provoking impulse in linking educational participation with the substantive and methodological changes in education that are necessary to support and advance the restructuring of human capital outlined above. The shared learning which he proposes, if successful, creates a school microcosm of a pluralistic society. It brings together students from different living environments with different lifestyles, ideas and values, different imprints from early childhood socialization and different everyday knowledge. However, this must not only happen formally, but must be implemented socially and methodically. Socially, this must be done by bringing these pupils together into a group. This will most probably first lead to conflicts which the group must solve sensibly with the help of their teachers. For this purpose, they should learn appropriate deliberative methods. This creates a lot of social competence and offers the chance to systematically use on a small scale the creative potential of an open and pluralistic society as outlined in chapter 1. Students learn a lot from each other and they learn a lot from "teaching" each other.[13]

Common learning presupposes that the students learn more by themselves and together and that less material is taught by the teachers. This places high demands on teachers and their social competence. They have to be less like lecturers and more like learning coaches. They must be allowed and able to act largely independently and hold their own responsibility within the framework of clear and continuously monitored targets. This is important because it is the only way they can respond to the demands, strengths, weaknesses and experiences of their students and to the composition of their group and its developing milieu.

One of the few school systems that systematically builds up on common learning is the Finnish one. It starts with early childhood education and care which is voluntary. Fees for this program are adjusted to families' income and size. This is followed by a year of compulsory pre-primary education which plays an important role in preparing kids for school. Compulsory school consists of nine years of comprehensive school and three years of upper secondary education. Upper secondary education may be either general, preparing students for academic education, or vocational. Separation of the two branches is not rigid. Graduates from the vocational branch may formally qualify for universities of applied science, and in some cases also for university. Conversely graduates from the general branch may enroll in advanced programs of vocational education. It is even possible to attend schools of both branches at the same time. There is also a range of adult education and training. The whole system is geared at balancing out social inequality.[14]

Learning in Finnish schools takes place in integrated learning groups and classes based on cooperation of students rather than competition. Students often have the same teacher for up to six years. In this way teachers become mentors who can account for each student's different conditions, learning styles and needs and guide students individually. This is supported by the absence of standardized testing. All students in Finnish schools are graded individually on grading systems set by their teacher. Finish schools provide a relaxed learning environment with little regulation and more care. Classes are longer but so is recreation time between classes. There is little homework. A simple but important element of this environment is that students start school between 09.00 and 09.45 and end school by 14.00 and 14.45. The World Economic Forum has declared the Finnish educational system the best in the World. If you look at Finland's economic and social performance, this seems to be wholly justified.

In many Western societies, and probably even more so in authoritarian societies, teaching content and methods are laid down in rather elaborate curricula by school policymakers and school authorities as well as by scientific experts and commissions. Often this is done with the intention of defining uniform national educational standards and creating uniform learning plans. This is intended to ensure that pupils throughout the country are exposed to uniform or at least comparable requirements, thus creating educational equity. The approach may be well-intentioned, but in reality it is not particularly wise because pupils have very different educational backgrounds and the individual schools often have to work in very different contexts as a result.

I had a colleague at the Ruhr University in Bochum, Karl-Peter Strohmeier, who investigates the social background of the pupils of the schools in the Ruhr area, a region in which about 6% of the German population lives.

He developed a social profile of the individual schools and presented it graphically. The proportion of pupils from educationally disadvantaged families and other problematic contexts is shown on a map as mountains above each school. So you could see at a glance the schools with an unfavorable profile. I was always surprised how different the social profiles of the individual schools and thus their working conditions were and how many schools with unfavorable profiles there were in the region. However, these schools are subject to the same curricula and are at best supplied with resources equal to those with a much more favourable profile although their task is much more difficult. This already comes close to industrial mass production, even though individual teachers can make big differences.

Especially in education, it is important to move away from mass production and introduce a strong "customer orientation" that puts the individual student in the focus. In Germany and Austria and the German-speaking part of Switzerland, the different abilities of students are supposed to be taken into account through separate school types after elementary school. Pupils are assigned to these types on the basis of their performance in primary school and the cognitive abilities assumed behind it. Only completion of the top level school type entitles students to university studies. However, this has nothing to do with "customer orientation" in the education system, but only with segregation.

As the Finnish school system demonstrates, caring for individuals' conditions, needs and learning styles is not a matter of different school types, but rather one of learning methods and dealing with students. Finland manages this well with its uniform school system, while Germany, Switzerland and Austria deliver a uniform mishmash in their structured school systems, which is also highly standardized. In prose: Segregation does not mean that the special abilities, aptitudes and skills of individual pupils are better catered for, but only that pupils are placed early and without regard to their individual situation in different types of schools. Rather than catering for individual situations, segregation assigns pupils on a certain educational path that for most defines their social chances for life. This is certainly not an education that gives children best possible chances nor one that contributes to a good human capital. It is far from what a modern knowledge society needs.

What is needed are forms and methods of teaching and working in schools that focus on the competencies and abilities of the students. This can, as the Finnish and Swedish school systems illustrate, be well combined with common learning because common learning offers unique opportunities of learning and teaching that can be tailored to individual students' competencies and abilities.[15]

What we have discussed so far requires far-reaching reforms of the education system which will be difficult to accomplish. A particularly difficult aspect of the reforms is that they must also take into account the handling of the uncertainty of the developing knowledge society discussed in the previous part of the chapter. Today's schools like to teach certainties, that is, knowledge and understandings that are widely accepted, and closed world views. This is to a large extent in the nature of the thing. Schools must convey to children and young people as high a capacity for action as possible. To do this, schools must impart a recognized and proven basic knowledge and understanding and a clear orientation. But this is no longer enough for the school of tomorrow.

The school of tomorrow must also teach the ability to deal with uncertainty and adapt to rapid change. This requires so-called disruptive thinking, i.e. thinking in alternatives and thinking that breaks out of established ways of thinking and worlds of experience and also thinks through the seemingly impossible. That is what creativity and innovation are all about. However, if there is too much focus on disruptive thinking and the uncertain, students will not be helped to cope with uncertainty, but will only be confused, disoriented and less able to act. Disruptive thinking must therefore be linked to the teaching of orientation and the ability to act. This can be done, for example, in history lessons by assigning students in their learning groups to imagine how Europe would have developed if Austria and Serbia had not fallen out over the assassination of Franz Ferdinand, heir to the Austrian throne, or if the German Emperor had refused to support Austria in a war against Serbia and the First World War had not broken out. Another example: In biology classes, learning groups could be assigned to systematically assess the pros and cons of biotechnology and to work out a strategy on how to deal with biotechnology in a sensible way.

For the second example, many people will probably say that this would overwhelm the students. But one should not underestimate the abilities of students who are taught well. At my institute, we organized together with a major German radio and television broadcast an event on the financial market crisis in 2006, entitled "Pupil Experts". We agreed with several schools that the schools organize a project in which students will engage intensively with the financial market crisis and its background. On this basis, they were to develop a strategy on how the financial market crisis could be solved and how they wanted it to be solved. To our surprise a "Hauptschule" – the "lowest" type of school in the structured German education system and mostly considered as a residual school for those who could not reach higher education – also wanted to take part. After some internal discussion we finally agreed to admit the Hauptschule although we had some uneasy feelings. The students of each school presented and discussed the results of their projects in a larger meeting with leaders from the financial sector and financial policy. The success was enormous. The class from the Hauptschule especially impressed participants with their knowledge and ideas. Based on this experience, I have no doubt that students can also be engaged with challenging topics, e.g. estimating biotechnology. This is all the more true as the pupils are dealing with important questions of their future and for this reason alone are mostly concerned with really well-founded and viable findings.

There is an urgent need for action for these reforms, because investments and innovations in education only take effect after years and decades. Therefore, if a sustainable development of a developed knowledge society is to be achieved by 2050, the reforms of the education system must take place as soon as possible. This is also and especially true for the economic strength and economic competitiveness of Western societies. The insight of the urgency of a school reform, however, does not make the reforms socially and politically any easier to implement. In the German-speaking countries, especially in Germany, there have been fierce and highly ideological disputes for years, which have so far inhibited any thoroughgoing reform. I am sure that if private schools were to be abolished, the same controversy would arise in the USA and the UK. The only thing that is likely to help is a patient reform strategy that relies on a growing number of successful examples and on the fact that these examples will prove so much more successful against the demands of the evolving knowledge society that they will prevail in the genesis of these societies.

There is another race that is important for the development of the knowledge society and the sustainable development of this society. This is a race between technology and culture. Culture is seen in the sense described in chapter 5 as a toolbox that helps people to construct their patterns and strategies of action. In concrete terms, this is about the individual and societal ability to use knowledge and technology sensibly and responsibly.

This ability seems to lag far behind technological progress. This is evidenced on the one hand by fears of new technologies that are either diffuse, scientifically unfounded or one-sided, or that are based on knowledge about outdated versions of this technology. This can often be observed in connection with biotechnology and genetic engineering, the latter with new versions of nuclear energy that are being developed. On the other hand, risks of new technologies are often not adequately investigated and assessed and no adequate risk precautions are taken. Sad examples of this are the handling of nuclear energy or of some chemical products, such as glyphosate.

The two sides often reinforce each other. Clumsy, mendacious or irresponsible actions by business and politics create or reinforce mistrust and rejection of new technologies. Diffuse or insufficiently justified rejection of new technologies promotes a dishonest or irresponsible approach to new technologies on the part of the business community, because it fears that this will destroy its investments in a new technology. However, there is a deliberative solution in the form of mini-publics for technology assessment.

The Fine Art of Social Learning

In the knowledge society, education is more important than ever for economic and social development as well as for individual life chances and participation opportunities. This also applies to schools. But especially in the knowledge society, education can no longer just mean school and university.

In view of the high knowledge dynamics of the knowledge society, school and university alone are no longer sufficient to impart and secure a high level of ability to act. A second phase of school education in the middle of working life would certainly make sense, but it could not fully solve the problem. What is needed instead is the institutional anchoring of learning in everyday life, at the work place, in politics and in civil society. Learning must simply go along with everyday life and offer people the opportunity to continuously develop their knowledge, skills and competences and thus secure and improve their social opportunities. Every day learning opportunities are provided, for example, by the economic structures and work organization which we described in chapter 4, participation in mini-publics on local and national levels and by many elements of the internet, for example by games which are not deliberatively designed as learning games but let you think and act strategically, think the unthinkable and create new worlds.

We are speaking here, however, not just about individual learning, but about organizational and other collective learning. The concept of a learning organization has been developed by Chris Argyris, a professor of education and organizational behavior at Harvard University, and David A. Schön, a professor of Urban Studies and Education at the Massachusetts Institute of Technology. It describes an organization that continuously reviews its actions and strategies, and the underlying goals and foundations and adapts them to changing circumstances. It is an organization that does not fix much and does not fall into routine. In a world as turbulent as the knowledge society, organizations of all kinds, i.e. companies, business associations, political parties, governments, bureaucracies and, last but not least, civil society organizations, as well as more complex organized systems, such as governments or cities, are usually required to have a high capacity for innovation and adaptation and thus a high capacity for learning. In highly organized societies, such as Western societies, organizational learning has long become a central issue. But in the modern knowledge society it has become an existential problem.[16]

In the introduction to the new edition of his successful book "The Fifth Discipline: The Art and Practice of the Learning Organization", Peter M. Senge, one of the masterminds of the learning organization, has written that many companies are still far from a learning organization and some are even moving away from it again. What he describes is the typical pattern of a rapid transformation process. Far-reaching changes usually also generate strong counterforces. It is not uncommon for the opposing forces to prevail at first.[17]

An illustrative example is work organization. In the late 1980s and early 1990s, there was a lot of discussion on anthropocentric production systems. The concept of anthropocentric production systems describes highly decentralized work systems with flat hierarchies and strong worker empowerment as we discussed in chapter 4. The model for such production systems was Toyota's lean production. At that time, this model was discussed in science and business as the future model for advanced manufacturing. In the prevailing causal way of thinking of science, this development seemed to be deeply anchored in the logic of globalization, the international division of labor and the competitive conditions of the developed economies, and thus compelling.

The scientists who thought this way, like myself, did not take into account the opposing forces. They were considerable because the production model we favored placed high demands on the leadership skills of managers. This overtaxed many managers, including those at the highest levels of management. But it also overtaxed many workers who did not want to assume so much self-responsibility as the model assumes. For these reasons, the model did not catch on in many companies, or only partially. In some companies, the hierarchy became even steeper. This can be seen, among other things, in the fact that in many companies the power of the chairperson of the board of directors, who previously had the role of a primus inter pares on the board, has been considerably increased. This is symbolized by the now widespread designation CEO.

It is quite widely shared in relevant literature that strongly hierarchical structures hinder rather than promote the learning ability of companies. Strong hierarchy tempts many managers to focus their actions primarily on securing their power. This in turn often leads to power being used primarily as a way of not having to learn. But this does not have to be the case. Leaders who combine a high level of professional competence with strong social competence can also develop companies with a pronounced hierarchical structure into a learning organization. They can also introduce and practice cooperative leadership styles, teamwork and other methods in hierarchical structures that promote organizational learning without endangering their power.[18]

I do not want to go into these further here, but limit myself to one way of developing and leading a learning organization that fits in with our overall concept of governance, namely the use of deliberative procedures, mini-publics in particular. While mini-publics are generally developed for politics and political administration, they can be adapted for companies in order to involve employees, customers or the general public in corporate decision-making or conflict resolution. Let us consider a fictive example: The top management of a company is determined to implement within a rather short time a strategy of sustainability, which satisfies the concept of threefold sustainability. In concrete terms, this would be a strategy that makes the company sustainable, increases the company's competitiveness and secures employment or compensates for job losses. In addition, the strategy would have to strengthen the corporate culture. In order to reach this ambitious goal, the top management could establish mini-publics to obtain suggestions for goals, ideas and measures for the design of the strategy and information on the consensus and acceptance of the strategy. A mini-public based on a stratified random sample of the entire workforce could work on the total strategy while another mini-public could discuss the possible impact of the strategy on employment and work in the company and probable measures to avoid or compensate undesirable effects. Another mini-public based on random-samples of the company's workforce, main clients and citizens could assess the impact of an effective strategy on the company's market positioning and public reputation. Finally, a mini-public of managers and other workers could discuss implementation strategies and propose strategies which will create least conflict in the company and can be best implemented. The results of the different mini-publics could be brought together in a consensus forum and later on communicated to the entire workforce in a consensus conference or a workforce conference according to the citizen conference. After the strategy is determined in broad outlines, more specific and narrow problems could be assigned to workforce juries. In the end, the final draft of strategy could again be discussed in a consensus forum.

For many traditional managers, this may seem like a planning process that is far too complex and takes far too much time. But this may be a big error. Deliberative procedures usually provide much more and broader information and induce often a strong and dynamic process of organizational learning. This is likely to enhance the quality of planning and the success of the strategy significantly. Deliberative procedures are also likely to increase acceptance of the strategy, reduce conflicts and mobilize support by the workforce. This may facilitate and speed up implementation significantly.

There are many other fields in which deliberative procedures may be reasonably applied in companies. An interesting field is quality control. To get a more profound understanding of or early warnings on serious problems, quality problems could be regularly discussed in a consensus conference. The conference could be based on hearings of quality managers, clients and experts by a workers' jury. This not only contributes to better problem solving by making the workers more familiar with the problems, but should sustainably strengthen quality awareness throughout the workforce.

Another example is continuous improvement of processes and products. This could be entrusted to workforce juries. Their task would be to receive suggestions for improvement from the workforce, evaluate them at regular intervals and develop consensual solutions with the support of experts. This could improve companies' suggestion schemes and increase acceptance of solutions. Workforce juries or consensus conferences could be used for early and forward-looking assessment of new production technology by either mini-publics or workforce juries.

In civil society too deliberative procedures may play an important role. NGOs, social movements, environmental groups, neighborhood organizations, labor unions, universities and research institutions, think tanks and other organizations may use them for a variety of different tasks and do so already. Environmental organizations and groups, for example, could use consensus forums to inform a wider public or to check and improve public acceptance of their major positions and strategy. They also could try to organize a mini-public with counterparts on the corporate side to look for possibilities of feasible solutions to their conflict and a joint longer-term strategy or project to implement these solutions. This could be a joint strategy to reach sustainability of the company by the year 2050. For that purpose, they could collaborate with management and workforce, or help the workforce to develop a strategy which secures their employment. With that kind of activity, environmental organizations and groups may greatly contribute to avoiding or resolving some of the conflicts which inhibit sustainable development so much. In the end, this may advance sustainable development much more than many spectacular protest actions.

Universities and other research institutions could use mini-publics for participative assessment of new technology on which they are working. The mini-publics could bring together the academics working on this technology and on technology assessment with a random sample of citizens. The mission of the mini-public would be to carefully assess chances and risks of the new technology and jointly develop a strategy which "maximizes" the exploitation of chances and "minimizes" risk. Moreover, they could identify applications of the new technology which would be particularly beneficial for society as a whole and for sustainable development. This could speed up desirable application of the new technology.

When viewed from an evolutionary perspective, mini-publics promote collective learning in society or organizations in two ways. Participation of randomly selected citizens in political or organizational decision-making often significantly increases variation in the system and intensifies debates. This promotes learning. The deliberative processes and the achievement of widely accepted understandings and solutions will in the end reduce the social complexity of the decision. This reduces conflict and promotes cohesion and decision-making capacity. Both learning and decision-making capacity are enhanced the more the citizens involved are actually accepted as trusted proxy.

In order to support and enhance deliberative procedures, government, some private foundations or other actors could install an organization like the Danish Technology Board Foundation. This is a non-profit foundation whose mission "is to work for society's development being shaped by informed and forward-looking collaboration between citizens, experts, stakeholders, and decision-makers". The Danish Board of Technology conducts mini-publics and other activities for participatory technology assessment of new technologies, such as biotechnology or robotics, participatory foresight on labor markets, nature and sustainable development, proposals for the Danish government's climate policy. It does research on a national and European scale on issues of social challenges, technology and public participation. It helps organizations to implement citizen participation.

The Deliberative Way: A New Enlightenment

The term Enlightenment describes an epoch, particularly in the eighteenth century, which is characterized above all by the appeal to reason as the universal authority of judgement. Its guiding was that people who use their reason can develop into mature personalities and attain freedom of action. This was associated with the idea that a society of reasonable citizens could gradually solve the important problems of society. Central ideas of the Enlightenment were freedom and equality for all people, and the common good as a state and civic duty. The right to education and the broad distribution of knowledge played an important role. This is manifested in one of the great projects of the Enlightenment, the 35 volume "Encyclopédie ou Dictionnaire raisonné des sciences, des arts et des métiers" (Encyclopedia or Reasoned Dictionary of Science, Arts and Crafts) by Jean le Rond d'Alembert and Denis Diderot, which was intended to bring the scientific knowledge of the time to a wider population. The Enlightenment shaped both the constitution of the United States and the French Revolution. It brought the bourgeoisie to power and fought for the development of a strong and informed public. For me, enlightenment is the first big step towards the development of a knowledge society, although it first brought about industrialization and the development of industrial society.

The Enlightenment changed a lot in Europe and America. It has triggered truly great upheavals in Western societies. Its principles and ideas have been reflected in democratic social orders in which tolerance has become a dominant principle. For a long time, it also seemed that it had initiated a state that was really based on broad social agreement in the sense of a social contract. It has created an enormous body of knowledge and is increasing this body of knowledge at sometimes breathtaking speed. It has led to the development of societies that seem particularly capable of solving their problems with reason and knowledge.

The Enlightenment was marked by a strong and unshakable belief in progress. From today's point of view, this belief in progress was naïve and it did not fully prove itself. Today in particular the ideas of the Enlightenment are experiencing severe setbacks in some Western societies. This is especially true for the country whose constitution and political system is based on the ideas of the Enlightenment, the United States of America. Today this country experiences social and political polarization which leaves little room for reasonable argument and sensible solutions to problems and conflicts. The two parties are engaged in ideological debates and an uncommitted quest for power. The social communication structures are characterized by a high degree of one-sided information and fake news, by low factuality of much information and news. Some news channels, such as Fox news, are often biased in their reporting and show little concern for journalistic objectivity. But even broadcasters with recognizably higher journalistic standards, such as CNN, are no strangers to a certain degree of partisanship. In the social media, there is often little evidence of the ideals of enlightenment, which however is no better in Europe. In some European countries, Poland and Hungary in particular, the actual political condition is not much better than in the United States. In the United Kingdom the conservative party seems to be leaning towards more authoritarian government. In case of Hungary and

Poland, the European Union is taking only half-hearted and hesitant action against clear violations of fundamental European principles and thus of the European Treaty.

It is easy to blame media and parties for the current political and social situation. But that is too easy. There is no doubt that media and parties have played an important and negative role in this development. There is no doubt that the actions of these actors must be reframed and changed. But one has to ask the question of chicken and egg, especially from an evolutionist perspective. Chickens are born from eggs, eggs are laid by chickens. Which came first? Transferred to our case, this means: media and parties not only cause these problems, but they also react to them. The occurrence of these problems also creates a potential demand for the media and parties and an opportunity to gain a unique selling position. With their polarizing actions, they fulfil an important need of many citizens. They create for these citizens a communicative cocoon in which they find certainty in an uncertain world. What one's own party and media report is the truth, what the opposing media and parties say is fundamentally wrong. Two conclusions follow from this insight. The first is that media and social media must be regulated according to their important social function. The second is that the material and social causes and problems of social and political polarization have to be eliminated.

Like many other important problems of Western societies, the problems we just discussed have been developing for a long time and have been discussed a lot by many experts and engaged citizens. Yet they are largely ignored or at best half-heartedly addressed in business and politics. Like so many unsolved problems, this is not due to a lack of knowledge or an underestimation of the scope of these problems. Rather, it manifests to a lack of willingness to use knowledge and solve problems. This a central issue of today's Western societies. It manifests that a very important goal of enlightenment has not yet been achieved or is no longer being achieved.

The great German philosopher and Enlightenment philosopher Immanuel Kant described the Enlightenment as the exit of human beings from self-inflicted immaturity. He described immaturity as the inability to use one's intellect without the guidance of another. Self-inflicted immaturity is when it is not based on a lack of understanding, but on the determination and courage to use one's own understanding, to form one's own judgement and to advocate it even if this meets with much opposition and rejection. In Kant's view, it is comfortable to be immature.

Judging from the way quite a number of companies and governments deal with important problems, many business and political leaders are also very much in this comfort zone. This can be criticized or complained about, but this is unlikely to help much. Here, too, the chicken-and-egg problem arises: Are the politicians and the top managers the ones who create the problems through inaction or weak action, or do they act that way because their conditions for action, their framing, suggest that to them? As the question suggests, I assume an important cause in the framing of elites. This is not to excuse the frequent failure of political and economic leadership, but it points to a fact that we have noted again and again in the preceding chapters: Western societies have lost common grounds. This has become a key issue of governance which cannot be solved within the current institutional framework of Western democracies but rather requires a deliberative switch. We will come back to this in the next chapter.

Notes

1 A stimulating philosophical view on contingency is offered in Richard Rorty (1989). Contingency, Irony and Solidarity. Cambridge UK: Cambridge University Press. For a social science approach to contingency see David Byrne, Gill Callaghan (2014). Complexity Theory and the Social Sciences: The State of the Art. London and New York: Routledge. Lex Donaldson (2001). The Contingency Theory of Organizations. London, Thousand Oaks and New Delhi: Sage. Alnoor Ebrahim (2019). Measuring Social Change: Performance and Accountability in a Complex World. Stanford: Stanford University Press. Euel Elliott, L. Douglas Kiel (2021). Complex Systems in Social and Behavioral Theory. Ann Arbor: University of Michigan Press. Robin Wagner-Pacifici (2000). Theorizing the Standoff: Contingency in Action. Cambridge UK: Cambridge University Press.

2 See Barbara Marx Hubbard (2015). Conscious Evolution: Awaking the Power of Our Social Potential. Novato, CA: New World Library

3 Simulation has become a key instrument to "predict" developments in a probabilistic way. See Nigel Gilbert, Klaus G. Troitzsch (2005). Simulation for the Social Scientist. Maidenhead UK and New York: Open University Press.

4 A stimulating evolutionary analysis of the importance of institutions for development of a knowledge economy is provided by Johann Peter Murmann (2003). Knowledge and Competitive Advantage: The Coevolution of firms, Technology and National Institutions. Cambridge UK and New York: Cambridge University Press.

5 For a broad description of structures and operation of modern public administration see Michiel S. de Vries (2016). Understanding Public Administration. London: Palgrave.

6 See Helga Nowotny (2016). The Cunning of Uncertainty. Cambridge UK: Polity Press. See also Nico Stehr (2001). Fragility of Modern Societies: Knowledge and Risk in the Information Age. London and Thousand Oaks, CA: Sage.

7 My understanding of science as a process of knowledge production has greatly profited from Karin Knorr Cetina (1981). The Manufacture of Knowledge: An Essay on the Constructivist and Contextual Nature of Science.

8 For a profound analysis of the inherent uncertainty in the knowledge society see Helga Nowotny, Peter Scott, Michael Gibbons (2001). Re-Thinking Science: Knowledge in an Age of Uncertainty. Cambridge UK and Malden, MA: Polity Press. Nico Stehr (2001). The Fragility of Modern Knowledge Societies: Knowledge and Risk in the Information Age. London and Thousand Oaks, CA: Sage.

9 A stimulating appeal to think the unthinkable is offered by Nik Gowing, Chris Langdon (2018). Thinking the Unthinkable. Melton UK: John Catt Educational Limited.

10 See Michael Gibbons, Camille Limoges, Helga Nowotny, Simon Schwartzman, Peter Scott, Martin Trow (1994). The New Production of Knowledge: The Dynamics of Science and Research in Contemporary Societies. London, Thousand Oaks and New Delhi: Sage.

   Helga Nowotny, Peter Scott, Michael Gibbons (2001). Rethinking Science: Knowledge and the Public in an Age of Uncertainty. Cambridge UK, Malden MA: Polity Press.

11 This is impressively described in Zygmunt Bauman (2007). Liquid Times: Living in an Age of Uncertainty. Cambridge UK: Polity Press. See also Gerd Gigerenzer (2002). Adaptive Thinking: Rationality in the Real World. Oxford and New York: Oxford University Press. Gerd Gigerenzer (2008). Rationality for Mortals: How People Cope with Uncertainty. Oxford and New York: Oxford University Press.

12 Cf. Claudia Goldin, Lawrence F. Katz (2008). The Race between Education and Technology. Cambridge, MA and London: Harvard University Press.

13 See Katie Martin (2021). Evolving Education: Shifting to a Learner-centered Paradigm. San Diego: IM Press. Jay Mctighe, Yong Zhao (2019). Leading Modern Learning: A Blueprint for Vision-driven Schools. Bloomington: Solution Tree.

14 For a comprehensive discussion of the Finnish school system see Eduardo Andere M. (2016). Teachers' Perspectives on Finnish School Education: Creating Learning Environments. Cham: Springer. See also https://www.weforum.org/agenda/2018/09/10-reasons-why-finlands-education-system-is-the-best-in-the-world

15 There is a range of literature on reforming education and schools. See for example Andreas Schleicher (2018). World Class: How to Build a 21st-century School System. Paris: OECD Publishing. Mark Prensky (2016). Education to Better their World. New York: Teachers College Press. Michael Young, David Lambert (2014). Knowledge and the Future School: Curriculum and Social Justice. London and New York: Bloomsbury Academic.

16 The great importance of a learning society for the economic development of Western societies is described in Joseph E. Stiglitz, Bruce C. Greenwald (2014). Creating a Learning Society: A New Approach to Growth, Development and Social Progress. New York: Columbia University Press.

17 Cf. Peter M. Senge (2006). The Fifth Discipline: The Art and Practice of the Learning Organization. New York: Crown Publishing Group.

18 A challenging approach to organizational learning based on a critical review of hierarchy is offered by Brian J. Robertson (2025). Holocracy: The New Way to Achieve Success by Distributing Authority. New York: Henry Holt.

7　The Deliberative Switch

In the subtitle of this book, I talk about an ambitious strategy to achieve a challenging goal. I can well imagine that some readers, after reading the six preceding chapters of this book, may doubt whether this strategy is not overambitious and unrealistic. But this is not the case. True, I propose in this book to achieve a far-reaching and difficult social change, namely sustainable development, with an equally far-reaching institutional change. But the necessary institutional change is entirely feasible if many people, networks and organizations from civil society, innovative companies and progressive cities join in.

In chapter 5, I cited the German journalist Petra Pinzler who said with regard to the Glasgow climate change conference in 2021 that she is wavering between hopeless despair and desperate hope. Her despair relates to politics, her desperate hope is based on the many companies, organizations, initiatives, networks, individuals and other actors who are working hard against climate change and for sustainable development. The only difference between us is that, to say it again, my hope is not desperate, but quite optimistic.

The reason for my optimism is that if many of the actors Petra Pinzler mentions, plus progressive cities, apply deliberative procedures in many smaller or larger projects on sustainable development, Western societies are likely to achieve sustainable development, including climate neutrality, by the middle of this century. There is already an impressive range of activities of cities, companies and initiatives and organizations in civil society. For these and hopefully many other activities, deliberative procedures, mini-publics in particular, provide them with a powerful toolbox. Cities and companies can use this toolbox to solve their sustainability problems and to develop a widely shared strategy for threefold sustainability. This will give them a competitive advantage which will provide incentives for other cities and companies to engage in similar activities. NGOs and similar actors may use the toolbox to expand their scope of activities by initiating and organizing projects for sustainable development with companies, cities and other actors.

There are five reasons for the feasibility of this approach. First, a deliberative switch is the best, probably even the only way to practically implement the concept of threefold sustainability. The concept of threefold

DOI: 10.4324/9781003261421-7

sustainability, in turn, is the best, probably even the only way to permanently resolve the many conflicts which are inevitably associated with sustainable development and which strongly impede it. Second, a deliberative switch may be implemented by a gentle revolution. The revolution is gentle because the deliberative switch can be accomplished within the existing institutions but nevertheless transform the way the existing institutions function and their ability to cope with complexity. Third, a deliberative switch fundamentally increases Western societies' ability to cope with complexity without compromising the openness and diversity of society. On the contrary, deliberative procedures, mini-publics in particular, gain their power precisely by making systematic use of openness and diversity. Mini-publics in particular resolve the major deficiencies of pluralism and, through the representative participation of citizens rebuild trust in the established institutions. Fourth, mini-publics offer a good, probably the best way to solve another core problem of Western societies, the reframing of governance that has gotten out of hand. Fifth, the versatile applicability of mini-publics creates many opportunities to drive sustainable, bottom-up development. This is an indispensable condition for achieving sustainable development in Western societies by the middle of this century. It makes this development a matter for society as a whole, not just politics. However, taking advantage of this great opportunity requires fundamental rethinking on the part of many of the avant-gardists of sustainable development.

The Implementation of Threefold Sustainability

Threefold sustainability is a complex concept that reflects the real complexity of sustainable development. In the second chapter I define threefold sustainability as the ability of a society to secure and improve in the long term, firstly, its natural bases of life by a high level of resource productivity, secondly, a fair standard of living of the vast majority of the population, and thirdly its social cohesion, that is its ability to make and maintain widely accepted collective decisions. Each of these issues is both substantially and socially complex. Their interplay and coevolution are naturally even more complex. Systematic consideration of this interplay is an indispensable prerequisite for the success of any sustainable development strategy. This inevitably makes any strategy for sustainable development a complex matter.

Mini-publics are a good vehicle for managing this complexity. On the one hand, they reduce the social complexity of sustainable development through the inclusion of all relevant social interests and development of shared understandings of problems and the principle way to solve them, and of a common knowledge base. Inclusion of many different interests first increases the complexity of collective decision-making and renders development of joint solutions and a common knowledge base more difficult. But if this is successful, the complexity of further proceedings will be significantly reduced. Reaching a common solution that is effective and durable is thus greatly facilitated in the end.

On the other hand, mini-publics use the rich knowledge and the great potential of an open and diverse society for creativity and social learning to cope with substantial complexity of sustainable development. They bring together many players with their knowledge and ideas. In this way, they can create a strong knowledge base and a creative milieu in which this knowledge base is put to good use. This provides good conditions for solving even complex problems amicably.

To the point: Mini-publics exploit the comparative advantage of the openness and diversity of Western societies without failing at the specific problems that openness and diversity pose for collective decision-making.

Application of mini-publics for the implementation of the concept of threefold sustainability can build on significant synergies between this concept and the proceeding of mini-publics. The concept focuses the attention of panels first on the conflicts associated with sustainable development and then on properties of the underlying problems and social conditions. It also focuses the discussions of the panels first on their members' dissenting views of the concerned problem and its possible solution, and on the goals and interests underlying these views. Dissenting views are understood as manifestations of conflicts. This is an important condition for the successful work of mini-publics.

Groups of people tasked with developing a mutually agreeable solution to a problem are usually tempted to define the problem in such a way that a mutually agreeable solution can be easily achieved. In the case of mini-publics, this could be reflected in emphasizing consensus rather than disagreement even in the initial discussion of the panelists' views of their own ideas and their background, and in that they look for compromises to resolve dissent. The result would be the same kind of weak compromises that politicians or other actors can adopt without mini-publics. These are solutions that meet with broad approval and are easy to implement only because they largely exclude conflicts. Mini-publics thus would deprive themselves of their effectiveness and their raison d'être.

But with the opposite approach which the concept of threefold sustainability suggests they can outperform the established structures. By first emphasizing conflicts and their substantial and social context they can reach an understanding of conflicts which enhances constructive resolution of the conflict in accordance with the concept of threefold sustainability.

I would like to illustrate this abstract argument with the fictive example of a mini-public commissioned with the drafting of a strategy leading to sustainable development by the middle of this century. One of the central themes of this strategy is to be mobility. In the first meetings of the panel of this mini-public, its members reveal their ideas of sustainable mobility and the goals and interests associated with it. In the process, as in the city's population, considerable divergences and sometimes fierce conflicts become apparent. A fierce conflict develops in particular between a committed environmentalist who wants to ban individual motorized traffic from the city to a large extent and a philosophy professor for whom this represents an inadmissible encroachment on individual liberties. In the debate other members of the panel take sides. On the environmentalist's side is a member who lives on busy road with a lot of traffic and a regular user of public transportation who simply wants higher investment in public transportation at the expense of investments in streets, parking lots and other facilities. On the philosopher's side were two members living in suburban areas and in a neighborhood with bad supply of public transportation who need their cars or motorcycles to commute to their place of work or to bring their kids to school.

After the initial round of discussion, the panel suggests that the environmentalist and the philosopher discuss the nature and deeper causes of the conflict. After a short exchange of arguments, the two agree that their conflict is not disagreement on the importance of sustainability, but on the principles which should guide sustainable development. The environmentalist states that for him the common good must take precedence over individual liberty; the philosopher, on the other hand, rejects this, arguing that the state must not interfere with the liberties of citizens in order to achieve a state defined by somebody as the common good, but only to prevent the exercise of its liberties by one citizen from interfering with the equal rights of other citizens. At this point, the panelist who lives on busy road speaks up, an IT-mechanic, saying that the exhaust gases and the noise are nothing else than such an interference. The philosopher accepts the validity of this argument. To cut a long story short, after further discussing the case the panel decides that with respect to mobility, the guideline of their work shall be to reach sustainable mobility by infringing individual liberty as little as possible.

The implementation of this principle is reflected in the sustainability concept which the mini-public finally proposes in three parts. The first is to better link public and individual transportation and create better solutions for the "last mile" between stations of public transportation and peoples' places of living or work. Such solutions are for example offered by LA metropolitan transportation. The second one is to regulate individual transportation by introducing a road toll and congestion charge. The toll could create significant incentives to reduce traveling into and within the city. It could stimulate formation of car pools or carsharing by many people. More importantly even, it could pressure relevant companies to drastically reduce the many delivering services which currently congest many cities. They could do this, for example, by cooperation in a joint delivery service. Online retailers could also be incentivized to curb returns of ordered goods. As a desirable side-effect, this may increase local retailers' competitive position in relation to Amazon and other big online retailers. The third is to invest the income from the toll in effective measures to drastically reduce the burden of motorized road traffic on citizens. This could for example be done by concentrating much of the traffic in and out of the city on a few traffic axes. These axes could be designed in a way which minimizes the negative impact on citizens. For this purpose, some axes could even be relocated in tunnels.

The concept of threefold sustainability provides a systematic theoretical framework and already much practical knowledge and experience for such an approach and enhances the application of mini-publics. On the other hand, the synergy between mini-publics and the concept of threefold sustainability also runs the other way. The mini-publics working on the basis of the concept of threefold sustainability will make a smaller or larger contribution to improving and expanding the knowledge base of this concept. While the existing knowledge base of the concept can provide them with a good foundation for their work, it will often not be sufficient. Solving the problem with which they are concerned will often require additional and more specialized knowledge. Thus, the knowledge base for applying the concept of threefold sustainability is getting better, broader and more differentiated. This also makes the concept increasingly more easily and more widely applicable.

Beyond that, the more the concept of threefold sustainability is applied by mini-publics, the more the knowledge base of the concept will become part of the knowledge base of society. This should enhance the understanding of many people and other social actors of the complex environmental, economic, and social interrelationships of sustainable development. It is also likely to promote an understanding that the challenges of sustainable development can only be met if these interrelationships are systematically taken into account. It should also show them that this is possible. This would be an important contribution to the reframing of the governance of Western societies.

At this point, we should poor some cold water on the matter. Even if, as I claim, threefold sustainability is the best, probably even the only way to permanently resolve the many conflicts which are inevitably associated with sustainable development and even if a deliberative switch is the best, probably even the only way to practically implement this concept, there is no guarantee that both will prevail in Western societies. Social evolution is not characterized by a survival of the fittest that is of the best possible solution, as an analogy to biological evolution may suggest. Precisely because social evolution can be influenced by human actor, it is also subject to power and power is the ability not to learn. The hope, however, is that deliberative procedures, mini-publics in particular, and threefold sustainability prevail despite much accumulated power in Western societies because both can be rather easily implemented and may be widely applied decentrally and from the bottom up. They could therefore profit from the fact that development of open and pluralistic society is difficult to control, even by much power.

Deliberation: A Gentle Revolution

Designing the deliberative switch as a gentle revolution follows the insight that those who want big changes should change as little as possible. That sounds like a contradiction in terms, but it's not. It simply calls for achieving the greatest possible effect with as few precisely targeted interventions as possible. This is partly a question of the complexity of interventions and of their contingency. The more interventions change, the less controllable their impact and the greater the likelihood that they will miss their targets in whole or in part. But above all it is a question of acceptance and enforcement of change. Many people are distant and skeptical about change, or even afraid of it. For many, probably most people, the existing has the charm of the familiar and known. Even if they find some things wrong with the existing, it still gives them a sense of security and orientation. The existing is their framing. This is the downside of framing. It binds people to the existing and creates path dependencies.

The new, on the other hand, is foreign and uncertain. Many people do not know what it will bring and what it will mean for them in concrete terms. It thus deprives them of orientation and certainty of action. It damages their framing. Contingency is not just a theoretical category, but an everyday experience. It is the everyday experience that things do not work as expected. For many people, this generates fear of change, resistance to change or a hesitant response to change. Revolutions or, more generally, far-reaching changes thus create uncertainty, fears, defensiveness, restraint and retreat into "safe" spaces and routines among many actors. This is exactly what should be avoided if sustainable development should be achieved by the middle of this century. Far-reaching change must therefore be integrated into a familiar institutional framework. Deliberative procedures fit this principle perfectly. They can be very effective even though, or rather because, they "only" complement the established institutional structures. I will illustrate this with two particularly difficult cases.

The first case is abortion. Abortion is precisely the kind of issue that creates deep and abiding divisions in some societies. Majority decisions on these issues create just that. To avoid divisions, solutions must be found that are widely accepted. To this end, a deliberative procedure can be built into existing political decision-making structures. This has been done in case of the Irish reform of abortion legislation and the underlying constitutional rule in 2018. In the Republic of Ireland, abortion is a along and bitterly disputed issue. To end the dispute over the abortion ban, which was also enshrined in the Constitution of the Irish Republic in 1983, the Irish government appointed a citizens' assembly with a mandate to submit a consensual proposal for reform of relevant law and constitutional rule. The citizens' assembly fulfilled its mission in 2016–17 and in 2017 a parliamentary committee discussed the matter. Both recommended a constitutional and legislative reform making abortion under some conditions legal. The proposal was accepted in 2018 in a referendum with a majority of 66%. Before that, this kind of majority had been reached on proposals to restrict abortion.

A critical issue with respect to sustainable development is trust in science and acceptance of technology. Without intensive use of science and technology, sustainable development and even climate neutrality are out of reach. Distrust in science and refusal of scientific knowledge or technology by smaller or larger groups of society creates social and political conflict which may significantly impede application of science. Knowledge on climate change or on Covid-19 or genetic engineering and nuclear technology illustrate this.

The Danish Technology Board Foundation has developed deliberative procedures for technology assessment and for framing science to solve this problem. One of the proven formats of the foundation is its participatory consensus conference which has a representative selection of 120–150 citizens as active listeners, a representative panel of 14 citizens and a group of experts. The core of the 4-day event is a hearing of the citizen panel with the experts, which is integrated into a broader discussion with the audience. On the basis of the hearing and the discussion, the panel prepares a statement which is discussed with the experts and the audience on the last day. Through this procedure, difficult, complex scientific and technical situations are presented in a way that is understandable to the general public, and are worked up into a statement that is written by "normal" citizens and voted on by a representative audience of "normal" citizens. For many citizens, this builds more confidence than pure expert opinions. It prevents them from being completely at the mercy of experts and scientists. But it also may enrich the understanding of scientists and other experts.

These examples as well as examples in previous chapters show that simply adding deliberative procedures to the established institutional structures of Western democracies can fundamentally improve Western democracies' ability to cope with complexity and resolve conflict in a lasting way. As we discussed in chapter 1, reduction of complexity is the major function of institutions and systems. While the existing institutional structures of Western democracies often fail to reasonably reduce complexity of problems, deliberative procedures are particularly good at it.

In the existing structures, complexity is, firstly, reduced by rules and understandings which are decided by majority rule and enforced by government power. In effect, this means that in the existing structures complexity is reduced by fading out a smaller or larger number of social interests. The second way to reduce complexity is structural differentiation of the government machinery, bureaucracy in particular. This is associated with a strong influence of special interest groups which fades out even more social interest, especially the more general interests of larger parts of society. As we discussed earlier in this book, fading out interests by political decision-making triggers follow-up conflicts and in the end increases rather than decreases complexity of problems.

Deliberatives procedure on the other hand reduce complexity by common agreement. They are designed to include all relevant interests and create a concise shared knowledge base. The latter combines scientific knowledge with experience, social knowledge, artistic knowledge, and in some cases even religious knowledge.

A no less important effect of deliberative procedures is the promotion of collective learning. Collective learning is an integral foundation of all deliberative procedures. I will further explain this in the following section. The established institutions of Western societies often inhibit rather than advance collective learning. The major reason for this is the paramount role of power in collective decision-making of Western societies. This applies mainly to politics, to a lesser degree to civil society and even to the market.

With politics, this seems to be the nature of things. After all, democratic politics is usually seen as a competition for government power. Parliamentary majority decisions are then simply the manifestation of democratically acquired power. In the pluralistic Western societies, however, this often creates conflicts and dissatisfaction. Even worse in this respect is the great power of small but well-organized interest groups. As we know, conflicts and dissatisfaction significantly lower governments' capacity to successfully cope with the challenges of our time, sustainable development in particular.

In civil society, collective decisions are, for the most part, implicitly made as a result of spontaneous development. But this has to a considerable degree become a myth. "Spontaneous" development is regularly influenced and even manipulated by powerful organizations and influencers. This often leads to hardened conflicts and social divisions. This is an important reason for the more or less severe erosion of social cohesion in most Western societies.

Even markets whose effective functioning theoretically requires the absence of power, are regularly influenced by economic power. This includes many big or small monopolies, but also banks and many other companies which are considered "systemic important". The latter can, thanks to government assistance, time and again evade the market's punishment of economically wrong actions. In this way, they do not override the market any less than many monopolists.

As was briefly mentioned at the end of the previous part of this chapter, mini-publics offer good chances to contain the paramount role of power. First of all, membership in mini-publics evades influence by powerful actors because it is established by accepted principles of random selection. Second, their proceedings cannot easily be influenced by power because they make such influence always visible and by this stimulate opposing forces. Third, consensual proposals from a representative sample of citizens make it harder for policymakers to follow the influence of well-organized interest groups. However, the fate of the French citizen assembly on climate change shows that this is by no means impossible. Fourth, perhaps most importantly, a multiplicity of mini-publics in many different places and on many different issues defy controlling by social power just as much as the social pluralism this multiplicity represents. All this will not eliminate power, but contain and even nullify it in many cases.

Making Pluralism Work

The great achievement of deliberative procedures, mini-publics in particular, is that they make pluralism a vital component of Western societies and their democratic systems. They do so, firstly, because by their mode of operation they achieve in reality what in the neat model of polyarchy only works theoretically – they check and balance social interests. This is above all achieved because preparation of political or important administrative decisions by mini-publics largely nullifies special interest groups' power. Secondly, they do so because they make systematic use of great potential for creativity and social learning inherent in the openness and social diversity of Western societies. We have discussed this earlier in this chapter and also in earlier chapters. So there is no need for a long discussion here. I am only highlighting it again because it is existential for Western societies and their democratic systems in two ways. It is existential in terms of their ability to meet the great challenges of this century, transformation of industrial to knowledge society and sustainable development. It is no less existential for their ability to survive in the economic and political competition of systems. But here again, we must pour cold water onto the matter.

In academic literature and political discussions development of the knowledge society is presented as firstly a compelling and secondly also a positive development. The first is wrong, the second describes only one possibility. The first contradicts not only the findings of the theory of social evolution, but above all historical and present experiences. In Europe much of the knowledge of ancient Greece and of the Roman Empire was forgotten in the Middle Ages. In the Islamic world the wealth of knowledge and technology of the Golden Ages of Islam from the eighth to the fourteenth century fell into oblivion afterwards. In more recent times, a civil war abruptly ended the economic and social flourishing of Lebanon, which until then had often been referred to as the Switzerland of the Orient, and with it the development of a knowledge society. But even events of lesser historical magnitude, such as long periods of low investment in education or growing inequality of educational opportunity, anti-science and anti-intellectual populist regimes can at least stall the development of the knowledge society.

In the fourth chapter, I presented the horrible scenario of the Israeli historian Yuval Noah Harari. This scenario describes development of a knowledge society that few people would end up judging as a positive development. It is a knowledge society dominated by a rather small class of super-intelligent people, the class of Homo Deus, the god-like man. Unfortunately, this scenario is not as unlikely as most of us would probably like it to be. We are already seeing that people who drive the development of information technology and, even more so, those who drive and then control its application gain much, some even huge power. We can also already observe growing inequality based on access to knowledge and the availability of knowledge. We also can foresee that digitalization may replace a lot of human work with algorithms already in the next few years. Beyond that, we may realize that singularity and self-expression of people are becoming products of new industrial mass consumerism. Last not least, we even today observe that organized communication of fake news and fake knowledge, and unconstrained communication in social media endanger social diversity and individual liberty.

All this indicates that we not only have to discuss how we may master the problems associated with the pluralism of modern Western societies and how we may exploit the potential for creativity and social learning inherent in the pluralism, but how we can maintain this pluralism. The only way to maintain it is to make it work well. It works well if, first, the conflicts associated with it can be accommodated to a degree that they are no longer a significant danger to Western societies' ability to reach widely accepted decisions. Due to their inclusiveness and their deliberative mode of operation, mini-publics accommodate conflict in a durable way which avoids follow-up conflicts. Second, it works well if its assets provide a strong base for Western societies' capacity to manage sustainable development. Mini-publics make knowledge provided by the emerging knowledge society a real common good of the whole society and do not leave it to the heads and hands of scientists and oligarchs that feel god-like. That is why a deliberative switch is urgently needed. If a deliberative switch is achieved, Western societies will also be capable of resolving their fundamental framing problems. I will show that in the following part.

Reframing Governance

A change process as complex as sustainable development can only be managed if not everything has to be planned and hierarchically controlled, but if many things unfold spontaneously. This, however, requires appropriate framing of societies. For Western societies, this particularly means that they have to resolve three particularly fundamental problems of framing, namely loss of common grounds, deficits of government regulation of markets and embedding of social communication.

Common grounds denotes, to remind, the basic values and principles which must be shared by (almost) all citizens so that social order can emerge and be maintained. The values and principles must be established in individuals' consciousness as an integral part of their individual construction of society. Common ground is, thus, primarily a matter of consciousness. Influencing consciousness is not easy because it is in principle intangible. It cannot be directly observed, but can only be captured indirectly via empirical methods. Yet, in modern Western societies, advertising campaigns, political campaigns, torrents of abuse and hate campaigns on the net and other campaigns change people's consciousness every day. But it is a very different thing, to change consciousness of many people in such a way that society develops common grounds again. Campaigns alone will hardly do the job.

The reason is that consciousness has to a large extent a material basis. We do not have to follow Karl Marx's thesis that being determines consciousness, but we must accept that the two are closely interrelated. In an evolutionary perspective, being and consciousness coevolve. This is particularly true for anchoring the values and principles that constitute the common grounds in the individual consciousness. As we have discussed in detail in the previous chapters, common grounds remain common grounds only as long as they are confirmed in the everyday experiences and communication of the members of society.

In the past three or four decades many material problems emerged which may have permanently changed political and social consciousness of many people. These problems include social inequality that has been growing for years and now is very high, the deterioration of working conditions for many, a large number of "nickel-and-dime" jobs, the social deprivation of a considerable part of the middle class, the financial market crisis, the many smaller and larger scandals in the financial industry, the automotive industry and other sectors, the tax evasion of many large corporations and wealthy citizens, and, last but not least, the often all too obvious inability or unwillingness of politicians to address and consistently solve long-known problems.

Against this backdrop, there are two ways to regain viable common grounds. Both use the insight into the co-evolution of being and consciousness in different ways. One way is slower but probably safer because it relies mainly on a spontaneous development of new or stronger common grounds. The second way can be much faster, but is riskier because it relies on hierarchical control. For both ways, the broad use of mini-publics is at least very helpful, maybe even necessary,

The first way builds upon the insight of French sociologist Émile Durkheim that modern societies are no longer held together by common values and norms, but by functional interdependence. We discussed this view in chapter 2. I define functional interdependence here somewhat different than Durkheim; not by division of labor but more generally by the existence of problems which social actors in a certain context cannot solve alone or whose solution affects different actors. The application of this insight is to stimulate many smaller or larger activities which aim at solving many smaller and larger problems which people in a certain social context, e.g. a city, a company, a social group or society at large, perceive as an important common problem.

The other way is to press government, business and other concerned actors to take strong action to solve the material problems that have led and continue to lead to a loss of common grounds. This has not happened yet although the problems are mostly known for a long time and could have been solved long ago. Most probably this will not change until higher awareness of the public for the problems and for feasible solutions creates strong political pressure and strong economic incentives to finally do it.

A promising way to accomplish this is the combination of strong awareness campaigns with mini-publics which work out widely acceptable model solutions to problems addressed by the campaign. The campaigns should regularly report on the proceedings of related mini-publics. In this way campaigns let their addressees indirectly participate in the development of a solution and share in the experiences of the participants in the mini-public. The campaign thus can not only highlight the problem and the need to solve it but also show an effective solution which most likely will be widely accepted.

The second framing problem, the regulation of markets, is less fundamental but not less important than the loss of common grounds. In my view, this problem is one of the worst manifestations of government failure in Western societies. It concerns the most important task of government, namely securing social order. Markets are a supporting institutional pillar of Western societal order, whether they remain capitalist societies or not. They are the only spontaneous mechanism of economic coordination which works on a large scale. This mechanism could and should also play an important role in sustainable development.

But in order for markets to function properly, government regulation must safeguard effective competition, the proper working of so-called natural monopolies and, last not least, the prevention of negative externalities. Negative externalities are, as we discussed in chapter 4, negative effects of economic activity on uninvolved third parties, e.g. pollution or other environmental damage. Most governments fail at the regulation of competition and externalities although related problems have been known for a long time. Possible solutions to the problems have also been known for long time. Yet the problems remain unsolved. I will not further discuss the problems of competition and externalities here, but rather focus on a problem which is at the root of both, to wit the accumulation of economic power.

It is well established in academia and politics that efficient operation of market competition requires absence of power. All Western governments have established legislation against the accumulation and misuse of economic power. This legislation provides an effective toolbox for the control and containment of economic power. But today we can observe in the global economy and the economies of most Western countries a probably unprecedented concentration of economic power. The power of the Silicon Valley bosses and of Google, Facebook or Amazon, or of large institutional investors like BlackRock, may easily match that of Standard Oil and the Rockefellers in the second half of the nineteenth and the early years of the twentieth century. The big difference is that Standard Oil was broken up in 1911 after Congress adopted the first anti-trust regulation in 1890, the Sherman Antitrust Act. The same fate was endured between 1974 and 1982 by the telephone company AT&T, whose power certainly was much lower than today's power of Google, Facebook or Amazon. The latter have not yet been broken up, although they have been proven to have carried out anti-competition practices and violations of law. They merely had to pay some millions of dollars or euros in fines. So far, these fines seem not to be very effective.[1]

Since the problem and its possible solutions have been known for a long time, it will probably not be brought to a solution until it is perceived as an important problem in the public consciousness and thus moves to a higher place on the political agenda. For that purpose, the combination of an awareness campaign and a citizens' assembly organized preferably by NGOs and progressive business actors would be particularly helpful. The mission of the citizens' assembly should be no less than working out with the support of a prestigious group of experts a rather detailed proposal for a new regulatory framework.

This is a difficult task because the campaign must address actors whose ideas and interests could hardly be further apart. These are on one side environmentalists and other actors engaged in working for the common good. For many of these actors, the market is a deeply capitalist institution, which they therefore reject or mistrust. They would first have to be convinced that market forces can be used to promote sustainable development and human development through appropriate framing. They have to be convinced that the use of this instrument is important when politics does too little.

On the other side, the campaign must convince many neoliberal economists and politicians who keep invoking the danger of too strong a state, but overlook the great economic and political power of a few super-rich oligarchs who now wield an economic and political power that is almost beyond any control. They use this power to create large monopolies and, like PayPal founder Peter Thiel, claim that monopolies are much better for society than a competitive economy. As I will further discuss in the last part of this chapter, bringing together such diverse actors is an important success factor of deliberative practices and of strategies for sustainable development.[2]

An even more important, but also more difficult, issue with regard to sustainable development, the development of the knowledge society and a deliberative switch is the regulation of social communication. In 1963 Karl W. Deutsch whom we mentioned already above, published a groundbreaking book with the telling title "The Nerves of Government: Models of Political Communication and Control". As the title suggests, mass communication is not merely an instrument for exchanging opinions, but key institution of political and social systems.

The nervous system of human beings links all the organs of their body by means of signals, thereby relating them to each other and making the body capable of acting. In addition, the nervous system adopts stimuli (signals) from the environment and forwards them to the "responsible" organs of the body. This alone makes it possible for people to act meaningfully in their environment and to adapt to changes in the environment. The reception and sending of signals, in other words communication, is what makes the body of humans properly functioning.

This applies analogously to the social interactions of people and to society. If people want to interact and to establish a reliable social order, they have to communicate with each other. This can happen through language, gestures, postures, the wearing of badges or other symbols. But this only works if communication is reliable and trustworthy. Through reliable and trustworthy communication between people, common understandings and common rules and regulations are formed, and social order evolves. As we have repeatedly emphasized in this book, common understandings and rules, and thus social order, only retain their validity if they are repeatedly confirmed by the everyday experiences and everyday communication of citizens. Experience is nothing other than communication through sensory experience, especially through observation, and its cognitive (intellectual) processing.

To put it in a nutshell: Without reliable and social communication, there can be no peaceful coexistence of people and no functioning society. There-fore, social communication cannot be left to arbitrary use, but must be designed according to its existential social function. If such a framing of communication does not arise and is not maintained spontaneously, it must be created and secured by government regulation. This is similar to the reg-ulation of the market.

This seems to be a very clear and simple case. However, in democratic societies, regulation of social communication amounts for a difficult tight-rope walk. The regulation of social communication on one hand must ensure that citizens can trust social communication and that it does not violate the rights of other people. On the other hand, regulation of social communication must respect freedom of expression.

A reasonable regulation of social communication need not to cut deeply into freedom of expression. In the case of broadcasting and newspapers, it must ensure that news is as objective as possible in all important aspects, including the associated controversies. Commenting on the news in con-tributions or taking sides in conflicts that are clearly recognizable as opinion, on the other hand, must not be restricted as long as other actors are thereby not denigrated, insulted or even threatened. For a long time, these were completely self-evident basic rules of good journalism. They were the rules that came completely naturally to Walter Cronkite, one of the greats of American journalism, and whose observance made him one of the most trusted men in the US. Since these rules are no longer self-evident today, they must formally be prescribed and enforced by government. As social communication is a politically highly sensitive issue, government should leave the design and execution of the rules to representative bodies of jour-nalism. For the design of the rules this could be a body similar to a citizens' assembly which is composed of a random sample of all journalists in the country. The assembly should be advised by a prestigious group of experts. The execution of the rules could be commissioned to a journalists' jury similar to a citizens' jury or a body of journalists similar to the citizen council of the German community of Belgium. The government role should be restricted to that of guarantor of the process.

In the case of social media, a lot would be gained if users of social media have to be registered with their real names and can thus be prosecuted for slurs, incitement to hatred and violence and other illegal activities. A first step to prevent such activities could be registration of all participants in social media with their full name and address. This should mean that they are allowed to use nicknames, but that their anonymity can easily be removed in case of violations of law. This would be a minimal, but effective regulation which maintains the freedom of the internet while preventing misusing the freedom of internet for slurs, incitement to hatred and violence and for criminal activity.

From Deliberative Democracy to Deliberative Society

By all our experience and knowledge, governments of Western society can neither reach sustainable development nor a deliberative switch single-handedly. This is on one side a matter of the existing institutional conditions and framing of government and on the other one a matter of the huge complexity of sustainable development. Of course, governments could and should also use deliberative procedures to break the institutional boundaries of their actions and to reduce the complexity of sustainable development.

A determined and strong democratic government could for example commission a citizens' assembly with developing a viable and long-termed strategy for achieving sustainable development by the middle of this century. A well-made proposal of a citizens' assembly would reduce social complexity and drastically reduce the influence of well-organized special interest groups. It also would be widely accepted in society which could make government very strong and which could send strong signals to the market. Since this is a very complex task, the citizens' assembly could be supported at different stages by a number of specialized mini-publics concerned with particular problems. This increases structural differentiation of the procedure, but reduces the complexity of tasks. In order to keep the complexity of the procedure within a manageable range, it could be carried out over a longer period of time, which may well be a few years. This delays sustainable development only temporarily. In the longer run, it will rather shorten the time until sustainable development is finally reached. Extension of the procedure allows for a more intensive pervasion of the problems and the conflicts associated with them, and thus may produce even better thought-out solutions. Moreover, a procedure extending over few years may initiate a much broader learning process than the same procedure over a few months. This would probably lead to an ever broader mobilization of political, economic and civil society forces.

Yet, such a long-term process is, under the present institutional conditions of Western societies, politically very difficult to implement. The decision to implement the process requires a broad parliamentary majority. This is the only way to reasonably ensure that the procedure and, even more importantly, the implementation of its proposal would be pursued even if the parliamentary majority were to change. To reach such a decision a large variety of different interests would have to be accommodated. Even a determined and strong government will have to fight a long battle with uncertain outcomes here.

What a strong and determined government can do more easily is to establish a few, well-focused measures to drive sustainability and to create favorable conditions for decentralized activities. This includes, in particular, the implementation of the dynamic, socially balanced resource tax and the environmental and social standards described in chapter four. It also includes establishing an environmentally and socially sound regulatory framework for the market. Both would drive sustainable development through market competition and locational competition. The government could commission citizens' assemblies to work at widely accepted proposals for these measures.

But even if there would be a strong government which could apply deliberative procedures in this way, it will not be enough to reach sustainable development. Such a complex development that requires so many changes must be set in motion at many points in society at the same time. It, thus, must be driven by a large variety of activities of economic and civil society actors, and of cities and other decentral political actors. For such an approach, the versatile uses of deliberative procedures offer huge opportunities.

At the beginning, this does not need to mobilize a large proportion of relevant actors in the different areas of society. Rather it may first be driven by a relatively small number of progressive actors. This is the way in which progress, or more broadly speaking, far-reaching social change, comes about. At the first glance, this may appear to be a rather easy way because as deliberative procedures, mini-publics offer so many versatile opportunities to drive sustainable development. But it may not be quite so simple at first. The reason is that a deliberative switch must come out of the established structures. The structures are strongly shaped by competitive rather than collaborative interest intermediation, realization of interests through power rather than amicable agreement, and by a strong quest for power. They include many actors who fight for the common good and sustainable development.

Many of these actors first have to be brought out of this mode of conflict and have to be convinced that deliberative processes are more likely to achieve sustainable development than endless conflicts. I can understand that many people who are strongly committed to environmental protection and sustainable development, and who have been and are still involved in fierce disputes with their opponents, find it difficult to imagine sitting down at the same table with these opponents and working out a joint solution for sustainable development. As we have discussed in this book, however, it is the only way. The path is certainly rocky in many cases, but if environmentalists openly look for ways to go down this path, they can also find allies in areas where they never expected to.

A very interesting example of this are the leading representatives of the classic enemy image of capitalism, namely institutional investors. These are the actors who probably decide where capital goes more than most other actors. Many of the institutional investors have been responsible in the past, and continue to be responsible today, for many investments that cause great environmental and social harm. But many are now on the way to becoming important drivers of sustainable development through their financial power.

I came to the realization that a genuinely capitalist entity, namely institutional investors, may be a driver of sustainable development through conversations with three friends working as financial executives. Heinz-Peter Heidrich, the former head of a church-related bank, told me early on about his efforts and problems in aligning his bank with investments that are environmentally and socially sustainable. For him, this was a fundamental question of his bank's identity and lasting commercial success. Hanspeter Sauter, the head of a German branch of a Swiss private bank, has demonstrated to me that sustainability has become a must for institutional investors for economic reasons alone – investments in non-sustainable activities will not have a good chance of survival if sustainable development is really taken seriously. Ludger Wibbeke, managing director of one of Germany's largest capital management companies, confirmed this and told me an interesting story. His company, which manages many funds for institutional investors and invests a lot in real estate, made a strategy change a few months ago. While it used to acquire old buildings mostly to demolish them and build new ones, it is now increasingly acquiring buildings in good condition. These buildings are being renovated and several floors added. The additions are made using a timber construction method and materials that are as sustainable as possible. This is a prime example of high resource productivity. The life span of the existing building has been sustainably extended, its productivity per unit area increased by the addition of the floors, which significantly reduces the material intensity of the building. The building's value and utility were significantly increased by the addition of new floors. In short, this investment generated much more benefit with a much lower use of resources. If such examples are replicated, much more private capital will flow into the sustainable development of the real estate sector without the need for government regulation or subsidies.

Former adversaries that turn into partners will significantly add to the wealth of opportunities which deliberative procedures offer to actors such as companies, NGOs, cities and neighborhoods, universities and other research institutions, and even political parties to sustainably shape their development or the development of society at large. The more these opportunities are exploited the more sustainable development becomes a matter of the whole society and not only of politics. The more this is the case, Western societies become deliberative societies which solve the problems associated with sustainable development and other social problems by amicable agreement rather than by conflict and power. This will make them strong societies which are competitive in any respect.

Notes

1 A worrying vision of Western societies being controlled by concentrated economic power is provided by Shoshana Zuboff (2019). The Age of Surveillance Capitalism: The Fight for the Future at the New Frontier of Power. New York: Public Affairs.
2 See Peter Thiel (2014). Zero to One: Notes on Startups or How to Build the Future. New York: Crown Business.

Index

activating government 38, 61, 63
agriculture 55, 60, 69, 71, 75, 80, 87–90,
    102, 108
Argyris, Chris 180
awareness 13, 91, 133, 182, 198, 200

Beck, Ulrich 3, 34
Bentham, Jeremy 96
Berger Peter L. 137
Bessette, Joseph 26
biodiversity 48, 58, 63, 68, 72, 81, 87, 90,
biotechnology 11, 16, 29, 32, 60, 71,
    83–85, 89, 96, 110, 112–113, 116
Böge, Stefanie 47, 64
bureaucracy 20, 27, 30, 39, 67, 100, 102,
    121, 140, 159–161, 166, 194

capitalism, capitalist societies xii, xiii, 4,
    9–11, 14–17, 31–37, 43–44, 49, 53, 84,
    77, 113–114, 123–126, 144, 151–152,
    199–200, 203–204
citizen assembly 28–29, 195
citizen council 29–30, 201
city xi, 5, 16, 23, 25, 28, 30, 31, 41–43,
    55, 59–60, 68, 86–92, 115–116, 131,
    150, 180, 188–191,198, 203–204
civil society ix–x, 17, 23, 40–43, 57, 61,
    67, 85–86, 92, 124, 126, 137, 141–142,
    150, 167, 170–171, 180, 182, 188, 195,
    202–203
climate ix, 1, 3, 5, 17–18, 22, 28–29,
    33, 39, 41–43, 45–46, 48, 58, 61, 64,
    66–74, 76, 80, 90, 116, 133, 150, 174,
    183, 188, 193–195
climate change 3, 17, 29, 33, 41, 45–48,
    58, 61, 66, 69, 71, 116, 150, 188,
    194–195
Club of Rome 9–10
CO_2 24, 46, 55, 72–74

cohesion xi–xii, 2, 15, 25, 32, 37, 43–45,
    48–50, 53–58, 69, 117, 124–126, 132,
    144, 146–149, 167, 175, 183, 189, 195
collective decision 26, 57, 63, 104, 146,
    189–190, 195
collective good 5, 37, 41–43
common good x, xii, 2–6, 30, 37–43,
    54–55, 63, 78, 86, 104, 126, 129, 175,
    191, 197, 200, 203
competition x, 2, 4, 7, 10, 19–20, 40–41,
    49, 54, 58, 68, 79–80, 86, 96–97,
    100–101, 104–107, 114, 120, 131,
    142–143,153, 155, 162–163, 176,
    195–196, 199, 203
Competitiveness Policy Council 49, 64,
    63, 104, 146, 189–190, 195,
complexity 21–22, 31, 45, 48, 53, 67,
    70–72, 87, 92, 103–106, 112, 129, 142,
    158, 160–161, 166, 183, 186, 189–190,
    193–194, 202
communication ix, 8, 21,37, 40, 111,
    113, 126, 130, 145–146, 149, 170,
    172–173, 184, 196–198, 200–201
conflict ix–xii, 1–6, 9, 11, 17–20, 22,
    25, 28–29, 31–33, 38–41, 43–44, 49,
    52–56, 61–62, 66–67, 70–71, 86, 98,
    102–104, 106,109–110, 116, 118, 127,
    132,137–139, 142–147, 150–151, 156,
    163, 166, 170, 175, 181–184, 189–191,
    192, 194–195, 197, 201–204
consciousness 197–199
consensus conference 28–29, 62,
    182, 194
consensus forum 29, 182
contingency 106, 157–159, 161, 162,
    164–167, 193
cooperative 11, 17, 30, 36, 62, 76–78, 88,
    114, 117, 171, 181
Cowen, Tyler 98

creativity x, 15, 18, 63, 68, 70, 77, 86,
91, 93, 96, 98, 104, 132, 156, 166,
171–174, 178, 190, 196–197
culture 17–18, 26, 55, 57, 78, 93, 100,
105, 125, 129–145, 149, 152, 162, 169,
173, 179, 181

Dahrendorf, Ralf 128
Danish Technology Board 183, 194
Darwin, Charles 7–8, 12, 148, 163, 167
decoupling 10, 32, 43, 50–51, 82, 98, 120
deliberation 26–27, 31, 116, 151, 169, 192
deliberative switch 26, 31, 151, 171, 186,
188–204
dematerialization 14, 58, 68, 75, 82–85
Despommier, Dickson 87
Deutsch, Karl W. 76, 200
digitalization 15, 44, 76, 84, 103, 113,
116, 159, 170–174, 196
distribution ix, 3–4, 6, 15–17, 44, 52–53,
68, 73, 88, 95, 97–99, 104, 109–111,
125, 127, 135, 137–138, 184
distributive state 95, 100–103, 106
diversity x–xi, 7, 13, 15, 18–19, 22, 39,
91–93, 104, 114, 126–127, 132–133,
142, 158–159, 166, 189–190, 196–197
division 5, 8, 11, 16, 53, 55, 66, 69, 73,
75, 86, 89, 108–109, 131–132, 141,
145–146, 148–150, 159, 181, 193,
195, 198
Drucker, Peter F. 13–14, 16
Durkheim, Émile 24–25, 55–57, 198

ecosystem 46, 48, 68–69, 72, 82, 87
Ehrenreich, Barbara 4
employment 3, 11, 25, 38, 41, 44, 49, 52, 60,
85, 96, 98, 104–105, 108, 114, 116–117,
119, 140–141, 170–175, 181, 183
Emscher Cooperative 30, 62
Enlightenment 124, 145, 157, 183–185

factor 10 xi, 32, 66–67, 70, 73–74
Festinger, Leon 45
footprint 66, 73–76, 87, 93
framing 124–130, 133, 149–150, 185, 189,
192–194, 197, 199–202
Friedman, Milton 81, 125, 137, 139–140

genesis 155, 157–162, 179
Gibbons, Michael 187
Goldin, Claudia 174–175
greatest happiness principle 95–97, 101
growth xii, 3–4, 9–10, 17, 32, 38, 43–45,
48, 50–53, 59–60, 68, 82, 87, 90, 94,

96–98, 105, 109, 113, 115, 117,
119–120, 137, 174

Habermas, Jürgen 26
Hambacher Forst 3, 22, 44
Harari, Yuval Noah 118, 196
hierarchical coordination 78, 129–130
Hubbard, Barbara Marx 158
human capital 15, 66, 98, 156, 170–177

inequality 4, 10–11, 15–16, 44–45, 50–53,
8, 95, 98–100, 108–110, 117, 124–127,
131–133, 137–141, 174–176, 196, 198
information technology 16, 60, 71, 82,
84, 89, 118, 159, 168, 171, 196
Inglehart, Ronald 108–109, 132, 134–135
institutional investor 11, 31, 113, 116,
151, 199, 203–204
interest groups 2, 6, 19–20, 31, 39, 43,
61, 71–72, 99–102, 105–106, 128, 165,
194–196, 202
Jackson, Tim 50–51
justice 21, 42, 56–57, 71, 75, 97, 124,
126, 131–132, 135

Kant, Immanuel 185
Katz, Lawrence 174–175

legitimacy 21, 105–106, 142, 164
lifestyle 2, 7, 18, 38–39, 45, 52–53, 66, 175
living standard 5, 7, 37, 44, 48–60, 81,
103, 110, 117, 132, 135–136, 138
Locke, John 97, 125
Luhmann, Niklas 8, 145

Marx, Karl 98, 197
microsystems technology 11, 16, 32, 84,
96, 112–114, 116, 120, 170–171
milieu xii–xiii, 8, 55–56, 86–87, 90–92,
115, 133, 176, 190
Mill, John Stewart 97
mini-public 27–30, 93, 116, 151–152,
157, 179–183, 189–190, 192, 195–198,
202–203
minimal state 101–103, 133
MIPS 74, 80, 110
mode of knowledge production 16,
167–170

negative income tax 81, 125, 139–140
nickel-and-dime economy 4, 10, 24–25,
33, 45, 51, 95–96, 106–110, 115, 120,
171, 198
Nowotny, Helga 162, 167

Offe, Claus 100
Olson, Mancur 20, 105
Ostrom, Elinor 61

Piketty, Thomas 51–53, 98
Pinzler, Petra 150, 188
planetary boundaries 32, 50, 58, 68, 77
pluralism 19, 22–34, 132, 144, 189, 195–197
polarization 5, 25, 70, 125, 136, 148, 157, 184–185
post-materialism 105, 109, 134–135
property rights 95, 101–103, 126–127, 131, 160

radical innovation 26, 58, 60–61, 79, 118
Rawls, John 26, 124, 126, 133
rebound effect 46, 77
Reckwitz, Andreas 23, 25
recycling 46, 59, 73–75, 82, 87
regulation ix–x, 6, 17, 21, 25, 27–28, 53–54, 61, 63, 67–68, 71–72, 74, 78–79, 92, 97, 99–106, 108, 115–116, 124–125, 129, 131–133, 159–160, 162, 165–166, 169, 176, 185, 191, 197, 199–204
regulatory capture 99–100, 105, 108
Reich, Robert B. 52, 135
representation x, 57, 124–126, 137, 142–143, 162
resource productivity xi–xii, 32–33, 37, 43–49, 60, 66–81, 110, 113, 131, 138, 189
resource tax 44, 51, 67, 78–82, 104, 110, 119, 131, 138–139, 203
Rifkin, Jeremy 77–78, 174
risk society 3
Rockström, Johann 56
Rolff, Hans-Günther xiii, 175
rucksack, ecological 47–48, 60, 66–67, 72–76, 85, 88, 104

Schmidt-Bleek, Friedrich xi–xii, 47–48, 70, 74, 110
Schön, David A. 180
school 16, 48, 85, 97–98, 144, 148, 156, 163, 166, 175–180, 191
Schumacher, Ernst Friedrich 120
Schumpeter, Joseph A. 12, 60, 86, 157
Scott, Peter 167
self-employment 77–78, 99, 114–117, 138, 171–173

self-organization 8, 17, 23, 38, 41, 43, 57, 61, 63, 68, 78, 92, 129, 174
Senge, Peter 180
skills 60, 62, 115, 117, 145, 149, 166, 170–175, 177, 180–181
SME 67, 78, 81, 96, 113–116, 121–122, 130, 138, 141, 171
social change 1, 3, 9–10, 69, 106, 145–146, 148, 155, 166, 188, 203
social contract 124–128, 133, 137, 142, 150–151, 184
social deprivation 51–52, 126, 135, 198
Spencer, Herbert 6–8, 12, 158, 167
spontaneous coordination 129–131
Steffen, Will 58
Stehr, Nico 16
Steiner, Jürg xi, xiii, 26
Stiglitz, Joseph E. 98–99, 101
Stone, Brad 108
Strohmeier, Karl-Peter 176
Swidler, Ann 145

Tapscott, Don 117
Taylor, Frederick W. 14
technological progress 9–10, 13, 32, 58, 128, 179
telesis 155, 158, 161, 166, 170
threefold sustainability xi–xii, 31–33, 37, 43, 48, 58, 60, 62–63, 67–68, 77, 106, 110, 116, 132, 156, 181, 188–192,
Tirole, Jean 54, 63, 96
Tönnies, Ferdinand 55–56
top runner program 79–81
transformation 6, 11, 13–14, 17, 22–23, 26, 52–53, 55, 66, 91, 116, 119, 155–156, 170, 180, 196

uncertainty 12, 16, 18, 59, 78, 155–156, 162, 164, 167, 171, 174, 177–178, 193
unconditional basic income 118, 141–142
urban agriculture 60, 75, 87–90
utilitarianism 95–98

Ward, Lester Frank 155–158, 166
Weber, Max 160, 166
Wickens, Peter 111
Witt, Ulrich 8, 12, 163
World Commission on Environment and Development 37, 64

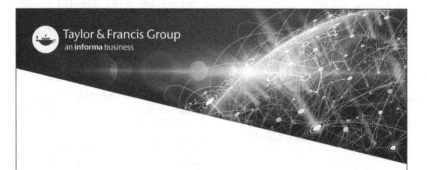